Fairy Mythology

Fairy Mythology
Romance and Superstition of Various Countries 2
Author: Thomas Keightley

Original publication: The Fairy Mythology, Illustrative of the Romance and Superstition of
Various Countries (1870)
Cover image: *Lily Fairy* (1888), Luis Ricardo Falero (1851 – 1896)
Lay-out: www.burokd.nl

ISBN 978-94-92355-10-2

VAMzzz Publishing
P.O. Box 3340
1001 AC Amsterdam
The Netherlands
www.vamzzz.com
contactvamzzz@gmail.com

FAIRY
MYTHOLOGY
Romance and Superstition
of Various Countries 2

VAMzzz PUBLISHING

contents

GREAT BRITIAN *9*

  England *10*

    The Green Children—*11*   The Fairy-Banquet—*14*

    The Fairy-Horn—*16*   The Portunes—*18*   The Grant—*19*

    The Luck of Eden Hall—*27*   The Fairy-Fair—*30*

    The Fairies' Caldron—*32*   The Cauld Lad of Hilton—*33*

    The Pixy-Labour—*40*   Pixy-Vengence—*43*   Pixy-Gratitude—*44*

    The Fairy Thieves—*46*   The Boggart—*48*

    Addlers and Menters—*50*   The Fairy-Nursling—*53*

    The Fairy-Labour—*54*   Ainsel and Puck—*56*

  Scottish Lowlands *102*

    The Fairies' Nurse—*107*   The Fairy Rade—*109*

    The Changeling—*110*   Departure of the Fairies—*112*

    The Brownie—*113*

CELTS AND CYMRY *119*

  Ireland *121*

    Clever Tom and the Leprechaun—*135*

    The Leprechaun in the Garden—*139*   The Three Leprechauns—*143*

    The Little Shoe—*148*

  Scottish Highlands *150*

    The Fairy's Inquiry—*152*   The Young Man in the Shian—*153*

    The Two Fiddlers—*155*   The Fairy-Labour—*157*

    The Fairy borrowing Oatmeal—*158*   The Fairy-Gift—*159*

    The Stolen Ox—*160*   The Stolen Lady—*162*   The Changeling—*164*

    The Wounded Seal—*166*   The Brownies—*168*   The Urisk—*169*

Isle of Man *170*

The Fairy-Chapman—*172*   The Fairy-Banquet—*173*
The Fairies' Christening—*174*   The Fairy-Whipping—*175*
The Fairy-Hunt—*176*   The Fiddler and the Fairy—*177*
The Phynodderee—*178*

Wales *180*

Tale of Elidurus—*181*   The Tylwyth Teg—*185*
The Spirit of the Van—*187*   Rhys at the Fairy Dance—*194*
Gitto Bach—*196*   The Fairies Banished—*198*

Brittany *200*

Lai D'Ywenec—*204*   Lord Nann and the Korrigan—*219*
The Dance and Song of the Korred—*225*

SOUTHERN EUROPE *231*

Greece *232*
Italy *237*
Spain *248*

The Daughter of Peter de Cabinam—*249*
Origin of the House of Haro—*251*   La Infantina—*253*
Pepito el Corcovado—*255*

France *260*

Legend of Melusina—*280*

EASTERN EUROPE *289*

Finns *290*
Slaves *294*

Vilas—*297*   Deer and Vila—*298*

AFRICANS, JEWS *301*

Africans *302*
Jews *304*

The Broken Oaths—*306*   The Moohel—*317*   The Mazik-Ass—*322*

CONCLUSION *325*

APPENDIX *329*

   The Harvest Dinner—*330*   The Young Piper—*343*
   The Soul Cages—*352*   Barry of Cairn Thierna—*367*
   Aileen a Roon—*375*   Rousseau's Dream—*377*
   Alexander Selkirk's Dream—*379*   A Moonlight Scene—*382*
   Lines —*383*   To Amanda—*385*   Lines—*386*   A Farewell—*387*
   Verses—*390*   Father Cuddy's Song—*391*
   The Praises of Mazenderan—*392*

INDEX   *395*

GREAT BRITIAN

In old wives dates that in old time did live,
To whose odde tales much credit men did give,
Great store of goblins, fairies, bugs, nightmares,
Urchins and elves to many a house repaires.
Old Poem.

WE USE the term Great Britain in a very limited sense, as merely inclusive of those parts of the island whose inhabitants are of
Gotho-German origin—England and the Lowlands of Scotland.

We have already seen that the Anglo-Saxon conquerors of
Britain had in their language the terms from which are derived Elf
and Dwarf, and the inference is natural that their ideas respecting
these beings corresponded with those of the Scandinavians and
Germans. The same may be said. of the Picts, who, akin to the Scandinavians, early seized on the Scottish Lowlands. We therefore close
our survey of the Fairy Mythology of the Gotho-German race with
Great Britain.

ENGLAND

Merry elves, their morrice pacing,
To aërial minstrelsy,
Emerald rings on brown heath tracing,
Trip it deft and merrily.
—SCOTT.

The Fairy Mythology of England divides itself into two branches, that of the people and that of the poets. Under the former head will be comprised the few scattered traditions which we have been able to collect respecting a system, the belief in which is usually thought to be nearly extinct; the latter will contain a selection of passages, treating of fairies and their exploits, from our principal poets.

The Fairies of England are evidently the Dwarfs of Germany and the North, though they do not appear to have been ever so denominated. [a] Their appellation was Elves, subsequently Fairies; but there would seem to have been formerly other terms expressive of them, of which hardly a vestige is now remaining in the English language.

They were, like their northern kindred, divided into two classes—the rural Elves, inhabiting the woods, fields, mountains, and caverns; and the domestic or house-spirits, usua called Hobgoblins and Robin Goodfellows. But the Thames, the Avon, and the, other English streams, never seem to have been the abode of a Neck or Kelpie.

The following curious instances of English superstition, occur in the twelfth century.

NOTE

[a] The Anglo-Saxon Dweorg, Dworh, and the English Dwarf; do not seem ever to have had any other sense than that of the Latin *nanus*.

The Green Children

"Another wonderful thing," says Ralph of Coggeshall, [a] "happened in Suffolk, at St. Mary's of the Wolf-pits. A boy and his sister were found by the inhabitants of that place near the mouth of a pit which is there, who had the form of all their limbs like to those of other men, but they differed in the colour of their skin from all the people of our habitable world; for the whole surface of their skin was tinged of a green colour. No one could understand their speech. When they were brought as curiosities to the house of a certain knight, Sir Richard de Caine, at Wikes, they wept bitterly. Bread and other victuals were set before them, but they would touch none of them, though they were tormented by great hunger, as the girl afterwards acknowledged. At length, when some beans just cut, with their stalks, were brought into the house, they made signs, with great avidity, that they should be given to them. When they were brought, they opened the stalks instead of the pods, thinking the beans were in the hollow of them; but not finding them there, they began to weep anew. When those who were present saw this, they opened the pods, and showed them the naked beans. They fed on these with great delight, and for a long time tasted no other food. The boy, however, was always languid and depressed, and he died within a short time. The girl enjoyed continual good health; and becoming accustomed to various kinds of food, lost completely that green colour, and gradually recovered the sanguine habit of her entire body. She was afterwards regenerated by the layer of holy baptism, and lived for many years in the service of that knight (as I have frequently heard from him and his

11

family), and was rather loose and wanton in her conduct. Being frequently asked about the people of her country, she asserted that the inhabitants, and all they had in that country, were of a green colour; and that they saw no sun, but enjoyed a degree of light like what is after sunset. Being asked how she came into this country with the aforesaid boy, she replied, that as they were following their flocks, they came to a certain cavern, on entering which they heard a delightful sound of bells; ravished by whose sweetness, they went for a long time wandering on through the cavern, until they came to its mouth. When they came out of it, they were struck senseless by the excessive light of the sun, and the unusual temperature of the air; and they thus lay for a long time. Being terrified by the noise of those who came on them, they wished to fly, but they could not find the entrance of the cavern before they were caught."

This story is also told by William of Newbridge, [b] who places it in the reign of King Stephen. He says he long hesitated to believe it, but he was at length overcome by the weight of evidence. According to him, the place where the children appeared was about four or five miles from Bury St. Edmund's: they came in harvest-time out of the Wolf-pits; they both lost their green hue, and were baptised, and learned English. The boy, who was the younger, died; but the girl married a man at Lenna, and lived many years. They said their country was called St. Martin's Land, as that saint was chiefly worshiped there; that the people were Christians, and had churches; that the sun did not rise there, but that there was a bright country which could be seen from theirs, being divided from it by a very broad river.

[a] As quoted by Picart in his Notes on William of Newbridge. We could not find it in the Collection of Histories, etc., by Martens and Durand,—the only place where, to our knowledge, this chronicler's works are printed.

[b] *Guilelmi Neubrigensis, Historia, sive Chronica Rerum Anglicarum*, Oxon. 1719, lib. i. c. 27.

The Fairy-Banquet

In the next chapter of his history, William of Newbridge relates as follows:—

"In the province of the Deiri (Yorkshire), not far from my birth-place, a wonderful thing occurred, which I have known from my boyhood. There is a town a few miles distant from the Eastern Sea, near which are those celebrated waters commonly called Gipse ... A peasant of this town went once to see a friend who lived in the next town, and it was late at night when he was coming back, not very sober; when lo! from the adjoining barrow, which I have often seen, and which is not much over a quarter of a mile from the town, he heard the voices of people singing, and, as it were, joyfully feasting. He wondered who they could be that were breaking in that place, by their merriment, the silence of the dead night, and he wished to examine into the matter more closely. Seeing a door open in the side of the barrow, he went up to it, and looked in; and there he beheld a large and luminous house, full of people, women as well as men, who were reclining as at a solemn banquet. One of the attendants, seeing him standing at the door, offered him a cup. He took it, but would not drink; and pouring out the contents, kept the vessel. A great tumult arose at the banquet on account of his taking away the cup, and all the guests pursued him; but he escaped by the fleetness of the beast he rode, and got into the town with his booty. Finally, this vessel of unknown material, of unusual colour, and of extraor-dinary form, was presented to Henry the Elder, king of the English, as a valuable gift, and was then given to the queen's brother David, king of the Scots, and was kept for several years in the treasury of Scotland; and a few years ago (as I have heard from good authority), it was given by William, king of the Scots, to Henry the Second, who wished to see it."

The scene of this legend, we may observe, is the very country in which the Danes settled; and it is exactly the same as some of the legends current at the present day among the Danish peasantry. It is really extraordinary to observe the manner in which popular traditions and superstitions will thus exist for centuries.

Gervase of Tilbury, the Imperial Chancellor, gives the following particulars respecting the Fairy Mythology of England in the thirteenth century.

The Fairy-Horn

"There is," says he, [a] "in the county of Gloucester, a forest abounding in boars, stags, and every species of game that England produces. In a grovy lawn of this forest there is a little mount, rising in a point to the height of a man, on which knights and other hunters are used to ascend when fatigued with heat and thirst, to seek some relief for their wants. The nature of the place, and of the business, is, however, such, that whoever ascends the mount must leave his companions, and go quite alone.

"When alone, he was to say, as if speaking to some other person, 'I thirst,' and immediately there would appear a cupbearer in an elegant dress, with a cheerful countenance, bearing in his stretched-out hand a large horn, adorned with gold and gems, as was the custom am~mg the most ancient English. In the cup [b] nectar of an unknown but most delicious flavour was presented, and. when it was drunk, all heat and weariness fled from the glowing body, so that one would be thought ready to undertake toil instead of having toiled. Moreover, when the nectar was taken, the servant presented a towel to the drinker, to wipe his mouth with, and then having performed his office, he waited neither for a recompense for his services, nor for questions and enquiry.

"This frequent and. daily action had for a very long period of old times taken place among the ancient people, till one day a knight of that city, when out hunting, went thither, and having called for a drink and gotten the horn, did not, as was the custom, and as in good manners he should have done, return it to the cup-bearer, but kept it for his own use. But the illustrious Earl of Gloucester, when he learned the truth of the matter, condemned the robber to death, and presented the horn to the most excellent King Henry the Elder, lest he should be thought to have approved of such wickedness, if he had added the rapine of another to the store of his private property."

NOTES
[a] Otis Imperiaila *apud Leibnitz Scriptores rerum Brunsvicarum,* vol.i. p. 981.
[b] Vice calicis.

The Portunes

In another part of this work the Chancellor says, [a]—

"They have in England certain demons, though I know not whether I should call them demons or figures of a secret and unknown generation, which the French call Neptunes, the English Portunes. [b] It is their nature to embrace the simple life of comfortable farmers, and when, on account of their domestic work, they are sitting up at night, when the doors are shut, they warm themselves at the fire, and take little frogs out of their bosom, roast them on the coals, and eat them. They have the countenance of old men, with wrinkled cheeks, and they are of a very small stature, not being quite half-an-inch high. [c] They wear little patched coats, and if anything is to be carried into the house, or any laborious work to be done, they lend a hand, and finish it sooner than any man could. It is tbeir nature to have the power to serve, but not to injure. They have, however, one little mode of annoying. When in the uncertain shades of night the English are riding any where alone, the Portune sometimes invisibly joins the horseman; and when he has accompanied him a good while, he at last takes the reins, and leads the horse into a neighbouring slough; and when he is fixed and floundering in it, the Portune goes off with a loud laugh, and by sport of this sort he mocks the simplicity of mankind.

NOTES

[a] Otis Imperiaila *apud Leibnitz Scriptores rerum Brunsvicarum,* vol.i. p. 980

[b] There is, as far as we are aware, no vestige of these names remaining in either the French or English language, and we cannot conceive how the Latin names of sea-gods came to be applied to the Gotho-German Kobolds, etc.

[c] Dimidium *pollicis.* Should we not read *pedis?*

The Grant

"There is," says he, again [a] "in England a certain kind of demon whom in their language they call Grant, [b] like a yearling foal, erect on its hind legs, with sparkling eyes. This kind of demon often appears in the streets in the heat of the day, or about sunset. If there is any danger impending on the following day or night, it runs about the streets provoking the dogs to bark, and, by feigning flight, draws the dogs after it, in the vain hope of catching it. This illusion warns the inhabitants to beware of fire, and the friendly demon, while he terrifies those who see him, puts by his coining the ignorant on their guard."

* * *

Thus far the Chancellor of the Holy Roman Empire, and, except in the poets, we have met with no further account of, or allusion to, fairies, until the reign of Elizabeth, when a little work appeared, named, The mad Pranks and merry Jests of Robin Goodfellow, [c] from which Shakespeare seems in a good measure to have derived his Puck.

This work consists of two parts. In the first we are informed that Robin was the offspring of a "proper young wench by a hee-fay-rie, a king or something of that kin among them." By the time he was six years old he was so mischievous and unlucky that his mother found it necessary to promise him a whipping. He ran away and engaged with a tailor, from whom also he soon eloped. When tired he sat down and fell asleep, and in his sleep he had a vision of fairies; and when he awoke he found lying beside him a scroll, evidently left by his father, which, in verses written in letters of gold, informed him that he should have any thing he wished for, and have also the power of turning himself "To horse, to hog, to dog, to ape," etc., but he was to harm none but knaves and queans, and was to "love those that honest be, and help them in necessity." He made trials of his power and found that be really possessed it. His first exploit was to turn himself into a horse, to punish a churlish clown, whom he induced to mount him, and gave him a fall that went well nigh to break his neck. The fellow then went to ride him through a great plash of water, "and in the middle of it he found himself with nothing but a pack-saddle between his legs, while Robin went off laughing, *Ho, ho, hoh!* He next exerted himself in the cause of two young lovers, and secured their happiness.

In the Second Part we find him more in the character of the Nis or Brownie. Coming to a farmer's house, he takes a liking to a "good handsome maid," that was there, and in the night does her work for her, at breaking hemp and flax, bolting meal, etc. Having watched one night and seen him at work, and observed that he was rather bare of clothes, she provided him with a waistcoat against the next night. But when he saw it he started and said:-

> Because thou layest me himpen hampen
> I will neither bolt nor stampen:
> 'Tis not your garments, new or old,
> That Robin loves: I feel no cold.
> Had you left me milk or cream,
> You should have had a pleasing dream:
> Because you left no drop or crum,
> Robin never more will come.

He went off laughing *Ho, ho, hoh!* and the maid in future had to do all the work herself.

A company of young fellows who had been making merry with their sweethearts were coming home over a heath. Robin met them, and to make himself merry took the form of a *walking fire,* and led them up and down till daylight, and then went off saying:—

> Get you home, you merry lads:
> Tell your mammies and your dads,
> And all those that news desire,
> How you saw a walking fire.
> Wenches that do smile and lispe,
> Use to call me Willy Wispe.
> If that you but weary be,
> It is sport alone for me.
> Away: unto your houses go,
> And I'll go laughing, *Ho, ho, hoh!*

A fellow was attempting to offer violence to a young maiden. Robin came to her aid, ran between his legs in the shape of a hare, then turning himself into a horse, carried him off on his back, and flung him into a thick hedge.

Robin fell in love with a weaver's pretty wife, and for her sake took service with her husband. The man caught them one day kissing, and next night he went and took Robin as he was sleeping, up out of his bed, and went to the river and threw him in. But instantly he heard behind him—

> For this your service, master, I you thank.
> Go swim yourself; I'll stay upon the bank;
> and was pushed in by Robin, who had put a bag of yarn in his bed,
> and now went off with, *Ho, ho, hoh!*

Robin went as a fiddler to a wedding. When the candles came he blew them out, and giving the men boxes in the ears he set them a-fighting. He kissed the prettiest girls, and pinched the others, till he made them scratch one another like cats. When the posset was brought forth, he turned himself into a bear, and frightening them away, had it all to himself.

At length his father who we now find, was king Obreon (i. e. Oberon), [d] called him up out of his bed one night, and took him to where the fairies were dancing to the music of Tom Thumb's bag-pipe, and thence to Fairy-land, where he "did show him many secrets which he never did open to the world."

In the same work Sib says of the woman-fairies:

"To walk nightly as do the men-fairies we use not; but now and then we go together, and at good housewives' fires we warm our fairy children. [e] If we find clean water and clean towels we leave them money, either in their basins, or in their shoes; but if we find no clean water in their houses, we wash our children in their pottage, milk, or beer, or whatever we find: for the sluts that have not such things fitting, we wash their faces and hands with a gilded child's clout, or else carry them to some river and duck them over head and ears. We often use to dwell in some great hill, and from thence we do lend money to any poor man or woman that hath need; but if they bring it not again at the day appointed, we do not only punish them with pinching, but also in their goods, so that they never thrive till they have paid us."

The learned and strong-minded Reginald Scot, thus notices the superstitions of his own and the preceding age. [f]

"Indeed your grandams' maids were wont to set a bowl of milk before him (Incubus) and his cousin Robin Goodfellow, for grinding of malt or mustard, and sweeping the house at midnight; and you have also heard that he would chafe exceedingly if the maid or good-wife of the house, having compassion of his nakedness, laid any clothes for him besides his mess of white bread and milk, which was his standing fee; for in that case he saith,

What have we here? Hemten, hamten,
Here will I never more tread nor stampen.

Again: [8]

"The Faeries do principally inhabit the mountains and caverns of the earth, whose nature is to make strange apparitions on the earth, in meadows or on mountains, being like men and women, soldiers, kings, and lathes, children and horsemen, clothed in green, to which purpose they do in the night steal hempen stalks from the fields where they grow, to convert them into horses, as the story goes.

"Such jocund and facetious spirits," he continues, "are said to sport themselves in the night by tumbling and fooling with servants and shepherds in country houses, pinching them black and blue, and leaving bread, butter, and cheese, sometimes with them, which, if they refuse to eat, some mischief shall undoubtedly befal them by the means of these Faeries; and many such have been taken away by the said spirits for a fortnight or a month together, being carried with them in chariots through the air, over hills and dales, rocks and precipices, till at last they have been found lying in some meadow or mountain, bereaved of their senses, and commonly one of their members to boot."

Elsewhere [h] he gives the following goodly catalogue of these objects of popular terror:—

"Our mother's maids have so frayed us with Bull-beggars, Spirits, Witches, Urchins, Elves, Hags, Faeries, Satyrs, Pans, Faunes, Sylens, Kit-wi-the-Canstick, Tritons, Centaurs, Dwarfs, Gyants, Im-pes, Calcars, Coujurors, Nymphs, Changelings, Incubus, Robin Good-fellow, the Spoorn, the Mare, the Man-in-the-Oak, the Hell-wain, the Firedrake, the Puckle, Tom-thombe, Hob-goblin, Tom-tumbler, Boneless, and such other Bugs, that we are afraid of our shadow." [i]

Burton, after noticing from Paracelsus those which in Ger-many "do usually walk in little coats, some two foot long," says, [j] "A bigger kind there is of them called with us Hobgoblins and Robin Goodfellows, that would, in those superstitious times, grind corn for a mess of milk, cut wood, or do any manner of drudgery work." And again: "Some put our Fairies into this rank (that of terrestrial devils), which have been in former times adored with much supersti-tion, with sweeping their houses, and setting of a pail of clean water, good victuals, and the like, and then they should not be pinched, but find money in their shoes, and be fortunate in their enterprises." In another place (p. 30,) he says, "And so those which Miyaldus calls *Ambulones,* that walk about midnight, on heaths and desert places, which (saith Lavater) draw men out of the way and lead them all night a by-way, or quite barre them of their way; these have several names, in several places; we commonly call them *Pucks.*"

Harsenet thus speaks of them in his Declaration: [k]

"And if that the *bowl* of curds and *cream* were not *duly set* out for Robin Goodfellow, the *friar,* and Sisse the dairy-maid, why then, either the pottage was burned the next day in the pot, or the cheeses would not curdle, or the butter would not come, or the ale in the fat never would have good head. But if a Peter-penny or a Housle-egge [l] were behind, or a patch of tythe unpaid—then 'ware of bull-beggars, spirits, &c."

Nash thus describes them: [m]

"Then ground they malt, and had hempen shirts for their la-bours; daunced in rounds in green meadows; pincht maids in their sleep that swept not their houses clean, and led poor travellers out of their way."

As the celebrated Luck of Eden Hall is supposed to have been a chalice, due respect for the piety of our forefathers will not allow of our placing the desecration of it any higher than the reign of Eliza-beth, or that of her father at farthest. We will therefore introduce its history in this place.

NOTES

[a] Otis Imperiaila *apud Leibnitz Scriptores rerum Brunsvicarum,* vol.i. p. 980.

[b] Can this name be connected with that of Grendel, the malignant spirit in Beowulf?

[c] Edited for the Percy Society by J. P. Collyer, Esq., 1841. Mr. Collyer says there is little doubt but that this work was printed before 1588, or even 1584. We think this is true only of the First Part; for the Second, which is of a different texture, must have been added some time after tobacco had come into common use in England: see the verses in p. 34.

[d] Mr. Collyer does not seem to have recollected that Huon de Bordeaux had been translated by Lord Berners

[e] It It is, according to this authority the man-fairy Gunn that steals children and leaves changelings.

[f] Discoverie of Witchcrafte, iv. ch. 10.

[g] R. Scot, Discoverie of Witchcrafte, ii. ch. 4.

[h] *Ib.* vii. 15.

[i] This appears to us to be rather a display of the author's learning than an actual enumeration of the objects of popular terror; for the maids hardly talked of Satyrs, Pans, etc. *Hag* is the Anglo-Saxon ..., German *here,* "witche," and hence the Nightmare which was ascribed to witches; we still say *Hag-ridden.* Calcar and Sporn (spurs?) may be the same, from the idea of riding: the French call the Nightmare, *(Cauchemare,* from *Caucher, calcare.* Kit-wi-the-canstick is Jack-with-the-Lanthorn. The Man in the Oak is probably Puck, "Turn your cloakes, quoth hee, for Pucke is busy in these oakes."—Iter Boreale. The Hell-wain is perhaps the Death-coach, connected with Northern and German superstitions, and the Fire-drake an Ignis Fatuus. Boneless may have been some impalpable spectre; the other terms seem to be mere appellations of Puck.

[j] Anat. of Mel. p. 47.

[k] Chap. xx. p. 134. Lond. 1604.

[l] This is, we apprehend, an egg at Easter or on Good Friday. *Housle* is the Anglo-Saxon ...; Goth. *hunsl,* sacrifice or offering, and thence the Eucharist.

[m] Terrors of the Night, 1594.

The Luck of Eden Hall

In this house (Eden Hall, a seat of the Musgraves,) are some good old-fashioned, apartments. An old painted drinking-glass, called the *Luck of Eden Hall, is* preserved with great care. In the garden near to the house is a well of excellent spring water, called St. Cuthbert's Well. (The church is dedicated to that saint.) This glass is supposed to have been a sacred chalice; but the legendary tale is, that the butler, going to draw water, surprised a company of Fairies, who were amusing themselves upon the green near the well; he seized the glass which was standing upon its margin. They tried to recover it; but, after an ineffectual struggle, flew away, saying,—

If that glass either break or fall,
Farewell the luck of Eden Hall [a]

"In the year 1633—4 (says Aubrey [b]) soon after I had entered into my grammar, at the Latin schoole of Yatton-Keynel, [near Chippenham, Wilts,] our curate, Mr. Hart, was annoyed one night by these elves or fayeries. Comming over the downes, it being neere darke, and approaching one of the faiery dances, as the common people call them in these parts, viz, the greene circles made by those sprites on the grasse, he all at once saw an innumerable quantitie of pigmies, or very small people, dancing rounde and rounde, and singing and making all maner of small odd noyses. He, being very greatly amazed, and yet not being able, as he says, to run away from them, being, as he supposes, kept there in a kinde of enchantment, they no sooner perceave him but they surround him on all sides, and what betwixte feare and amazement he fell down, scarcely knowing what he did; and thereupon these little creatures pinched him all over, and made a quick humming noyse all the tyme; but at length they left him, and when the sun rose he found himself exactly in the midst of one of these faiery dances. This relation I had from him myselfe a few days after he was so tormented; but when I and my bed-fellow, Stump, wente soon afterwards, at night time, to the dances on the downes, we sawe none of the elves or faieries. But, indeed, it is saide they seldom appeare to any persons who go to seeke for them."

The next account, in order of time, that occurs, is what Sir Walter Scott calls the Cock Lane narrative of Anne Jefferies, who was born in 1626, in the parish of St. Teath, in Cornwall, and whose wonderful adventures with the Fairies were, in 1696, communicated by Mr. Moses Pitt, her master's son, to Dr. Fowler, bishop of Glouces-ter. [c]

According to this account, Anne described the Fairies, who she said came to her, as "six small people, all in green clothes." They taught her to perform numerous surprising cures; they fed her from harvest-time till Christmas; they always appeared in even numbers. When seen dancing in the orchard among the trees, she said she was dancing with the fairies. These fairies scorned the imputation of being evil spirits, and referred those who termed them such to Scripture.

The following "relation of the apparition of Fairies, their seem-ing to keep a fair, and what happened to a certain man that endeav-oured to put himself in amongst them," is given by Bovet. [d]

NOTES

[a] Hutchinson, History of Cumberland, vol. 1. p. 269.

[b] As quoted by Thoms in his Essay on Popular Songs, in the Athenaeum for 1847.

[c] Morgan, Phoenix Britannicus, Loud. 1732.

[d] Pandemonium, n. 207. Lond. 1684.

The Fairy-Fair

"Reading once the eighteenth of Mr. Glanvil's relations, p. 203, concerning an Irishman that had like to have been carried away by spirits, and of the banquet they had spread before them in the fields, etc., it called to mind a passage I had often heard, of Fairies or spirits, so called by the country people, which showed themselves in great companies at divers times. At some times they would seem to dance, at other times to keep a great fair or market. I made it my business to inquire amongst the neighbours what credit might be given to that which was reported of them, and by many of the neighbouring inhabitants I had this account confirmed.

"The place near which they most ordinarily showed themselves was on the side of a hill, named Black-down, between the parishes of Pittminster and Chestonford, not many miles from Tanton. Those that have had occasion to travel that way have frequently seen them there, appearing like men and women, of a stature generally near the smaller size of men. Their habits used to be of red, blue, or green, according to the old way of country garb, with high crowned hats. One time, about fifty years since, a person living at Comb St. Nicholas, a parish lying on one side of that hill, near Chard, was riding towards his home that way, and saw, just before him, on the side of the hill, a great company of people, that seemed to him like country folks assembled as at a fair. There were all sorts of commodities, to his appearance, as at our ordinary fairs; pewterers, shoemakers, pedlars, with all kind of trinkets, fruit, and drinking-booths. He could not remember anything which he had usually seen at fairs but what he saw there. It was once in his thoughts that it might be some fair for Chestonford, there being a considerable one at some time of the year; but then again he considered that it was not the season for it. He was under very great surprise, and admired what the meaning of what he saw should be. At length it came into his mind what he had heard concerning the Fairies on the side of that hill, and it being near the road he was to take, he resolved to ride in amongst them, and see what they were. Accordingly he put on his horse that way, and, though he saw them perfectly all along as he came, yet when he was upon the place where all this had appeared to him, he could discern nothing at all, only seemed to be crowded and thrust, as when one passes through a throng of people. All the rest became invisible to him until he came to a little distance, and then it appeared to him again as at first. He found himself in pain, and so hastened home; where, being arrived, lameness seized him all on one side, which continued on him as long as he lived, which was many years; for he was living in Comb, and gave an account to any that inquired of this accident for more than twenty years afterwards; and this relation I had from a person of known honour, who had it from the man himself.

"There were some whose names I have now forgot, but they then lived at a gentleman's house, named Comb Farm, near the place before specified: both the man, his wife, and divers of the neighbours, assured me they had, at many times, seen this *fair-keeping* in the summer-time, as they came from Tanton-market, but that they durst not adventure in amongst them; for that every one that had done so had received great damage by it."

The Fairies' Caldron

"In the vestry of Frensham church, in Surrey, on the north side of the chancel, is an extraordinary great kettle or caldron, which the inhabitants say, by tradition, was brought hither by the fairies, time out of mind, from Borough-hill, about a mile hence. To this place, if anyone went to borrow a yoke of oxen, money, etc., he might have it for a year or longer, so he kept his word to return it. There is a cave where some have fancied to hear music. In this Borough hill is a great stone, lying along the length of about six feet. They went to this stone and knocked at it, and declared what they could borrow, and when they would repay, and a voice would answer when they should come, and that they should find what they desired to borrow at that stone. This caldron, with the trivet, was borrowed here after the manner aforesaid, and not returned according to promise; and though the caldron was afterwards carried to the stone, it could not be received, and ever since that time no borrowing there." [a]

NOTE
[a] Aubrey, Natural History of Surrey, iii, 366, *ap*. Ritson, Fairy Tales, p. 166

The Cauld Lad of Hilton

"Hilton Hall, in the vale of the Wear, was in former times the resort of a Brownie or House-spirit called The Cauld Lad. Every night the servants who slept in the great hall heard him at work in the kitchen, knocking the things about if they had been set in order, arranging them if otherwise, which was more frequently the case. They were resolved to banish him if they could, and the spirit, who seemed to have an inkling of their design, was often heard singing in a melancholy tone:

> Was 'a me! was 's me!
> The acorn is not yet
> Fallen from the tree,
> That's to grow the wood,
> That's to make the cradle,
> That's to rock the bairn,
> That's to grow to a man,
> That's to lay me.

The servants, however, resorted to the usual mode of banishing a Brownie: they left a green cloke and hood fbr hini by the kitchen fire, and remained on the watch. They saw him come in, gaze at the new clothes, try them on, and, apparently in great delight, go jumping and frisking about the kitchen. But at the first crow of the cock he vanished, crying—

> Hero 'a a cloak, and here's a hood!
> The Cauld Lad of Hilton will do no more good;

and he never again returned to the kitchen; yet it was said that he might still be heard at midnight singing those lines in a tone of melancholy.

There was a room in the castle long called the Cauld Lad's Room, which was never occupied unless the castle was full of company, and within the last century many persons of credit had heard of the midnight wailing of the Cauld Lad, who some maintained was the spirit of a servant whom one of the barons of Hilton had killed unintentionally in a fit of passion." [a]

In the beginning of the last century Bourne thus gives the popular belief on this subject:

"Another part of this (winter's evening) conversation generally turns upon Fairies. These, they tell you, have frequently been seen and heard; nay, that there are some still living who were stolen away by them, and confined seven years. According to the description they give of them, who pretend to have seen them, they are in the shape of men exceeding little: they are always clad in green, and frequent the woods and fields. When they make cakes (which is a work they have been often heard at), they are very noisy; and when they have done, they are full of mirth and pastime. But generally they dance in moonlight, when mortals are asleep, and not capable of seeing them; as may be observed on the following morning, their dancing places being very distinguishable: for as they dance hand in hand, and so make a circle in their dance, so next day there will be seen rings and circles on the grass." [b]

The author of "Round about our Coalfire" says [c]:

"My grandmother has often told me of Fairies dancing upon our green, and they were *little little creatures, clothed in green.*

"The moment any one saw them, and took notice of them, they were struck blind of an eye. They lived under ground, and generally came out of a mole-hill.

"They had fine music always among themselves, and danced in a moonshiny night around, or in a ring, as one may see at this day upon every common in England, where mushrooms grow.

"When the master and mistress were laid on their pillows, the men and maids, if they had a game at romp, and blundered upstairs, or jumbled a chair, the next morning every one would swear it was the fairies, and that they heard them stamping up and down stairs all night, crying 'Water 's locked! Water 's locked!' when there was not water in every pail in the kitchen."

To come to the present times. There is no stronger proof of the neglect of what Mr Thoms has very happily designated "Folk-lore" in this country, than the fact of there having been no account given anywhere of the Pixies or Pisgies [d] of Devonshire and Cornwall, till within these last few years. In the year 1836, Mrs. Bray, a lady well known as the author of several novels, and wife of a clergyman at Tavistock, published, in a series of letters to Robert Southey, interesting descriptions of the part of Devonshire bordering on the Tamar and the Tavy. In this work there is given an account of the Pixies, from which we derive the following information:

According to the Devon peasant, the Pixies are the souls of infants who died before they were baptised. They are of small dimensions, generally handsome in their form. Their attire is always green. Dancing is their chief amusement, which they perform to the music of the cricket, the grasshopper, and the frog,—always at night; and thus they form the fairy-rings. The Pixy-house is usually in a rock. By moon-light, on the moor, or under the dark shade of rocks, the Pixy-monarch, Mrs. Bray says, holds his court, where, like Titania, he gives his subjects their several charges. Some are sent to the mines, where they will kindly lead the miner to the richest lode, or maliciously, by noises imitating the stroke of the hammer, and by false fires, draw him on to where the worst ore in the mine lies, and then laugh at his disappointment. Others are sent

> To make the maids their sluttery rue,
> By pinching them both black and blue.

On this account, says Mrs. Bray, "the good dames in this part of the world are very particular in sweeping their houses before they go to bed; and they will frequently place a basin of water beside the chimney-nook, to accommodate the Pixies, who are great lovers of water; and sometimes they requite the good deed by dropping a piece of money into the basin. A young woman of our town, who declared she had received the reward of sixpence for a like service, told the circumstance to her gossips; but no six-pence ever came again, and it was generally believed that the Pixies had taken offence by her chattering, as they do not like to have their deeds, good or evil, talked over by mortal tongues."

The office of some is to steal children; of others, to lead travellers astray, as Will-o'-the-wisps, or to *Pizxy-lead* them, as it is termed. Some will make confusion in a house by blowing out the candle, or kissing the maids "with a smack, as they 'shriek Who 'a this?' as the old poet writes, till their grandams come in and lecture them for allowing unseemly freedoms with their bachelors." Others will make noises in walls, to frighten people. In short, everything that is done elsewhere by fairies, boggarts, or other like beings, is done in Devon by the Pixies.

It is said that they will sometimes aid their favourites in spinning their flax. "I have heard a story about an old woman in this town," says Mrs. Bray, "who suspected she received assistance of the above nature; and one evening, coming suddenly into the room, she spied a ragged little creature, who jumped out of the door. She thought she would try still further to win the services of her elfin friend, and so bought some smart new clothes, as big as those made for a doll. These pretty things she placed by the side of her wheel. The Pixy returned, and put them on; when, clapping her tiny hands, she was heard to exclaim—

> Pixy fine, Pixy gay,
> Pixy now will run away;

and off she went. But the ungrateful little creature never spun for the poor old woman after."

Mrs. Bray has been assured that mothers used frequently to pin their children to their sides, to prevent their being stolen by the Pixies; and she heard of a woman in Tavistock who avowed that her mother had a child which was stolen by them, as she was engaged banging out clothes to dry in her garden. She almost broke her heart when she discovered it; but she took great care of the changeling, which so pleased the Pixy, that she soon after gave the woman back her child, who proved eminently lucky in after life.

The being *Pixy-led* is a thing very apt to befall worthy yeomen returning at night from fair or market, especially if they sat long at the market-table; and then, says our authority, "he will declare, and offer to take his Bible-oath upon it, that, as sure as ever he 'a alive to tell it, whilst his head was running round like a mill-wheel, be heard with his own ears they bits of Pisgies a-laughing and *a-tacking* their hands, all to see he led-astray, and never able to find the right road, though he had travelled it scores of times long agone, by night or by day, as a body might tell." Mr. Thoms, too, was told by a Devon girl, who had often beard of the Pixies, though she had never seen any, that "she once knew a man who, one night, could not find his way out of his own fields, all he could do, until he recollected to *turn his coat;* and, the moment he did so, he heard the Pixies all fly away, up into the trees, and there they sat and laughed. Oh! how they did laugh! But the man then soon found his way out of the field."

This turning of the coat, or some other article of dress, is found to be the surest remedy against Pixy-illusion. Mrs. Bray says that the old folk in Tavistock have recourse to it as a preventive against being *Pixy-led,* if they have occasion to go out after sundown. It appears to have been formerly in use in other parts of England also; for Bishop Corbet thus notices it in his "Iter Boreale:"

> William found
> A mean for our deliverance, *Turne your cloakes*
> Quoth hee, for Puoke is busy in these oakes;
> If ever wee at Bosworth will be found
> Then *turne your cloake,* for this is fairy ground.

In Scandinavia, also, we learn the remedy against being led

astray by the Lygtemand, Lyktgubhe, or Will-o'-the-Wisp, is to turn one's cap inside out.

Mrs. Bray gives, in addition, the following-legends, which we have taken the liberty of abridging a little.

NOTES

[a] The Local Historian's Table-Book, by M. A. Richardson, iii. 239. Newcastle-upon-Tyne, 1846.
[b] Bourne, Antiquitates Vulgares, 1725.
[c] Quoted by Brand in his Popular Antiquities, an enlarged edition of Bourne's work.
[d] This word Pixy, is evidently Pucksy, the endearing diminutive *sy* being added to Puck, like Betsy, Nancy, Dixie. So Mrs. Trimmer in her Fabulous Histories—which we read with wonderful pleasure in our childhood, and would recommend to our young readers— calls her hen-robins Pecksy and Flapsy. Pisgy is only Pixy transposed. Mrs. Bray derives Pixy from Pygmy. At Truro, in Cornwall, as Mr. Thorns informs us, the *moths,* which some regard as departed souls, others as fairies, are called *Pisgies.* He observes the curious, but surely casual, resemblance between this and the Greek ψυχή, which is both soul and moth. Grimm (p. 430) tells us from an old glossary, that the caterpillar was named in Germany, *Alba,* i. e. *Elbe,* and that the Alp often takes the form of a butterfly.

The Pixy-Labour

One night, about twelve o'clock in the morning, as the good folks say, who tell this good tale, Dame—the *sage femme* of Tavistock, had just got comfortably into bed, when rap, rap, rap, came on her cottage door, with such bold and continued noise, that there was a sound of authority in every individual knock. Startled and alarmed by the call, she arose from her bed, and soon learnt that the summons was a hasty one to bid her attend on a patient who needed her help. She opened her door, when the summoner appeared to be a strange, squint-eyed, little, ugly old fellow, who had a look, as she said, very like a certain dark personage, who ought not at all times to be called by his proper name. Not at all prepossessed in favour of the errand by the visage of the messenger, she nevertheless could not, or dared not, resist the command to follow him straight, and attend on "his wife."

"Thy wife!" thought the good dame; "Heaven forgive me, but as sure as I live I be going to the birth of a little divil." A large coal-black horse, with eyes like balls of fire, stood at the door. The ill-looking old fellow, without more ado, whisked her up on a high pillion in a minute, seated himself before her, and away went horse and riders as if sailing through the air rather than trotting on the ground. How she got to the place of her destination she could not tell; but it was a great relief to her fears when she found herself set down at the door of a neat cottage, saw a couple of tidy children, and remarked her patient to be a decent looking woman, having all things about her fitting the time and occasion. A fine bouncing babe soon made its appearance, who seemed very bold on its entry into life, for it gave the good dame a box on the ear, as, with the coaxing and cajolery of all good old nurses, she declared the "sweet little thing to be very like its father." The mother said nothing to this, but gave nurse a certain ointment, with directions that she should *strike* (i. e. *rub)* the child's eyes with it. The nurse performed her task, considering what it could be for. She thought that, as no doubt it was a good thing, she might just as well try it upon her own eyes as well as those of the baby; so she made free to *strike* one of them by way of trial, when, O ye powers of fairy land! what a change was there!

The neat, but homely cottage, and all who were in it, seemed all on a sudden to undergo a mighty transformation; some for the better, some for the worse. The new-made mother appeared as a beautiful lady attired in white; the babe was seen wrapped in swaddling clothes of a silvery gauze. It looked much prettier than before, but still maintained the elfish cast of the eye, like his father, whilst two or three children more had undergone a strange metamorphosis. For there sat on either side the bed's head, a couple of little flat-nosed imps, who with "mops and mows,' and with many a grimace and grin, were busied to no end in scratching their own polls, or in pulling the fairy lady's ears with their long and hairy paws. The dame who beheld all this, fearing she knew not what, in the house of enchantment, got away as fast as she could, without saying one word about *striking* her own eye with the magic ointment and what she had seen. The sour-looking old fellow once more handed her up on the coal-black-horse, and sent her home in a *whip sissa* [a] much faster than she came.

On the next market-day, when she sallied forth to sell her eggs, she saw the same old fellow busy pilfering sundry articles from stall to stall, and going up to him she enquired about his wife and child. "What!" exclaimed he, "do you see me to-day?" "See you! to be sure I do, as plain as I see the sun in the sky; and I see you are busy, too." "Do you?" says he, "and pray with which eye do you see all this?" "With the right eye to be sure."

"The ointment! the ointment!" cried he. "Take that, for meddling with what did not belong to you; you shall see me no more."

He struck her eye as he spoke, and from that hour till the day of her death she was blind of that eye.

NOTE
[a] *Whip says he,* as Mrs. Bray conjectures.

Pixy-Vengence

Two serving-girls in Tavistock said that the Pixies were very kind to them, and used to drop silver for them into a bucket of fair water which they took care to place for them in the chimney-nook every night. Once it was forgotten, and the Pixies forthwith came up to the girls' room, and loudly complained of the neglect. One of them, who happened to be awake, jogged the other, and proposed going down to rectify the omission, but she said, "for her part she would not stir out of bed to please all the pixies in Devonshire." The other went down and filled the bucket, in which, by the way, she found next morning a handfull of silver pennies. As she was returning, she heard the Pixies debating about what they would do to punish the other. Various modes were proposed and rejected; at last it was agreed to give her a lame leg for a term of seven years, then to be cured by an herb growing on Dartmoor, whose name of seven syllables was pronounced in a clear and audible tone. This the girl tried by every known means to fix in her memory. But when she awoke in the morning, it was gone, and she could only tell that Molly was to be lame for seven years, and then be cured by an herb with a strange name. As for Molly, she arose dead lame, and so she continued till the end of the period, when one day, as she was picking up a mushroom, a strange-looking boy started up and insisted on *striking* her leg with a plant which he held in his hand. He did so, and she was cured and became the best dancer in the town.

Pixy-Gratitude

An old woman who lived near Tavistock had in her garden a splendid bed of tulips. To these the Pixies of the neighbourhood loved to resort, and often at midnight might they be heard singing their babes to rest among them. By their magic power they made the tulips more beautiful and more permanent than any other tulips, and. they caused them to emit a fragrance equal to that of the rose. The old woman was so fond of her tulips that she would never let one of them be plucked, and thus the Pixies were never deprived of their floral bowers.

But at length the old woman died; the tulips were taken up, and the place converted into a parsley-bed. Again, however, the power of the Pixies was shown; the parsley withered, and nothing would grow even in the other beds of the garden. On the other hand, they tended diligently the grave of the old woman, around which they were heard lamenting and singing dirges. They suffered not a weed to grow on it; they kept it always green, and evermore in sprng-time spangled with wild flowers.

Thus far for the Pixies of Devon; as for the adjoining Somerset, all we have to say is, that a good woman from that county, with whom we were acquainted, used, when making a cake, always to draw a cross upon it. This, she said, was in order to prevent the Vairies from dancing on it. She described these Vairies as being very small people, who, with the vanity natural to little personages, wear high-heeled shoes, and if a new-made cake be not duly crossed, they imprint on it in their capers the marks of their heels. Of the actual existence of the Vairies, she did not seem to entertain the shadow of a doubt.

In Dorset also, the Pixy-lore still lingers. The being is called *Pexy* and *Colepexy;* the fossil belemnitos are named Colepexies'-fingers; and the fossil echini, Colepexies'-heads. The children, when naughty, are also threatened with the Pexy, who is supposed to haunt woods and coppices. [a]

"In Hampshire," says Captain Grose, "they give the name of Colt-Pixy to a supposed spirit or fairy, which in the shape of a horse *wickers,* i. e. neighs, and misleads horses into bogs, etc."

The following is a Hampshire legend: [b]

NOTES
[a] Brand, Popular Antiquities, ii. 513. Bohn's edit.
[b] Given in the Literary Gazette for 1825. No. 430.

The Fairy Thieves

A farmer in Hampshire was sorely distressed by the unsettling of his barn. However straightly over-night he laid his sheaves on the threshing-floor for the application of the morning's flail, when morning came, all was topsy-turvy, higgledy-piggledy, though the door remained locked, and there was no sign whatever of irregular entry. Resolved to find out who played him these mischievous pranks, Hodge couched himself one night deeply among the sheaves, and watched for the enemy. At length midnight arrived, the barn was illuminated as if by moonbeams of wonderful brightness, and through the key-hole came thousands of elves, the most diminutive that could be imagined. The immediately began their gambols among the straw, which was soon in a most admired disorder. Hodge wondered, but interfered not; but at last the supernatural thieves began to busy themselves in a way still less to his taste, for each elf set about conveying the crop away, a straw at a time, with astonishing activity and perseverance. The key-hole was still their port of egress and regress, and it resembled the aperture of a bee-hive, on a sunny day in June. The farmer was rather annoyed at seeing his grain vanish in this fashion, when one of the fairies said to another in the tiniest voice that ever was heard—"*I weat, you weat?* Hodge could contain himself no longer. He leaped out crying, "The devil sweat ye. Let me get among ye!" when they all flew away so frightened that they never disturbed the barn any more.

In Suffolk the fairies are called *farisees*. Not many years ago, a butcher near Woodbridge went to a farmer's to buy a calf; and finding, as he expressed it, that "the cratur was all o' a muck," he desired the farmer to hang a flint by a string in the crib, so as to be just clear of the calf's head. "Becaze," said he, "the calf is rid every night by the *farisees,* and the stone will brush them off" [a]

We once questioned a girl from Norfolk on the subject of Fairy-lore. She said she had often heard of and even seen the *Frairies.* They were dressed in white, and lived under the ground, where they constructed houses, bridges, and other edifices. It is not safe, she added, to go near them when they appear above ground.

We now proceed to Yorkshire, where the Boggart and the Barguest used to appear in by-gone days. The former, whose name we will presently explain, is the same as the Brownie or Kobold; the latter, whose proper name perhaps is Barn-ghaist, or Barn-spirit, keeps without, and usually takes the form of some domestic animal.

NOTE
[a] Brand, Popular Antiquities, ii. 503. Bohn's edit.

The Boggart

In the house of an honest farmer in Yorkshire, named George Gilbertson, a Boggart had taken up his abode. He here caused a good deal of annoyance, especially by tormenting the children in various ways. Sometimes their bread and butter would be snatched away, or their porringers of bread and milk be capsized by an invisible hand; for the Boggart never let himself be seen; at other times, the curtains of their beds would be shaken backwards and forwards, or a heavy weight would press on and nearly suffocate them. The parents had often, on hearing their cries, to fly to their aid. There was a kind, of closet, formed by a wooden partition on the kitchen-stairs, and a large knot having been driven out of one of the deal-boards of which it was made, there remained a hole. [a] Into this one day the farmer's youngest boy stuck the shoe-horn with which he was amusing himself when immediately it was thrown out again, and struck the boy on the head. The agent was of course the Boggart, and it soon became their sport (which they called *larking* [b] *with Boggart)* to put the shoe-horn into the hole and have it shot back at them.

The Boggart at length proved such a torment that the farmer and his wife resolved to quit the house and let him have it all to himself. This was put into execution, and the farmer and his family were following the last loads of furniture, when a neighbour named John Marshall came up—"Well, Georgey," said he, "and soa you 're leaving t'ould hoose at last? "—"Heigh, Johnny, my lad, I 'm forced tull it; for that damned Boggart torments us soa, we can neither rest neet nor day for't. It seems loike to have such a malice again t'poor bairns, it ommost kills my poor dame here at thoughts on't, and soa, ye see, we're forced to flitt loike." He scarce had uttered the words when a voice from a deep upright churn cried out, "Aye, aye, Georgey, we're flitting ye see."—"Od damn thee," cried the poor farmer, "if I d known thou'd been there, I wadn't ha' stirred a peg. Nay, nay, it 's no use, Mally," turning to his wife, "we may as weel turn back again to t'ould hoose as be tormented in another that's not so convenient." [c]

NOTES

[a] The *Elfbore* of Scotland, where it is likewise ascribed to the fairies, Jamieson, *s v.* The same opinion prevails in Denmark, where it is said that any one who looks through it will see things he would not otherwise have known: see Thiele, ii. 18.

[b] from the Anglo-Saxon word to *play*.

[c] We have abridged this legend from a well-written letter in the Literary Gazette, No. 430 (1825), the writer of which says, he knew the house in which it was said to have occurred. He also says he remembered an old tailor, who said the horn was often pitched at the head of himself and his apprentice, when in the North-country fashion they went to work at the farm-house. its identity with other legends will be at once perceived.

Addlers and Menters

An old lady in Yorkshire related as follows:—My eldest daughter Betsey was about four years old; I remember it was on a fine summer's afternoon, or rather evening, I was seated in this chair which I now occupy. The child had been in the garden, she came into that entry or passage from the kitchen (on the right side of the entry was the old parlour-door, on the left the door of the common sitting-room; the mother of the child was in a line with both the doors); the child, instead of turning towards the sitting-room made a pause at the parlour-door, which was open. She stood several minutes quite still; at last I saw her draw her hand quickly towards her body; she set up a loud shriek and ran, or rather flew, to me crying out "Oh! Mammy, green man will hab me! green man will hab me!" It was a long time before I could pacify her; I then asked her why she was so frightened. "O Mammy," she said, "all t'parlour is full of *addlers* and *menters."* Elves and fairies (spectres?) I suppose she meant. She said they were dancing, and a little man in a green coat with a gold-laced cocked hat on his head, offered to take her hand as if he would have her as his partner in the dance. The mother, upon hearing this, went and looked into the old parlour, but the fairy vision had melted into thin air. "Such," adds the narrator, "is the account I heard of this vision of fairies. The person is still alive who witnessed or supposed she saw it, and though a well-informed person, still positively asserts the relation to be strictly true. [a]

Ritson, who was a native of the bishoprick of Durham, tells us [b] that the fairies frequented many parts of it; that they were described as being of the smallest size, and uniformly habited in green. They could, however, change their size and appearance. "A woman," he says, "who had been in their society challenged one of the guests whom she espied in the market selling fairy-butter. [c] This freedom was deeply resented, and cost her the eye she first saw him with. Some one informed him that an acquaintance of his in Westmoreland, wishing to see a fairy, was told that on such a day on the side of such a hill, he should be gratified. He went, and there, to use his own words, "the hobgoblin stood before him in the likeness of a green-coat lad," but vanished instantly. This, he said, the man told him. A female relation of his own told Mr. Ritson of Robin Goode fellow's, it would seem, thrashing the corn, churning the butter, drinking the milk, etc., and when all was done, lying before the fire " *like a great rough hurgin* (hugging?) *bear.*" [d]

The Menyn Tylna Têg or Fairy-butter of Wales, we are told in the same place, is a substance found at a great depth in cavities of limestone-rocks when sinking for lead-ore.

The Barguest used also to appear in the shape of a mastiff-dog and other animals, and terrify people with his *skrikes.* (shrieks). There was a Barguest named the Pick-tree Brag, whose usual form was that of a little galloway, "in which shape a farmer, still or lately living thereabouts, reported that it had come to him one night as he was going home; that he got upon it and rode very quietly till it came to a great pond, to which it ran and threw him in, and *went laughing away.*"

In Northumberland the belief in the fairies is not yet extinct. The writer from whom we derive the following legends tells us [e] that he knew an old man whose dog had *pointed* a troop of fairies, [f] and though he could not see them he plainly heard their music sounding like a fiddle and a *very small* pair of pipes. He also tells us, that many years ago a girl who lived near Nether Witton, as she was returning from milking with her pail on her head, saw the fairies playing in the fields, and though she pointed them out to her companions they could not see them. The reason it seemed was her *weise* or pad for bearing the pail on her head was composed of four-leaved clover, which gives the power of seeing fairies. Spots are pointed out in sequestered places as the favourite haunts of the elves. A few miles from Alnwick is a fairy-ring, round which if people run more than nine times, some evil will befall them. The children constantly run this number, but nothing will induce them to venture a tenth run.

NOTES

[a] And true no doubt it is, *i.e.* the impression made on her imagination was as strong as if the objects had been actually before her. The narrator is the same person who told the preceding Boggart story.

[b] Fairy Tales, pp. 24, 56.

[c] In Northumberland the common people call a certain fungous excrescence, sometimes found about the roots of old trees, Fairy-butter. After great rains and in a certain degree of putrefaction, it is reduced to a consistency, which, together with its colour, makes it not unlike butter, and hence the name. Brand, Popular Antiquities, ii. 492, Bohn's edit.

[d] Comp. Milton, L'Allegro, 105 *seq.*

[e] Richardson, Table-book, iii. 45

[f] This word, as we may sea, is spelt *faries* in the following legends; so we may suppose that *fairy* is pronounced *farry* in the North, which has a curious coincidence with *Peri.*

The Fairy-Nursling

A cottager and his wife residing at Nether Witton were one day visited by a *fary* and his spouse with their young child, which they wished to leave in their charge. The cottager agreed to take care of the child for a certain period when it had to be taken thence. The fary gave the man a box of ointment with which to anoint the child's eyes; but he had not on any account to touch himself with it, or some misfortune would befal him. For a long time he and. his wife were 'very careful to avoid the dangerous unction; but one day when his wife was out curiosity over-came his prudence, and he anointed his eyes without any noticeable effect; but after a while, when walking through Long Horsley Fair, he met the male fary and accosted him. He started back in amazement at the recognition; but instantly guessing the truth, blew on the eyes of the cottager, and instantly blinded him. The child was never more seen.

The Fairy-Labour

Another tale relates that a messenger having visited a country-mid-wife or *howdie* requested her professional assistance in a case where so much secrecy was required that she must be conducted to and from the destined place blindfolded; she at first hesitated, but her scruples were overcome by a handsome present, the promise of a future reward, and assurance of perfect personal safety. She then submitted to the required condition, mounted behind the messenger on a fleet charger, and was carried forward in an unaccountable manner. The journey was not of long continuance, the steed halted, she dismounted, and was conducted into a cottage where the band-age was removed from her eyes; everything appeared neat and com-fortable. She was shown the woman "in the straw," and performed her office; but when ready to dress the babe, an old woman, (who, according to the narration, appears to have been the nurse,) put a box of ointment into her hand, requiring her to anoint the child all over with it, but to be careful that it dld not touch her own person; she prudently complied, though wondering at the motive. Whilst this operation was going on, she felt an itching in one of her eyes, and in an unguarded moment rubbed it with a finger which had touched the mysterious ointment. And now a new scene forced itself upon her astonished vision, and she saw everything in a different light; instead of the neat cottage, she perceived the large overhanging branches of an ancient oak, whose hollow and moss-grown trunk she had before mistaken for the fire place, glow-worms supplied the place of lamps, and, in short, she found herself in the abode of a family of faries, with faries was she surrounded, and one of their number reposed on her lap. She however retained her self-possession, finished her task, and was conducted homeward in the same manner as she was brought. So far all went well, and the *howdie* might have carried the secret to her grave, but in after time, on a market-day (in what town the legend saith not,) forgetful of her former caution, she saw the old. nurse among the countrywomen, gliding about from one basket to another, passing a little wooden scraper along the rolls of butter, and carefully collecting the particles thus purloined into a vessel hung 'by her side. After a mutual but silent recognition, the nurse addressed her thus, "Which eye do you see me with?"' "With this," innocently answered the other. No sooner had she spoken than a puff from the withering breath of her unearthly companion extinguished the ill-fated orb for ever, and the hag instantly vanished.

Another version says the Doctor is presented with a box of eye-salve by his conductor; on using it he sees a splendid portico in the side of a steep hill, through this he is shown into the faries' hall in the interior of the mountain: he performs his office, and on coming out receives a second box; he rubs one eye, and with it sees the hill in its natural shape; then thinking to cheat the devil, feigns to rub the other, and gallops off. Afterwards he sees the fary's husband stealing corn in the market, when similar consequences befal him as those which occurred unto the woman.

Ainsel and Puck

A widow and her son, a little boy, lived, together in a cottage in or near the village of Rothley, Northumberland. One winter's evening the child refused to go to bed with his mother, as he wished to sit up for a while longer, "for," said he, "I am not sleepy." The mother finding remonstrance in vain, at last told him that if he sat up by himself the faries would most certainly come and take him away. The boy laughed as his mother went to bed, leaving him sitting by the fire; he had not been there long, watching the fire and enjoying its cheerful warmth, till a beautiful little figure, about the size of a child's doll, descended the chimney and alighted on the hearth! The little fellow was somewhat startled at first, but its prepossessing smile as it paced to and fro before him soon overcame his fears, and he inquired familiarly, "What do they ca' thou?" "Ainsel," answered the little thing haughtily, at the same time retorting the question, "And what do they ca'*thou?*" "*My* ainsel'," answered the boy; and they commenced playing together like two children newly acquaint- ed. Their gambols continued quite innocently until the fire began to grow dim; the boy then took up the poker to stir it, when a hot cinder accidentally fell upon the foot of his playmate; her tiny voice was instantly raised to a most terrific roar, and the boy had scarcely time to crouch into the bed behind his mother, before the voice of the old fary-mother was heard shouting, "Who's done it? 'Who's done it?" "Oh! it was my ainsel!" answered the daughter. "Why, then," said the mother, as she kicked her up the chimney, "what 's all this noise for: there's nyon (*i.e.* no one) to blame."

* * *

Such is the sum of what we have been able to collect respecting the popular fairy-lore of England, the largest and most complete collection that, to our knowledge, has ever been made. We might venture to add that little more is ever likely to be collected, for the sounds of the cotton-mill, the steam-engine, and, more than all, the whistle of the railway train, more powerful than any exorcists, have banished, or soon will banish, the fairy tribes from all their accustomed haunts, and their name and their exploits will in future be found in works like the present rather than in village tradition.

As the merry spirit, Puck, is so prominent an actor in the scenes forming our next division, this may be deemed no unfitting place for the consideration of his various appellations; such as Puck, Robin Good-fellow, Robin Hood, Hobgoblin.

Puck is evidently the same with the old word *Pouke,* [a] the original meaning of which would seem to be devil, demon, or evil spirit. We first meet with it in the Vision of Piers Ploughman, where it undoubtedly signifies 'the grand adversary of God and man.'

When, in this poem, [b] the Seer beholds Abraham, the personification of Faith, with his "wide clothes," within which lay a Lazar,

Amonges patriarkes and prophetes,
Pleying togideres,
and asks him what was there,
Loo! quod he, and leet me see.
Ne no buyrn be oure borgh,
Lord mercy! I seide;
Ne bringe us from his daunger;

This is a present of muche pris,
Out of the *pouke pondfold*
What prynce shal it have?
No maynprise may us fecche,
It is a precious present, quod he,
Til he come that I carpe of,
Ac the *pouke* it hath attached,
Crist is his name,
And me theremyde, quod that
That shall delivere us som day man,
Out of the *develes* power.
May no wed us quyte,

Golding also must have understood Pooke in the sense of devil, when in the ninth book of his translation of Ovid, unauthorised however by the original, he applies it to the Chimaera,

The country where Chymsara, that same *pooke*
Hath goatish body, lion's head and brist, and dragon's tayle.

Spenser employs the word, and he clearly distinguishes it from hob-goblin:

Ne let housefires nor lightnings helpless harms,
Ne let the *pouke* [c] nor other evil sprites,
Ne let mischievous witches with their charms,
No let *hob-goblins,* names whom sense we see not,
Fray us with things that be not—*Epithalamion,* v. 340.

These terms are also distinguished in the poem named The Scourge of Venus:

And that they may perceive the heavens frown,
The *poukes* and *goblins* pull the coverings down.

In Ben Jonson's play of *The Devil is an Ass,* the unlucky fiend who gives origin to its name is called Pug, and in the same author's Sad Shepherd the personage named Puck-hairy is, as Gifford justly observes, "not the Fairy or Oriental Puck, though often confounded with him." [d] In truth, it is first in Shakespeare that we find Puck confounded with the House-spirit, and having those traits of character which are now regarded as his very essence, and have caused his name Pug to be given to the agile mischievous monkey, and to a kind of little dog.

We will now discuss the origin of this far-famed appellation and its derivation.

In the Slavonic tongues, which are akin to the Teutonic, *Bôg* is God, and there are sleights of etymology which would identify the two terms; the Icelandic Puki is an evil spirit, and such we have seen was the English Pouke, which easily became Puck, Pug, and Bug; finally, in Friesland the Kobold is called Puk, and in old German we meet with Putt or Butz as the name of a being not unlike the original English Puck.[e] The Devonshire fairies are called Pixies, and the Irish have their Pooka, and the Welsh their Pwcca, both derived from Pouke or Puck. From Bug comes the Scottish Bogle, (which Gawin Douglas expressly distinguishes from the Brownie) and the Yorkshire Boggart. [f] The Swedish language has the terms *spöka, spöke;* the Danish *spöge, spögelse,* the German, *spuken, spuk,* all used of spirits or ghosts, and their apparitions. Perhaps the Scottish *pawkey,* sly, knowing, may belong to the same family of words. Akin to Bogle was the old English term Puckle, noticed above, which is still retained in the sense of mischievous, as in Peregrine Pickle and Little Pickle. It has been conjectured [8] that *Picklehäring,* the German term for zany or merry-andrew, may have been properly *Picklehärin, i.e.* the hairy sprite, answering to Jonson's Puck-hairy, and that he may have worn a vesture of hair or leaves to be rough like the Brownie and kindred beings.

From Bug also come Bugbear, and Bugleboo, or Bugaboo. They owe their origin probably to the Ho! Ho! Ho! given to Puck or Robin Goodfellow, as it was to the Devil *(i.e.,* Pouke) in the Mysteries. Bull-beggar may be only a corruption of Bugbear. [h]

The following passage from a writer of the present day proves that in some places the idea of Puck as a spirit haunting the woods and fields is still retained. "The peasantry" says Mr. Allies, [i] "of Alfrick and those parts of Worcestershire, say that they are some-times what they call *Poake-ledden,* that is, that they are occasionally waylaid in the night by a mischievous sprite whom they call Poake, who leads them into ditches, bogs, pools, and. other such scrapes, and then sets up a loud laugh and leaves them quite bewildered in the lurch." This is what in Devon is called being *Pixy-led.* We may observe the likeness here to the Puck of Shakspeare and Drayton, who were both natives of the adjoining county.

A further proof perhaps of Puck's rural and extern character is the following rather trifling circumstance. An old name of the fun-gus named *puffball* is *puck-fist,* which is plainly Puck's-fist, and not *puff-fist* as Nares conjectured; for its Irish name is *Cos-a-Phooka,* or Pooka's-foot, *i.e.,* Puck's-foot. We will add by the way, that the Anglo-Saxon, Wolf's-fist, is rendered in the dictionaries toadstool, mushroom, and we cannot help suspecting that as wolf and elf were sometimes confounded, and wolf and fist are, in fact, incompatible terms, this was originally Elf's-fist, and that the mushrooms meant were not the thick ugly toadstools, the "grislie todestooles," of Spenser, but those delicate fungi called in Ireland *fairy-mushrooms* and which perhaps in England also were ascribed to the fairies. [i]

So much then for Puck; we will now consider some other terms.

Robin Goodfellow, of whom we have given above a full account, is evidently a domestic spirit, answering in name and character to the Nisse God-dreng of Scandinavia, the Knecht Ruprecht, *i.e.,* Robin of Germany. He seems to unite in his person the Boggart and Barguest of Yorkshire.

Hob-goblin is, as we have seen, another name of the same spirit. Goblin is the French *gobelin,* German Kobold; Hob is Rob, Robin, Bob; just as Hodge is Roger. We still have the proper names Hobbs, Hobson, like Dix, Dixon, Wills, Wilson; by the way, Hick, *i. e.* Dick, from Richard, still remains in Hicks, Hickson.

Robin Hood, though we can produce no instance of it, must, we think, also have been an appellation of this spirit, and been given to the famed outlaw of merry Sherwood, from his sportive character and his abiding in the recesses of the greenwood. The hood is a usual appendage of the domestic spirit.

Roguery and sportiveness are, we may see, the characteristics of this spirit. Hence it may have been that the diminutives of proper names were given to him, and even to the Ignis Fatuus, which in a country like England, that was in general dry and free from sloughs and bog-holes, was mischievous rather than dangerous. [k] But this seems to have been a custom of our forefathers, for we find the devil himself called Old Nick, and Old Davy is the sailor's familiar name for Death.

In the Midsummer Night's Dream the fairy says to Puck "Thou Lob of spirits;" Milton has the *lubber-fiend,* and Fletcher says, [l] "There is a pretty tale of a witch that had a giant to be her son that was called Lob Lie-by-the-fire." This might lead us to suppose that *Lob,* whence *loby* (looby), *lubbard, lubber,* [m] and adding the diminutive *kin,* Lubberkin, a name of one of the clowns in Gay's Pastorals, was an original name of some kind of spirit. We shall presently see that the Irish name of the Leprechaun is actually Lubberkin. As to the origin of the name we have little to say, but it may have had a sense the very opposite of the present one of *lubber,* and have been connected with the verb *to leap.* [n] Grimm [o] tells of a spirit named the Good Lubber, to whom the bones of animals used to be offered at Mansfield in Germany; but we see no resemblance between him and our Lob of spirits; we might rather trace a connexion with the French Lutin, Lubin. [p] The phrase of *being in* or *getting into Lob's Pound* (like the "Pouke's pondfold,") is easy of explanation, if we suppose Lob to be a sportive spirit. it is equivalent to being *Poake-ledden* or *Pixy-led.*

Wight, answering to the German *Wicht,* seems to have been used in the time of Chaucer for elf or fairy, most probably for such as haunted houses, or it may have had the signification of *witch,* which is evidently another form of it. In the Miller's Tale the carpenter says, l crouchè thee from elves and from *wights.*

And

Jesu Crist, and Seint Benedight,
Blisse this house from every wicked *wight.* [q]

Urchin is a term which, like *elf* and such like, we still apply to children, but which seems formerly to have been one of the appellations of the fairies. Reginald Scott, as we have seen, places it in his list, and we find it in the following places of the poets:

Urchins
Shall for the vast of night that they may work
All exercise on *thee.—Tempest,* i. 2.
His spirits hear me,
And yet l needs must curse; but they'll not pinch
Fright me with *urchin-shows,* pitch me i' the mire,
Nor lead me like a fire-brand in the dark
Out of my way, unless he bid '*em.—lb.* ii. 2.

Like *urchins,* ouphs, and fairies.
Merry Wives of Windsor, iv. 4.

Elves, *urchins,* goblins all, and little fairyes.
Mad Pranks, etc., p.38.

Great store of goblins, fairies, bugs, nightmares,
Urchins, and elves, to many a house repairs.
Old Poem, in Brand, ii. 514.

Trip it, litttle *urchins* all.
Maid's Metamorphosis.
Helping all *urchin-blasts* and ill-luck signs,
That the shrewd meddling elfe delights to make.
Comas, 845.

Urchin is a hedgehog, as Stevens has justly observed,[r] and in these lines of Titus Andronicus (ii. 3.)

> A thousand fiends, a thousand hissing snakes,
> Ten thousand swelling toads, as many *urchins,*

it probably has this sense. We still call the *echinus marinus* the Sea-urchin. Still as we have no analogy, but rather the contrary, for transferring the name of an animal to the elves, we feel inclined to look for a different origin of the term as applied to these beings. The best or rather only hypothesis we have met with [s] is that which finds it in the hitherto unexplained word *Orcneas* in Beówulf which may have been *Orcenas,* and if, as we have supposed [t] the Anglo-Saxons sometimes pronounced *c* before *e* and *i* in the Italian manner, we should have, if needed, the exact word. We would also notice the old German *urkinde,* which Grimm renders *nanus.* [u]

We now come to the poets.

In Beówulf, an Anglo-Saxon poem, supposed not to be later than the seventh century, we meet with the following verse,

> "Eotenas, and Ylfe,
> And Orcneas."

The first of these words is evidently the same as the lötunn or Giants of the northern mythology; the second is as plainly its Alfar, and we surely may be excused for supposing that the last may be the same as its Duergar.

Layamon, in the twelfth century, in his poetic paraphrase of Wace's Brut, [v] thus expands that poet's brief notice of the birth of

Arthur:

> "Ertur son nom; de sa bunte
> Ad grant parole puis este."
> So soon he came on earth,
> Elves received him.
> They enchanted that child
> With magic most strong.
> They gave him might
> To be the best of all knights.
> They gave him another king.
> They gave him the third
> That he should long live.
> They gave to that kingly child
> Virtues most good.
> That he was most generous
> Of all men alive.
> This the Elves him gave,
> vv 19254: *seq.*

If we have made any discovery of importance in the department of romantic literature, it is our identification of Ogier le Danois with the Eddaic Helgi. [w] We have shown among other points of resemblance, that as the Norns were at the birth of the one, so the Fées were at that of the other. With this circumstance Layamon was apparently acquainted, and when he wished to transfer it to Arthur as the Norns were no longer known and the Fées had not yet risen into importance, there only remained for him to employ the Elves, which had not yet acquired tiny dimensions. Hence then we see that the progress was Norns, Elves, Fées, and these last held their place in the subsequent Fairy tales of France and Italy.

These potent Elves are still superior to the popular Fairies which we first met with in Chaucer.

Yet nothing in the passages in which he speaks of them leads to the inference of his conceiving them to be of a diminutive stature. His notions, indeed, on the subject seem very vague and unsettled; and there is something like a confusion of the Elves and Fairies of Romance, as the following passages will show:—

The Wife of Bathes Tale is evidently a Fairy tale. It thus commences:

> In oldê dayès of the king Artoúr,
> Of which that Bretons speken gret honoúr,
> All was this lond fulfilled of faerie; [x]
> The Elf-quene with her joly compagnie,
> Danced ful oft in many a grenè mede.
> This was the old opinion as I rede;
> I speke of many hundred yeres ago.
> But now can no man see non elvès mo,
> For now the gretè charitee and prayéres
> Of limitoures, and other holy freres,
> That serchen every land and every streme,
> As thikke as motes in the sonnè-beme,
> Blissing halles, chambres, kichenès, and boures,
> Citees and burghès, castles highe, and toures,
> Thropès [y] and bernès, shepenes and dairiés,
> This maketh that there ben no faëries;
> For there as wont to walken was an elf,
> There walketh now the limitour himself,
> In undermelès, [z] and in morweninges,
> And sayth his matines and his holy thinges,
> As he goth in his limitatioun.
> Women may now go safely up and down;
> In every bush and under every tree
> There is none other incubus but he,
> And he ne will don hem no dishonoúr.

The Fairies therefore form a part of the tale, and they are thus introduced:

> The day was come that homward must he turne;
> And in his way it happed him to ride,
> In all his care, under a forest side,
> Wheras he saw upon a dancè go
> Of ladies foure and twenty, and yet mo:
> Toward this ilke dance he drow ful yerne,
> In hope that he som wisdom shuldè lerne;
> But certainly, er he came fully there,
> Yvanished was this dance, he n'iste not wher;
> No creäture saw he that barè lif,
> Save on the grene he saw sitting a wif,
> A fouler wight ther may no man devise.

These ladies bear a great resemblance to the Elle-maids of Scandinavia. We need hardly inform our readers that this "foul wight" becomes the knight's deliverer from the imminent danger he is in, and that, when he has been forced to marry her, she is changed into a beautiful young maiden. But who or what she was the poet sayeth not.

In the Marchantes Tale we meet the Faerie attendant on Pluto and Proserpina, their king and queen, a sort of blending of classic and Gothic mythology:

> for to tell
> The beautee of the gardin, and the well
> That stood under a laurer alway grene;
> Ful often time he Pluto, and his quene
> Proserpina, and alle hir faerie [aa]
> Disporten hem, and maken melodie
> About that well, and daunced, as men told.

Again, in the same Tale:
And so befel in that bright morwe tide,
That, in the gardin, on the ferther side,
Pluto, that is the king of Faerie,
And many a ladye in his compagnie,
Folwing his wif, the quene Proserpina,
Which that he ravisshed out of Ethná,
While that she gadred floures in the mede,
(In Claudian ye may the story rede,
How that hire in his grisely carte he fette);
This king of Faërie adoun him sette
Upon a benche of turvès, fresh and grene.

... to be continued ...

In the conversation which ensues between these august personages, great knowledge of Scripture is displayed; and the queen, speaking, of the "sapient prince," passionately exclaims—

I setè nat of all the vilanie
That he of women wrote a boterflie;
I am a woman nedès moste I speke,
Or swell unto that time min hertè breke.

Some might suspect a mystery in the queen's thus emphatically styling herself a woman, but we lay no stress upon it, as Faire Damoselle Pertelote, the hen, who was certainly less entitled to it, does the same.

In the Man of Lawes Tale the word Elfe is employed, but whether as equivalent to witch or fairy is doubtful.

This lettre spake, the quene delivered was
Of so horrible a fendliche creäture,
That in the castle, non so hardy was,
That any whilè dorste therein endure.
The mother was an *elfe* by áventure,
Y come, by charmès or by sorcerie,
And everich man hateth hire conlpagnie. [ab]

The Rime of Sir Thopas has been already considered as belonging to romance.

It thus appears that the works of manners-painting Chaucer give very little information respecting the popular belief in Fairies of his day. Were it not for the sly satire of the passage, we might be apt to suspect that, like one who lived away from the common people, he was willing to represent the superstition as extinct—"But now can no man see non elves mo." The only trait that he gives really characteristic of the popular elves is their love of dancing.

In the poets that intervene between Chaucer and the Maiden Reign, we do not recollect to have noticed anything of importance respecting Fairies, except the employment, already adverted to, of that term, and that of Elves, by translators in rendering the Latin *Nymphae*. Of the size of these beings, the passages in question give no information.

But in Elizabeth's days, "Fairies," as Johnson observes, "were much in fashion; common tradition had made them familiar, and Spenser's poem had made them great." A just remark, no doubt, though Johnson fell into the common error of identifying Spenser's Fairies with the popular ones.

The three first books of the Faerie Queene were published in

1590, and, as Warton remarks, Fairies became a familiar and fashionable machinery with the poets and poetasters. Shakspeare, well acquainted, from the rural habits of his early life, with the notions of the peasantry respecting these beings, and highly gifted with the prescient power of genius, saw clearly how capable they were of being applied to the production of a species of the wonderful, as pleasing, or perhaps even more so, than the classic gods; and in the Midsummer-Night's Dream he presented them in combination with the heroes and heroines of the mythic age of Greece. But what cannot the magic wand of genius effect? We view with undisturbed delight the Elves of Gothic mythology sporting in the groves of Attica,, the legitimate haunts of Nymphs and Satyrs.

Shakspeare, having the Faerie Queene before his eyes, seems to have attempted a blending of the Elves of the village with the Fays of romance. His Fairies agree with the former in their diminutive stature,—diminished, indeed, to dimensions inappreciable by village gossips,—in their fondness for dancing, their love of cleanliness, and their child-abstracting propensities. Like the Fays, they form a community, ruled over by the princely Oberon and the fair Titania. [ac] There is a court and chivalry: Oberon would have the queen's sweet changeling to be a "Knight of his train to trace the forest wild." Like earthly monarchs, he has his jester, "the shrewd and knavish sprite, called Robin Good-fellow."

The luxuriant imagination of the poet seemed to exult in pouring forth its wealth in the production of these new actors on the mimic scene, and a profusion of poetic imagery always appears in their train. Such lovely and truly British poetry cannot be too often brought to view; we will therefore insert in this part of our work several of these gems of our Parnassus, distinguishing by a different character such acts and attributes as appear properly to belong to the Fairy of popular belief.

MIDSUMMER-NIGHTS DREAM.   ACT II—SCENE I.

Puck and a Fairy.

Puck. How now, spirit! whither wander you?

Fai. Over hill, over dale,
Thorough bush, thorough briar,
Over park, over pale,
Thorough flood, thorough fire.
I do wander every where,
Swifter than the moonès sphere,
And I serve the Fairy-queen,
To dew her orbs upon the green.
The cowslips tall her pensioners be;
In their gold coats spots you see.
Those be rubies, fairy favours,
In those freckles live their savours.
I must go seek some dew-drops here,
And hang a pearl in every cowslip's ear. [ad]
Farewell, thou lob of spirits! I'll be gone;
Our queen and all her elves come here anon.

Puck. The king doth keep his revels here to-night
Take heed the queen come not within his sight;
For Oberon is passing fell and wroth,
Because that she, as her attendant, hath
A lovely boy stolen from an Indian king,—
She never had so sweet a changeling;
And jealous Oberon would have the child
Knight of his train, to trace the forests wild;
But she, perforce, withholds the loved boy,
Crowns him with flowers, and makes him all her joy;
And now they never meet in grove or green,
By fountain clear, or spangled star-light sheen,
But they do square; that all their elves, for fear,
Creep into acorn cups, and hide them there.

Fai. Either I mistake your shape and making quite,
Or else you are that shrewd and knavish sprite
Call'd Robin Good-fellow. Are you not he
That frights the maidens of the villagery,
Skims milk, and sometimes labours in the quern,
And bootless makes the breathless housewife churn;

And sometimes makes the drink to bear no barm;
Misleads night-wanderers, laughing at their harm?
Those that Hob-goblin call you, and sweet Puck.
You do their work, and they shall have good luck,
Are not you he?
Puck. Thou speakest aright,
I am that merry wanderer of the night.
I jest to Oberon, and make him smile,
When I a fat and bean-fed horse beguile,
Neighing in likeness of a filly-foal;
And sometimes lurk I in a gossip's bowl,
In very likeness of a roasted crab,
And when she drinks, against her lips I bob,
And on her withered dewlap pour the ale.
The wisest aunt, telling the saddest tale,
Sometimes for three-foot stool mistaketh me:
Then slip I from her bum,—down topples she,
And *tailor* cries, and falls into a cough;
And then the whole quire hold their hips and loffe,
And waxen in their mirth, and neeze, and swear
A merrier hour was never wasted there.

The haunts of the Fairies on earth are the most rural and romantic that can be selected. They meet

On hill, in dale, forest or mead,
By paved fountain, or by rushy brook,
Or on the beached margent of the sea,
To dance their ringlets to the whistling wind.
And the place of Titania's repose is
A bank whereon the wild thyme blows,
Where oxlips and the nodding violet grows,
Quite over-canopied with lush woodbine,
With sweet musk-roses, and with eglantine.
There sleeps Titania, some time of the night
Lull'd in these flowers with dances and delight;
And there the snake throws her enamell'd skin,
Weed wide enough to wrap a fairy in.

The powers of the poet are exerted to the utmost, to convey an idea of their minute dimensions; and time, with them, moves on lazy pinions. "Come," cries the queen,

> Come now, a roundel and a fairy song,
> Then for the third part of a minute hence:
> Some to kill cankers in the musk-rose buds;
> Some war with rear-mice for their leathern wings,
> To make my small elves coats.

And when enamoured of Bottom, she directs her Elves that they should

> Hop in his walks and gambol in his eyes;
> Feed him with apricocks and dewberries,
> With purple grapes, green figs, and mulberries.
> The honey-bags steal from the humble-bees,
> And for night-tapers crop their waxen thighs,
> And light them at the fiery glow-worm's eyes;
> To have my love to bed, and to arise
> And pluck the wings from painted butterflies,
> To fan the moon-beams from his sleeping eyes.

Puck goes "swifter than arrow from the Tartar's bow;" he says, "he'll put a girdle round about the earth in forty minutes;" and "We," says Oberon—

> We the globe can compass soon,
> Swifter than the wandering moon.

They are either not mortal, or their date of life is indeterminately long; they are of a nature superior to man, and speak with contempt of human follies. By night they revel beneath the light of the moon and stars, retiring at the approach of "Aurora's harbinger," [ae] but not compulsively like ghosts and "damned spirits."

But we (says Oberon) are spirits of another sort;
I with the morning's love have oft made sport,
And like a forester the groves may tread,
Even till the eastern gate, all fiery red,
Opening on Neptune with fair blessed beams,
Turns into yellow gold his salt-green streams.

In the Merry Wives of Windsor, we are introduced to mock-fairies, modelled, of course, after the real ones, but with such additions as the poet's fancy deemed itself authorised to adopt.

Act IV., Scene IV., Mrs. Page, after communicating to Mrs. Ford her plan of making the fat knight disguise himself as the ghost of Herne the hunter, adds—

Nan Page, my daughter, and my little son,
And three or four more of their growth, we'll dress
Like urchins, ouphes, [af] and fairies, green and white,
With rounds of waxen tapers on their heads,
And rattles in their hands.

* * *

Then let them all encircle him about,
And, *fairy-like, to-pinch* the unclean knight,
And ask him why that hour of fairy revel
In their so sacred paths he dares to tread
In shape profane.

And

My Nan shall be the queen of all the fairies,
Finely attired in a robe of white.

In Act V., Scene V., the plot being all arranged, the Fairy rout appears, headed by Sir Hugh, as a Satyr, by ancient Pistol as Hob-goblin, and by Dame Quickly.

Quick. Fairies black, grey, green, and white,
You moonshine revellers and shades of night,
You orphan heirs of fixed destiny, [ag]
Attend your office and your quality.
Crier Hob-goblin, make the fairy O-yes.
Pist. Elves, list your names! silence, you airy toys!
Cricket, to Windsor chimneys shalt thou leap;
Where fires thou findest unraked, and hearthe waswept,
There pinch the maids as blue as bilberry:
Our radiant queen hates slats and sluttery.
Fals. They are fairies; *he that speaks to them shall die.*
I'll wink and couch; no man their works must eye.
Pist. Where's Bead?—Go you, and where you find a maid
That, ere she sleep, has thrice her prayers said,
Raise up the organs of her fantasy,
Sleep she as sound as careless infancy;
But those as sleep and think not on their sins,
Pinch them, arms, legs, backs, shoulders, sides, and shins.
Quick. About, about,
Search Windsor castle, elves, within and out;
Strew good luck, ouphes, on every sacred room,
That it may stand till the perpetual doom,
In state as wholesome as in state 'tis fit;
Worthy the owner, and the owner it.
The several chairs of order look you scour
With juice of balm and every precious flower;
Each fair instalment, coat, and several crest,
With loyal blazon evermore be blest;
And nightly, meadow-fairies, look, you sing,
Like to the Garter's compass, *in a ring:*
The expressure that it bears green let it be,
More fertile-fresh than all the field to see;
And "Hony soit qui mal y pense" write,
In emerald tufts, flowers, purple, blue, and white;
Like sapphire, pearl, and rich embroidery,

Buckled below fair knighthood's bending knee:
Fairies use flowers for their charactery.
Away—disperse!—but, till 'tis one o'clock,
Our dance of custom, round about the oak
Of Herne the hunter, let us not forget.
Era. Pray you, lock hand in hand, yourselves in order set,
And twenty glow-worms shall our lanterns be,
To guide our measure round about the tree;
But stay, I smell a man of middle earth.
Fal. Heaven defend me from that Welsh fairy, lest
He transform me to a piece of cheese.
Pist. Vile worm! thou west o'erlook'd even in thy birth.
Quick. With trial fire touch we his finger-end:
If he be chaste the flame will back descend,
And turn him to no pain; but if he start,
it is the flesh of a corrupted heart.
Pist. A trial, come.
Eva. Come, will this wood take fire?
Fal'. Oh, oh, oh!
Quick. Corrupt, corrupt, and tainted in desire:
About him, fairies, sing a scornful rime;
And, as you trip, still pinch him to your time.

In Romeo and. Juliet the lively and gallant Mercutio mentions a fairy personage, who has since attained to great celebrity, and completely dethroned Titania, we mean Queen Mab, [ah] a dame of credit and renown in Faëry.

"I dreamed a dream to-night," says Romeo.
"O then," says Mercutio:
O then, I see Queen Mab hath been with you.
She is the fairies' midwife; and she comes,
In shape no bigger than an agate-stone
On the forefinger of an alderman,
Drawn with a team of little atomies,
Over men's noses as they lie asleep:
Her waggon-spokes made of long spinners' legs;

The cover, of the wings of grasshoppers;
The traces, of the smallest spider's web;
The collars of the moonshine's watery beams:
Her whip of cricket's bone; the lash of film:
Her waggoner, a small gray-coated gnat,
Not half so big as a round little worm
Prick'd from the lazy finger of a maid;
Her chariot is an empty hazel-nut,
Made by the joiner squirrel or old grub,
Time out of mind the fairies' coachmakers.

* * *

This is that very Mab
That pleats the manes of horses in the night;
And bakes the elf-locks in foul sluttish hairs,
Which once untangled, much misfortune bode.
This is the hag, [ai] *when maids lie on their backs,*
That *presses them.*

In an exquisite and well-known passage of the Tempest, higher and. more awful powers are ascribed to the Elves: Prospero declares that by their aid he has "bedimmed the noon-tide sun;" called forth the winds and thunder; set roaring war "twixt the green sea and the azured vault;" shaken promontories, and plucked up pines and cedars. He thus invokes them:—

Ye elves of hills, brooks, standing lakes, and groves; [ai]
And ye, that on the sands with printless foot
Do chase the ebbing Neptune, and do fly him,
When he comes back; you demi-puppets that
By moonshine do the green-sour ringlets make,
Whereof the ewe not bites; and you whose pastime
Is to make midnight-mushrooms, that rejoice
To hear the solemn curfew.

The other dramas of Shakspeare present a few more characteristic traits of the Fairies, which should not be omitted.

> Some say that ever 'gainst that season comes
> Wherein our Saviour's birth is celebrated,
> This bird of dawning singeth all night long;
> And then they say no spirit dares stir abroad;
> The nights are wholesome; then no planet strikes,
> *No fairy tales,* [ak] no witch hath power to charm,
> So hallow'd and so gracious is that time.
> *Hamlet,* Act i.sc. 1.

> King Henry IV. wishes it could be proved,
> *That some night-tripping fairy had exchanged*
> *In cradle-clothes our children where they lay,*
> And called mine—Percy, his—Plantagenet!

The old shepherd in the Winter's Tale, when he finds Perdita,
exclaims,

> It was told me, I should be rich, by the fairies: this is some
> changeling.

And when his son tells him it is gold that is within the "bear-
ing-cloth," he says,

> This is fairy-gold, boy, and 'twill prove so. We are lucky, boy, and
> *to be so still requires nothing but secresy.* [al]

In Cymbeline, the innocent Imogen commits herself to sleep
with these words:

> To your protection I commit me, gods!
> *From fairies and the tempters of the night,*
> *Guard me,* beseech ye!

And when the two brothers see her in their cave, one cries—

But that it eats our victuals, I should think
Here were a fairy.

And thinking her to be dead, Guiderius declares—

If he be gone, he'll make his grave a bed;
With female fairies will his tomb be haunted,
And worms will not come to thee.

The Maydes Metamorphosis of Lylie was acted in 1600, the year the oldest edition we possess of the Midsummer Night's Dream was printed. In Act II. of this piece, Mopso, Joculo, and Frisio are on the stage, and "Enter the Fairies singing and dancing."

By the moon we sport and play,
With the night begins our day;
As we dance the dew doth fall—
Trip it, little urchins all,
Lightly as the little bee,
Two by two, and three by three;
And about go we, and about go we.
Jo. What mawmets are these?
Fris. O they be the faieries that haunt these woods.
Mop. O we shall be pinched most cruelly!
1st *Fai.* Will you have any music, sir?
2d *Fai.* Will you have any fine music?
3d Fai. Most dainty music?
Mop. We must set a face on it now; there is no flying.
No, sir, we very much thank you.
1st Fai. O but you shall, sir.
Fris. No, I pray you, save your labour.
2d Fai. O, sir! it shall not cost you a penny.
Jo. Where be your fiddles?
3d Fai. You shall have most dainty instruments, sir?
Mop. I pray you, what might I call you?

1st Fai. My name is Penny.
Mop. I am sorry I cannot purse you.

Fris. I pray you, sir, what might I call you?

2d Fai. My name is Cricket.

Fris. I would I were a chimney for your sake.

Jo. I pray you, you pretty little fellow, what's your name?

3d Fai. My name is little little Prick.

Jo. Little little Prick? O you are a dangerous faierie!
I care not whose hand I were in, so I were out of yours.

1st Fai. I do come about the coppes.
Leaping upon flowers' toppes;
Then I get upon a fly,
She carries me about the sky,
And trip and go.

2d Fai. When a dew-drop falleth down,
And doth light upon my crown.
Then I shake my head and skip,
And about I trip.

3d Fai. When I feel a girl asleep,
Underneath her frock I peep,
There to sport, and there I play,
Then I bite her like a flea,
And about I skip.

Jo. I thought where I should have you.

1st Fai. Will 't please you dance, sir?

Jo. Indeed, sir, I cannot handle my legs.

2d Fai. O you must needs dance and sing,
Which if you refuse to do,
We will pinch you black and blue;
And about we go.

They all dance in a ring, and sing as followeth:
Round about, round about, in a fine ring a,
Thus we dance, thus we dance, and thus we sing a;
Trip and go, to and fro, over this green a,
All about, in and out, for our brave queen a.
Round about, round about, in a fine ring a,
Thus we dance, thus we dance, and thus we sing a;
Trip and go, to and fro, over this green a,
All about, in and out, for our brave queen a.
We have danced round about, in a fine ring a,
We have danced lustily, and thus we sing a;

All about, in and out, over this green a,
To and fro, trip and go, to our brave queen a.

The next poet, in point of time, who employs the Fairies, is worthy, long-slandered, and maligned Ben Jonson. His beautiful entertainment of the Satyr was presented in 1603, to Anne, queen of James I. and prince Henry, at Althorpe, the seat of Lord Spenser, on their way from Edinburgh to London. As the queen and prince entered the park, a Satyr came forth from a "little spinet" or copse, and having gazed the "Queen and the Prince in the face" with admiration, again retired into the thicket; then "there came tripping up the lawn a bevy of Fairies attending on Mab, their queen, who, falling into an artificial ring, began to dance a round while their mistress spake as followeth:"

> *Mab.* Hail and welcome, worthiest queen!
> Joy had never perfect been,
> To the nymphs that haunt this green,
> Had they not this evening seen.
> *Now they print it on the ground*
> *With their feet, in figures round;*
> Marks that will be ever found
> To remember this glad stound.
> *Satyr (peeping out of the bush).*
> Trust her not, you bonnibell,
> She will forty leasings tell;
> I do know her pranks right well.
> *Mab.* Satyr, we must have a spell,
> For your tongue it runs too fleet.
> *Sat.* Not so nimbly as your feet,
> When about the cream-bowls sweet
> You and all your elves do meet.

(Here he came hopping forth, and mixing himself with the Fairies, skipped in, out, and about their circle, while they made many offers to catch him.)

This is Mab, the mistress Fairy,
That doth nightly rob the dairy;
And can hurt or kelp the churning
As she please, without discerning.
1st Fai. Pug, you will anon take warning.
Sat. She that pinches country wenches,
If they rub not clean their benches,
And, with sharper nail, remembers
When they roke not up their embers;
But if so they chance to feast her,
In a shoe she drops a tester.
2d Fai. Shall we strip the skipping jester?
Sat. This is she that empties cradles,
Takes out children, puts in ladles;
Trains forth midwives in their slumber,
With a sieve the holes to number,
And then leads them from her burrows,
Home through ponds and water-furrows. [am]
1st Fai. Shall not all this mocking stir us?
Sat. She can start our Franklin's daughters
In her sleep with shouts and laughters;
And on sweet St. Anna's [an] night
Feed them with a promised sight
Some of husbands, some of lovers,
Which an empty dream discovers.
1st Fai. Satyr, vengeance near you hovers.
At length Mab is provoked, and she cries out,
Fairies, pinch him black and blue.
Now you have him make him rue.
Sat. O hold, mistress Mab, I sue!

Mab, when about to retire, bestows a jewel on the Queen, and concludes with,

Utter not, we you implore,
Who did give it, nor wherefore.
And whenever you restore
Yourself to us you shall have more.
Highest, happiest queen, farewell,
But, beware you do not tell.

The splendid Masque of Oberon, presented in 1610, introduces the Fays in union with the Satyrs, Sylvans, and the rural deities of classic antiquity; but the Fay is here, as one of them says, not

The coarse and country fairy,
That doth haunt the hearth and dairy;

it is Oberon, the prince of Fairy-land, who, at the crowing of the cock, advances in a magnificent chariot drawn by white bears, attended by Knights and Fays. As the car advances, the Satyrs begin to leap and jump, and a Sylvan thus speaks:

Give place, and silence; you were rude too late—
This is a night of greatness and of state;
Not to be mixed with light and skipping sport—
A night of homage to the British court,
And ceremony due to Arthur's chair,
From our bright master, Oberon the Fair,
Who with these knights, attendants here preserved
In Fairy-land, for good they have deserved
Of yond' high throne, are come of right to pay
Their annual vows, and all their glories lay
At's feet.
Another Sylvan says,
Stand forth, bright faies and elves, and tune your lay
Unto his name; then let your nimble feet
Tread subtile circles, that may always meet
in point to him.
In the Sad Shepherd, Alken says,
There in the stocks of trees white fays [ao] do dwell,

And span-long elves that dance about a pool,
With each a little changeling in their arms!

The Masque of Love Restored presents us "Robin Good-fellow, he that sweeps the hearth and. the house clean, riddles for the country maids, and does all their other drudgery, while they are at hot-cockles," and he appears therefore with his *broom* and his *canles.*

In Fletcher's Faithful Shepherdess we read of
A virtuous well, about whose flowery banks
The nimble-footed fairies dance their rounds,
By the pale moonshine; dipping oftentimes
Their stolen children, so to make them free
From dying flesh and dull mortality.

And in the Little French Lawyer (iii. 1), one says, "You walk like Robin Goodfellow all the house over, and every man afraid of you."

In Randolph's Pastoral of Amyntas, or the Impossible Dowry, a "knavish boy," called Dorylas, makes a fool of a "fantastique sheapherd," Jocastus, by pretending to be Oberon, king of Fairy. In Act i., Scene 3, Jocastus' brother, Mopsus, "a foolish augur," thus addresses him:

Mop. Jocastus, I love Thestylis abominably,
The mouth of my affection waters at her.
Jo. Be wary, Mopsus, learn of me to scorn
The mortals; choose a better match: go love
Some fairy lady! Princely Oberon
Shall stand thy Mend, and beauteous Mab, his queen,
Give thee a maid of honour.
Mop. How, Jocastus?
Marry a puppet? Wed a mote i' the sun?

Go look a wife in nutshells? Woo a gnat,
That's nothing but a voice? No, no, Jocastus,
I must have flesh and blood, and will have Thestylis;
A fig for fairies!

Thestylis enters, and while she and Mopsus converse, Jocastus muses. At length he exclaims,

Jo. It cannot choose but strangely please his highness.
The. What are you studying of Jocastus, ha?
Jo. A rare device; a masque to entertain
His Grace of Fairy with.
The. A masque! What is 't?
Jo. An anti-masque of fleas, which I have taught
To dance corrantos on a spider's thread.

* * *

And then a jig of pismires
Is excellent.

Enter Dorylas. *He salutes* Mossus, *and then*

Dor. Like health unto the president of the jigs.
I hope King Oberon and his joyall Mab
Are well.
Jo. They are. I never saw their Graces
Eat such a meal before.
Dor. E'en much good do 't them!
Jo. They're rid a hunting.
Dor. Hare or deer, my lord?
Jo. Neither. A brace of snails of the first head.

Act I.—SCENE 6.

Jo. Is it not a brave sight, Dorylas? Can the mortals Caper so nimbly?
Dor. Verily they cannot
Jo. Does not King Oberon bear a stately presence?
Mab is a beauteous empress.
Dor. Yet you kissed her
With admirable courtship.
Jo. I do think
There will be of Jocastus' brood in Fairy.

* * *

The. But what estate shall he assure upon me?
Jo. A royal jointure, all in Fairyland.

* * *

Dorylas knows it.
A curious park—
Dor. Paled round about with pickteeth.
Jo. Besides a house made all of mother-of-pearl,
An ivory tennis-court.
Dor. A nutmeg parlour.
Jo. A sapphire dairy-room.
Dor. A ginger hall.
Jo. Chambers of agate.
Dor. Kitchens all of crystal
Am. O admirable! This it is for certain.
Jo. The jacks are gold.
Dor. The spits are Spanish needles.
Jo. Then there be walks—
Dor. Of amber.
Jo. Curious orchards—
Dor. That bear as well in winter as in summer.
Jo. 'Bove all, the fish-ponds, every pond is full—
Dor. Of nectar? Will this please you! Every grove Stored with
delightful birds.

Act III—SCENE 2.
Dorylas says,
Have at Jocastus' orchard! Dainty apples,
How lovely they look! Why these are Dorylas' sweetmeats.
Now must I be the princely Oberon,
And in a royal humour with the rest
Of royal fairies attendant, go in state
To rob an orchard. I have hid my robes
On purpose in a hollow tree.

Act III—SCENE 4.

Dorylas with a bevy of Fairies.

Dor. How like you now, my Grace? Is not my countenance
Royal and full of majesty? Walk not I
Like the young prince of pygmies? Ha, my knaves,
We'll fill our pockets. Look, look yonder, elves;
Would not yon apples tempt a better conscience
Than any we have, to rob an orchard? Ha!
Fairies, like nymphs with child, must have the things
They long for. You sing here a fairy catch
In that strange tongue I taught you, while ourself
Do climb the trees., Thus princely Oberon
Ascends his throne of state.

Elves. Nos beata Fauni proles,
Quibus non eat magna moles,
Quamvis Lunam incolamus.
Hortos saepe frequentamus.
Furto cuncta magis bella,
Furto dulcior puella,
Furto omnia decora,
Furto poma dulciora.
Cum mortales lecto jacent,
Nobis poma noctu placent;
Illa tamen sunt ingrata
Nisi furto sint parata.

Jocastus and his man Bromius come upon the Elves while plundering the orchard: the latter is for employing his cudgel on the occasion, but Jocastus is overwhelmed by the condescension of the princely Oberon in coming to his orchard, when

His Grace had orchards of his own more precious
Than mortals can have any.
The Elves, by his master's permission, pinch Bromius, singing,
Quoniam per te violarnur,
Ungues hic experiamur;
Statim dices tibi datam

Cutem valde variatam.
Finally, when the coast is clear, Oberon cries,
So we are got clean off; come, noble peers
Of Fairy, come, attend our royal Grace.
Let's go and share our fruit with our queen Mab
And the other dairy-maids; where of this theme
We will discourse amidst our cakes and cream.
Cum tot poma habeamus,
Triumphos laeti jam canamus;
Faunos ego credam ortos,
Tantum ut frequentent hortos.
I domum, Oberon, ad illas,
Qum nos manent nunc, ancillas,
Quarum osculemur sinum,
Inter poma lac et vinum.
In the old play of Fuimus Troes are the following lines: [ap]
Fairies small,
Two foot tall,
With caps red
On their head,
Danse around
On the ground.

The pastoral poets also employed the Fairy Mythology. Had they used it exclusively, giving up the Nymphs, Satyrs, and all the rural rout of antiquity, and joined with it faithful pictures of the scenery England then presented, with just delineations of the manners and character of the peasantry, the pastoral poetry of that age would have been as unrivalled as its drama. But a blind admiration of classic models, and a fondness for allegory, were the beset. ting sins of the poets. They have, however, left a few gems in this way.

Britannia's Pastorals furnish the following passages: [aq]
Near to this wood there lay a pleasant mead,
Where fairies often did their measures tread,

Which in the meadows made such circles green,
As if with garlands it had crowned been;
Or like the circle where the signs we track,
And learned shepherds call 't the Zodiac;
Within one of these rounds was to be seen
A hillock rise, where oft the fairy-queen
At twilight sate, and did command her elves
To pinch those maids that had not swept their shelves;
And, further, if by maiden's oversight,
Within doors water was not brought at night,
Or if they spread no table, set no bread,
They should have nips from toe unto the head;
And for the maid who had perform'd each thing,
She in the water-pail bade leave a ring.
Song 2
Or of the faiery troops which nimbly play,
And by the springs dance out the summer's day,
Teaching the little birds to build their nests,
And in their singing how to keepen rests.
Song 4.
As men by fairies led fallen in a dream.
Ibid.

In his Shepherd's Pipe, also, Brown thus speaks of the Fairies:—

Many times he hath been seen
With the fairies on the green,
And to them his pipe did sound
While they danced in a round.
Mickle solace they would make him,
And at midnight often wake him
And convey him from his room
To a field of yellow-broom;
Or into the meadows where
Mints perfume the gentle air,
And where Flora spreads her treasure;
There they would begin their measure.

If it chanced night's sable shrouds
Mused Cynthia up in clouds,
Safely home they then would see him,
And from brakes and quagmires free him.

But Drayton is the poet after Shakespeare for whom the Fairies had the greatest attractions. Even in the Polyobion he does not neglect them. In Song xxi., Ringdale, in Cambridgeshire, says,

For in my very midst there is a swelling ground
About which Ceres' nymphs dance many a wanton round;
The frisking fairy there, as on the light air borne,
Oft run at barley-break upon the ears of corn;
And catching drops of dew in their lascivious chases.
Do cast the liquid pearl in one another's faces.
And in Song iv., he had spoken of
The feasts that underground the faery did him (Arthur) make,
And there how he enjoyed the Lady of the Lake.

Nymphidia is a delicious piece of airy and fanciful invention. The description of Oberon's palace in the air, Mab's amours with the gentle Pigwiggin, the mad freaks of the jealous Oberon, the pygmy Orlando, the mutual artifices of Puck and the Fairy maids of honour, Hop, Mop, Pip, Trip, and Co., and the furious combat of Oberon and the doughty Pigwiggin, mounted on their earwig chargers—present altogether an unequalled fancy-piece, set in the very best and most appropriate frame of metre.

It contains, moreover, several traits of traditionary Fairy lore, such as in these lines:

Hence shadows, seeming idle shapes
Of little frisking elves and apes,
To earth do make their wanton skapes

As hope of pastime hastes them;
Which maids think on the hearth they see,
When fires well near consumed be,
There dancing hays by two and three,
Just as their fancy casts them. [ar]
These make our girls their sluttery rue,
By pinching them both black and blue,
And put a penny in their shoe,
The house for cleanly sweeping;
And in their courses make that round,
In meadows and in marshes found,
Of them so call'd the fairy ground,
Of which they have the keeping.
These, when a child haps to be got,
That after proves an idiot,
When folk perceive it thriveth not,
The fault therein to smother,
Some silly, doating, brainless calf;
That understands things by the half;
Says that the fairy left this aulf;
And took away the other.

And in these:
Scarce set on shore but therewithal
He meeteth Puck, whom most men call
Hobgoblin, and on him doth fail
With words from frenzy spoken;
"Ho! ho!" quoth Puck, "God save your Grace!
Who drest you in this piteous case?
He thus that spoiled my sovereign's face,
I would his neck were broken.
This Puck seems but a dreaming dolt,
Still walking like a ragged colt,
And oft out of a bush doth bolt,
Of purpose to deceive us;
And leading us, makes us to stray
Long winter nights out of the way;
And when we stick in mire and clay,
He doth with laughter leave us.

In his Poet's Elysium there is some beautiful Fairy poetry, which we do not recollect to have seen noticed any where. This work is divided into ten Nymphals, or pastoral dialogues. The Poet's Elysium is, we are told, a paradise upon earth, inhabited by Poets, Nymphs, and the Muses.

> The poet's paradise this is,
> To which but few can come,
> The Muses' only bower of bliss,
> Their dear Elysium.
> In the eighth Nymphal,
> A nymph is married to a fay,
> Great preparations for the day,
> All rites of nuptials they recite you
> To the bridal, and invite you.

The dialogue commences between the nymphs Mertilla and Claia:

> M. But will our Tita wed this fay?
> C. Yes, and to-morrow is the day.
> M. But why should she bestow herself
> Upon this dwarfish fairy elf?
> C. Why, by her smallness, you may find
> That she is of the fairy kind;
> And therefore apt to choose her make
> Whence she did her beginning take;
> Besides he 's deft and wondrous airy,
> And of the noblest of the fairy, [as]
> Chief of the Crickets, [at] of much fame,
> In Fairy a most ancient name.

The nymphs now proceed. to describe the bridal array of Tita: her jewels are to be dew-drops; her head-dress the "yellows in the full-blown rose;" her gown

Of pansy, pink, and primrose leaves,
Most curiously laid on in threaves;

her train the "cast slough of a snake;" her canopy composed of "moons from the peacock's tail," and. "feathers from the pheasant's head;"

Mix'd with the plume (of so high price),
The precious bird of paradise;
and it shall be
Borne o'er our head (by our inquiry)
By elfs, the fittest of the fairy.

Her buskins of the "dainty shell" of the lady-cow. The musicians are to be the nightingale, lark, thrush, and other songsters of the grove.

But for still music, we will keep
The wren and titmouse, which to sleep
Shall sing the bride when she's alone,
The rest into their chambers gone;
And like those upon ropes that walk
On gossamer from stalk to stalk,
The tripping fairy tricks shall play
The evening of the wedding day.

Finally, the bride-bed is to be of roses; the curtains, tester, and all, of the "flower imperial;" the fringe hung with harebells; the pillows of lilies, "with down stuft of the butterfly;"

For our Tita is to-day,
To be married to a fay.
In Nymphal iii.,
The fairies are hopping,

The small flowers cropping,
And with dew dropping,
Skip thorow the greaves.
At barley-break they play
Merrily all the day:
At night themselves they lay
Upon the soft leaves.
And in Nymphal vi. the forester says,
The dryads, hamadryads, the satyrs, and the fawns,
Oft play at hide-and-seek before me on the lawns;
The frisking fairy oft, when horned Cynthia shines,
Before me as I walk dance wanton matachines.

Herrick is generally regarded as the Fairy-poet, *par excellence;* but, in our opinion, without sufficient reason, for Drayton's Fairy pieces are much superior to his. Indeed Herrick's Fairy-poetry is by no means his best; and we doubt if he has anything to exceed. in that way, or perhaps equal, the light and fanciful King Oberon's Apparel of Smith. [au]

Milton disdained not to sing
How faery Mab the junkets eat.
She was pinch'd and pull'd, she said;
And he, by friar's lantern led, [av]
Tells how the drudging Goblin sweat
To earn his *cream bowl duly set,*
When in one night, ere glimpse of morn,
His shadowy flail bath thresh'd the corn
That ten day-labourers could not end;
Then lies him down, the lubber fiend,
And stretch'd out all the chimney's length,
Beaks at the fire his hairy dtrength,
And, crop-full, out of doors he flings,
Era the first cock his matin rings.

Regardless of Mr. Gifford's sneer at "those who may undertake the unprofitable drudgery of tracing out the property of every word, and phrase, and idea in Milton," [aw] we will venture to trace a little here, and beg the reader to compare this passage with one quoted above from Harsenet, and to say if the resemblance be accidental. The truth is, Milton, reared in London, probably knew the popular superstitions chiefly or altogether from books; and almost every idea in this passage may be found in books that he must have read.

In the hands of Dryden the Elves of Chaucer lose their indefiniteness. In the opening of the Wife of Bath her Tale,

> The king of elves and *little* fairy queen
> Gamboled on heaths and danced on every green.

And

> In vain the dairy now with mint is dressed,
> The dairy-maid expects no fairy guest
> To skim the bowls, and after pay the feast.
> She sighs, and shakes her empty shoes in vain,
> No silver penny to reward her pain.

In the Flower and the Leaf, unauthorised by the old bard, he makes the knights and dames, the servants of the Daisy and of the Agnus Castus, Fairies, subject, like the Italian Fate, to "cruel Demogorgon."

Pope took equal liberties with his original, as may be seen by a comparison of the following verses with those quoted above:

> About this spring, if ancient fame say true,
> The dapper elves their moonlight sports pursae:
> Their pigmy king and little fairy queen
> In circling dances gamboled on the green,
> While tuneful sprites a merry concert made,
> And airy music warbled through the shade.

January and May, 459.
It so befel, in that fair morning tide,
The fairies sported on the garden's side,
And in the midst their monarch and his bride.
So featly tripp'd the light-foot ladies round,
The knight so nimbly o'er the greensward bound,
That scarce they bent the flowers or touch'd the ground.
The dances ended, all the fairy train
For pinks and daisies search'd the flowery plain. [ax]
Ibid., 617.

With the Kensington Garden [ay] of Tickell, Pope's contemporary, our Fairy-poetry may be said to have terminated. [az] Collins, Beattie, and a few other poets of the last century make occasional allusions to it, and some attempts to revive it have been made in the present century. But vain are such efforts, the belief is gone, and divested of it such poetry can produce no effect. The Fairies have shared the fate of the gods of ancient Hellas.

NOTES

[a] Probably pronounced *Poke,* as still in Worcestershire. Our ancestors frequently used *ou* or *oo* for the long *o* while they expressed the sound of *oc* by *o* followed by *e,* as *rote* root, *coke* cook,*more* moor, *pole* pool.

[b] Passus xvii. *v.* ll,323 *seq.* ed. 1842. Comp. *vv.* 8363, 9300, 10,902.

[c] *Mr.* Todd is right, in reading *pouke* for *ponke,* an evident typographic error: wrong in saying, " He is the Fairy, Robin Good-fellow, known by the name of Puck." Robin is the "hob-goblin" mentioned two lines after.

[d] We know nothing of the Oriental origin of Puck, and cannot give our full assent to the character of our ancestry, as expressed in the remaining part of Mr. Gifford's note: "but a fiend engendered in the moody minds, and rude and gloomy fancies of the barbarous invaders of the North." It is full time to have done with describing the old Gothic race as savages.

[e] *Der Putz würde uns über berg und thäler tragen.* To frighten children they say *Der Butz kommt!* see Grimm, Deut. Mythol. p. 474.

[f] The former made by adding the Anglo-Saxon and English *el,* ie; the latter by adding the English *art.*

[g] By Sir F. Palgrave, from whose article In the Quarterly Review, we have derived many of the terms named above. He adds that the Anglo-Saxon *paecan* is to deceive, seduce; the Low-Saxon*picken* to gambol; *pickeln* to play the fool; *pukra* in Icelandic to make a murmuring noise, to steal secretly; and *pukke* in Danish to scold. He further adds the Swedish *poika* boy, the Anglo-Saxon and Swedish *piga* and Danish *pige* girl. If, however, Pouke is connected with the Sclavonic Bog, these at the most can be only derivations from it. By the way *boy* itself seems to be one of these terms; the Anglo-Saxon *piga* was probably pronounced *piya,* and a is a masculine termination in that language.

[h] In Low German, however, the Kobold is called Bullmann, Bullermann, Bullerkater, from *bullen, bullern,* to knock: see Grimm, *et sup.* p.473.

[i] Essay on the Ignis Fatuus, quoted by Thoms.

[j] And you whose pastime
Is to make midnight *mushrooms.—Tempest,* v. 1.

[k] Jack-o'-the-lanthorn, Will-o'-the-wisp. In Worcestershire they call it Hob-and-his-lanthorn, and Hobany's—or Hobredy's-lanthorn. Allies, *ut sup.*

[l] Knight of the Burning Pestle

[m] *Ard* is the German *hart,* and is, like it, depreciatory. It is not an Anglo-Saxon termination, but from the Anglo-Saxon *dull,* we have *dullard.* May not *haggard* be *hawk-ard,* and the French*haggard* be derived from it, and not the reverse?

[n] For in Anglo-Saxon *áttorcoppe (Poison-head?)* is spider, and from *áttorcoppe-web,* by the usual aphoeresis of the two first syllables we put *coppeweb,* cobweb. May not the same have been the case with *lob?* and may not the nasty *bug* be in a similar manner connected with Puck? As *dvergsnat* is in Swedish a cobweb, one might be tempted to suppose that this last, for which no good etymon has been offered, was *lob-web;* but the true etymon is *cop-web,* from its usual site.
Upon the *cop* right of his nose he hedde
A wert .—Chaucer, *Cant. Tales, v.* 556.

[o] Deut. Mythol. p. 492.

[p] See *France. In* is a mere termination, perhaps. like *on,* a diminutive, as in *Catin* Kate, *Robin* Bob. *Lutin* was also spelt. *Luyton.*

[q] The two lines which follow

Fro the nightes mare the witè Paternoster!

Where wonest thou Seint Peter's suster?

are rather perplexing. We would explain them thus. Bergerac, as quoted by Brand (Pop. Antiq. i. 312. Bohn's edit.) makes a magician say "I teach the shepherds the wolf's paternoster," *i. e.* one that keeps off the wolf. *Wite may* then be *i. q. wight,* and *wight paternoster* be a safeguard against the wights, and we would read the verse thus: "Fro the nightes mare the wite paternoster" *ac. blisse it* or *us*. St. Peter's *suster, i. e.* wife (see 1 Cor. ix. 5) may have been canonised in the popular creed, and held to be potent against evil beings. The term *suster* was used probably to obviate the scandal of supposing the first Pope to have been a married man. This charm is given at greater length and with some variations byCartwright in his Ordinary, Act iii. sc.

[r] He derives it from the French *oursin*.

[s] Athenaeum, Oct. 9, 1847

[t] Hist. of England, 1. 478, 8vo edit.

[u] Deut. Mythol. p. 419

[v] Layamon's Brut, etc., by Sir Frederick Madden.

[w] Tales and Popular Fictions, ch. viii. We do not wonder that this should have eluded previous observation, but it is really surprising that we should have been the first to observe the resemblance between Ariosto's tale of Giocondo and the introductory tale of the Thousand and One Nights. It is also strange that no one should have noticed the similarity between Ossian's Carthon and the tale of Soohrab in the Shah-nameh.

[x] Both here and lower down we would take *faêrie* in its first sense.

[y] *Thrope, thorpe,* or *dorp,* is a village, the German *dorf;* Dutch *dorp;* we may still find it in the names of places, as Althorpe. *Dorp'* occurs frequently in Drayton's Polyolbion; it is also usell by Dryden, Hind and Panther, *v.* l905.

[z] *Undermeles,* i. e. *undertide* (p. 51), aftermeal, afternoon.

[aa] This is the third sense of *Faerie*. In the next passage it is doubtful whether it be the second or third sense; we think the latter.

[ab] This wife which is *fairie,*

Of such a childe delivered is,

Fro kindè which stante all amis.

Gower, *Legende of Constance*

[ac] The derivation of Oberon has been already given. The Shakspearean commentators have not thought fit to inform us why the poet designates the Fairy-queen, Titania. It, however, presents no difficulty. It was the belief of those days that the Fairies were the same as the classic Nymphs, the attendants of Diana: "That fourth kind of spiritis," says King James, "quhilk be the gentilis was called Diana, and her wandering court, and amongst us called the *Phairie*." The Fairy-queen was therefore the same as Diana, whom Ovid (Met. iii. 173) styles Titania; Chaucer, as we have seen, calls her Proserpina.

[ad] 'Twas I that led you through the painted meads,

Where the light Fairies danced upon the flowers,

Hanging on every leaf an orient pearl.

Wisdom of Dr. Dodypoll, 1600. *Stevens.*

Men of fashion, in that age, wore earrings.

[ae] And the yellow-skirted Fayes

Fly after the night-steeds, leaving their moon-loved maze.

MILTON, *Ode on the Nativity,* 235.

[af] *Ouph,* Steevens complacently tells us, in the Teutonic language, is a fairy; if by Teutonic he means the German, and we know of no other, he merely showed his ignorance. Ouph is the same as *oaf* (formerly spelt *aulf),* and is probably to be pronounced in the same manner. It is formed from *elf* by the usual change of *l* into *u.*

[ag] After all the commentators have written, this line is still nearly unintelligible to us. It may relate to the supposed origin of the fairies. For *orphan,* Warburton conjectured *ouphen,* from *ouph.*

[ah] The origin of Mab is very uncertain; it maybe a contraction of Habundia, see below *France.* "Mab," says Voss, one of the German translators of Shakspeare, "is not the Fairy-queen, the same with Titania, as some, misled by the word *queen,* have thought. That word in old English, as in Danish, designates the female sex." Voss is perhaps right and *elf-queen* may have been used in the same manner as the Danish *Elle-quinde, Elle-kone* for the female Elf. We find Phaer using *Fairy-queen,* as a translation for *Nympha.*

[ai] *i. e,* Night-mare. "Many times," says Gull the fairy, "I get on men and women, and so lie on their stomachs, that I cause them great pain; for which they call me by the name of Hagge or Night-mare." *Merry Pranks,* etc. p.42

[aj] Auraeque et venti, montesque, amnesque, lacuaque,
Dique omnes nemorum, dique omnes noctis, adeste.
Ovid, Met. 1. vii. 190.
Ye ayres and winds, ye *elves* of hills, of brooks, of woods, alone,
Of standing lakes, and of the night—approach ye everich one.
GOLDING.
Golding seems to have regarded, by chance or with knowledge, the Elves as a higher species than the Fairies. Misled by the word *elves,* Shakspeare makes sad confusion of classic and Gothic mythology.

[ak] *Take* signifies here, to strike, to injure.
And there he blasts the tree and *takes* the cattle.
Merry Wives of Windsor, iv. 4
Thou farest as fruit that with the frost is taken.
Surrey, *Poems,* p. 13, Ald, edit.
In our old poetry *take* also signifies, to give.

[al] But not a word of it,—'tis fairies' treasure,
Which but revealed brings on the blabber's ruin.
MASSINGER, *Fatal Dowry,* Act iv. sc. 1.
A prince's secrets are like fairy favours,
Wholesome if kept, but poison if discovered.
Honest Man's Fortune.

[am] We do not recollect having met with any account of this prank; but Jonson is usually so correct, that we may be certain it was a part of the popular belief.

[an] Whalley was certainly right in proposing to road Agnes. This ceremony is, we believe, still practised in the north of England on St. Agnes' night. See Brand, i. 34.

[ao] Shakespeare gives different colours to the Fairies; and in some places they are still thought to be white.

[ap] Act i. Sc. 5. Dodsley's Old Plays, vii. p. 394. We quote this as the first notice we have met of the red caps of the fairies.

[aq] Brown, their author, was a native of Devon, the Pixy region; hence their accordance with the Pixy legends given above.

[ar] This is perhaps the dancing on the hearth of the fairy-ladies to which Milton alludes: "Doth not the warm zeal of an Englishman's devotion make them maintain and defend the social hearth as the sanctuary and chief place of residence of the tutelary lares and household gods, and the only court where the *lady-fairies convene to dance and revel!*"— Paradoxical Assertions, etc. 1664, quoted by Brand, ii. p. 504.

[as] The reader will observe that the third sense of Fairy is the most usual one in Drayton. It occurs in its second sense two lines further on, twice in Nymphidia, and in the following passage of his third Eclogue,

For learned Colin (Spenser) lays his pipes to gage,
And is to *Fayrie* gone a pilgrimage,
The more our moan.

[at] Mr. Chalmers does not seem to have known that the Crickets were a family of note in Fairy. Shakapeare *(Merry Wives of Windsor)* mentions a Fairy named Cricket; and no hint of Shakspeare's was lost upon Drayton.

[au] In the Musarum Deliciae.

[av] This is a palpable mistake of the poet's. The Friar is the celebrated Friar Rush, who haunted houses, not fields, and was never the same with Jack-o'-the-Lanthorn. It was probably the name Rush, which suggested *rushlight,* that caused Milton's error. He is the Brüder Rausch of Germany, the Broder Ruus of Denmark. His name is either as Grimm thinks, *noise,* or as Wolf (Von Bruodor Rauschen, p. xxviii.) deems *drunkenness,* our old word, *rouse.* Sir Walter Scott in a note on Marmion, says also "Friar Rush, *alias* Wili-o'-the-Wisp. He was also a sort of Robin Goodfellow and Jack-o'-Lanthorn," which is making precious confusion. Reginald Scot more correctly describes him as being "for all the world such another fellow as this Hudgin," *i.e.* Hödeken.

[aw] Ben jonson's Works, vol. ii. p. 499. We shall never cease to regret that the state to which literature has come in this country almost precludes even a hope of our ever being able to publish our meditated edition of Milton's poems for which we have been collecting materials these five and twenty years. It would have been very different from Todd's. [Published in 1859.]

[ax] Evidently drawn from Dryden's Flower and Leaf.

[ay] We meet here for the last time with Fairy in its collective sense, or rather, perhaps, as the country:

All Fairy shouted with a general voice.

[az] In Mr. Halliwell's Illustrations of Fairy Mythology, will be found a good deal of Fairy poetry, for which we have not had space in this work.

SCOTTISH LOWLANDS

When from their hilly dens, at midnight hour,
Forth rush the airy elves in mimic state,
And o'er the moonlight heath with swiftness scour,
In glittering arms the little horsemen shine.
—ERSKINE.

The Scottish Fairies scarcely differ in any essential point from those of England. Like them they are divided into the rural and the domestic. Their attire is green, their residence the interior of the hills. They appear more attached than their neighbours to the monarchical form of government, for the Fairy king and queen, who seem in England to have been known only by the poets, were recognised by law in Caledonia, and have at all times held a place in the popular creed. They would appear also to be more mischievously inclned than the Southrons, and less addicted to the practice of dancing. They have, however, had the advantage of not being treated with contempt and neglect by their human countrymen, and may well be proud of the attention shown them by the brightest genius of which their country can boast. There has also been long due from them an acknowledgment of the distinction conferred on them by the editor of the Nithsdale and Galloway Song, [a] for the very fanciful manner in which he has described their attributes and acts.

The Scottish Fairies have never been taken by the poets for their heroes or machinery, a circumstance probably to be attributed to the sterner character of Scottish religion. We cannot, therefore, as in England, make a distinction between popular and poetic fairies.

The earliest notice we have met with of the Fairies is in Montgomery's Flyting against Polwart, where he says,

> In the hinder end of harvest, at All-hallowe'en,
> When our *good neighbours* [b] dois ride, if I read right,
> Some buckled on a beenwand, and some on a been,
> Ay trottand in troops from the twilight;
> Some saidled on a she-ape all graithed in green,
> Some hobland on a hempstalk hovand to the sight;
> The king of Phairie and his court, with the elf-queen,
> With many elfish incubus, was ridand that night.

Elf-land was the name of the realm ruled by the king of Phairie. King James [c] speaks of him and his queen, and "of sic a jolie court and traine as they had; how they had a teinde and a dewtie, as it were, of all guidis; how they naturally raid and yeid, eat and drank, and did all other actions lyke natural men and women. I think," concludes the monarch, "it is lyker Virgilis *Campi Elysii* nor anything that ought to be believed by Christianis." And one of the interlocutors in his dialogue asks how it was that witches have gone to death confessing that they had been "transported with the Phairie to such and such a hill, which, opening, they went in, and there saw a faire queene, who, being now lighter, gave them a stone which had sundry virtues."

According to Mr. Cromek, who, however, rather sedulously keeps their darker attributes out of view, and paints everything relating to them *couleur de rose*, the Lowland Fairies are of small stature, but finely proportioned; of a fair complexion, with long yellow hair hanging over their shoulders, and gathered above their heads with combs of gold. They wear a mantle of green cloth, inlaid with wild flowers; green pantaloons, buttoned with bobs of silk; and silver shoon. They carry quivers of "adder-slough," and bows made of the ribs of a man buried where *three lairds' lands meet;* their arrows are made of bog-reed, tipped with white flints, and dipped in the dew of hemlock; they ride on steeds whose hoofs "would not dash the dew from the cup of a harebell." With their arrows they shoot the cattle of those who offend them; the wound is imperceptible to common eyes, but there are gifted personages who can discern and cure it. [d]

In their intercourse with mankind they are frequently kind and generous. A young man of Nithsdale, when out on a love affair, heard most delicious music, far surpassing the utterance of 'any mortal mixture of earth's mould.' Courageously advancing to the spot whence the sound appeared to proceed, he suddenly found himself the spectator of a Fairy-banquet. A green table with feet of gold, was laid across a small rivulet, and supplied with the finest of bread and the richest of wines. The music proceeded from instruments formed of reeds and stalks of corn. He was invited to partake in the dance, and presented with a cup of wine. He was allowed to depart in safety, and ever after possessed the gift of second sight. He said he saw there several of his former acquaintances, who were become members of the Fairy society.

We give the following legend on account of its great similarity to a Swiss tradition already quoted:—

Two lads were ploughing in a field, in the middle of which was an old thorn-tree, a trysting place of the Fairy-folk. One of them described a circle round the thorn, within which the plough should not go. They were surprised, on ending the furrow, to behold a green table placed there, heaped up with excellent bread and cheese, and even wine. The lad who had drawn the circle sat down without hesitation, ate and drank heartily, saying, "Fair fa' the hands whilk gie." His companion whipped on the horses, refusing to partake of the Fairy-food. The other, said Mr. Cromek's informant, "thrave like a breckan," and was a proverb for wisdom, and an oracle for country knowledge ever after. [e]

The Fairies lend and borrow, and it is counted *uncanny* to refuse them. A young woman was one day sifting meal warm from the mill, when a nicely dressed beautiful little woman came to her with a bowl of antique form, and requested the loan of as much meal as would fill it. Her request was complied with, and in a week she returned to make repayment. She set down the bowl and breathed over it, saying, "Be never toom." The woman lived to a great age, but never saw the bottom of the bowl.

Another woman was returning late one night from a gossiping. A pretty little boy came up to her and said, "Coupe yere dish-water farther frae yere door-step, it pits out our fire." She complied with this reasonable request, and prospered ever after.

NOTES

[a] Mr. Cromek. There was, we believe, some false dealing on the pert of Allan Cunningham toward this gentleman, such as palming on him his owe verses as traditionary ones. But the legends are genuine.

[b] This answers to the *Deenè Máh,* Good People, of the Highlands and Ireland. An old Scottish name, we may add, for a fairy seems to have been Bogle, akin to the English Pouke, Puck, Puckle but differing from the Boggart. Thus Gawain Douglas says,
Of *Brownyis* and of *Boggles* full is this Beuk.

[c] Daemonologie, B. III. c. 5.

[d] These elf-arrows are triangular pieces of flint, supposed to have been the herds of the arrows used by the aborigines. Though more plentiful in Scotland they are also found in England and Ireland, and were there also attached to the fairies, and the wounds were also only to be discerned by gifted eyes

[e] "It was till lately believed by the ploughmen of Clydesdale, that if they repeated the rhyme
Fairy, fairy, bake me a bannock and roast me a collop,
And I'll gie ye a spurtle oft' my gadend!
three several times on turning their cattle at the terminations of ridges, they would find the said fare prepared for them on reaching the end of the fourth furrow."—Chambers' Popular Rhymes of Scotland, p. 83.

The Fairies' Nurse

The Fairies have a great fondness for getting their babes suckled by comely, healthy young women. A fine young woman of Nithsdale was one day spinning and rocking her first-born child. A pretty little lady in a green mantle, and bearing a beautiful babe, came into 'the cottage and said, "Gie my bonny thing a suck." The young woman did so, and the lady left her babe and disappeared, saying, "Nurse kin' and ne'er want." The young woman nursed the two children, and was astonished to find every morning, when she awoke, rich clothes for the children, and food of a most delicious flavour. Tradition says this food tasted like wheaten-bread, mixed with wine and honey.

When summer came, the Fairy lady came to see her child. She was delighted to see how it had thriven, and, taking it in her arms, desired the nurse to follow her. They passed through some scroggy woods skirting the side of a beautiful green hill, which they ascended half way. A door opened on the sunny side—they went in, and the sod closed after them. The Fairy then dropped three drops of a precious liquid on her companion's left eyelid, and she beheld a most delicious country, whose fields were yellow with ripening corn, watered by *looping burnies,* and bordered by trees laden with fruit. She was presented with webs of the finest cloth, and with boxes of precious ointments. The Fairy then moistened her right eye with a 'green fluid, and bid her look. She looked, and saw several of her friends and acquaintances at work, reaping the corn and gathering the fruit. "This," said the Fairy, "is the punishment of evil deeds!" She then passed her hand over the woman's eye, and restored it to its natural power. Leading her to the porch at which she had entered, she dismissed her; but the woman had, secured the wonderful salve. From this time she possessed the faculty of discerning the Fairy people as they went about invisibly; till one day, happening to meet the Fairy-lady, she attempted to shake hands with her. "What ee d'ye see me wi'?" whispered she. "Wi' them baith," said the woman. The Fairy breathed on her eyes, and the salve lost its efficacy, and could never more endow her eyes with their preternatural power. [a]

NOTE
[a] Graham also relates this legend in his Picturesque Sketches of Perthshire.

The Fairy Rade

The *Fairy Rade,* or procession, was a matter of great importance. It took place on the coming in of summer, awl the peasantry, by using the precaution of placing a branch of rowan over their door, might safely gaze on the cavalcade, as with music sounding, bridles ringing, and voices mingling, it pursued its way from place to place. An old woman of Nithadale gave the following description of one of these processions:

"In the night afore Roodmass I had trysted with a neebor lass a Scots mile frae hame to talk anent buying braws i' the fair. We had nae sutten lang aneath the haw-buss till we heard the loud laugh of fowk riding, wi' the jingling o' bridles, and the clanking o' hoofs. We banged up, thinking they wad owre us. We kent nae but it was drunken fowk ridin' to the fair i' the forenight. We glowred roun' and roun', and sune saw it was the *Fairie-fowks Rade.* We cowred down till they passed by. A beam o' light was dancing owre them mair bonnie than moonshine: they were a' wee wee fowk wi' green scarfs on, but ane that rade foremost, and that ane was a good deal larger than the lave wi' bonnie lang hair, bun' about wi' a strap whilk glinted like stars. They rade on braw wee white naigs, wi' unco lang swooping tails, an' manes hung wi' whustles that the win' played on. This an' their tongue when they sang was like the soun' o' a far awa psalm. Marion an' me was in a brade lea fiel', where they came by us; a high hedge o' haw-trees keepit them frae gaun through Johnnie Corrie's corn, but 'they lap a' owre it like sparrows, and gallopt into a green know beyont it. We gaed i' the morning to look at the treddit corn; but the fient a hoof mark was there, nor a blade broken."

The Changeling

But the Fairies of Scotland were not, even according to Mr. Cromek, uniformly benevolent. Woman and child abstraction was by no means uncommon with them, and the substitutes they provided were, in general, but little attractive.

A fine child at Caerlaveroc, in Nithsdale, was observed on the second day after its birth, and before it was baptised, to have become quite ill-favoured and deformed. Its yelling every night deprived the whole family of rest; it bit and tore its mother a breasts, and would lie still neither in the cradle nor the arms. The mother being one day obliged to go from home, left it in charge of the servant girl. The poor lass was sitting bemoaning herself—"Were it nae for thy girning face, I would knock the big, winnow the corn, and grun the meal."—"Lowse the cradle-band," said the child, "and tent the neighbours, and I'll work yere work." Up he started—the wind arose—the corn was chopped—the outlyers were foddered—the hand-mill moved around, as by instinct—and the knocking-mill did its work with amazing rapidity. The lass and child then rested and diverted themselves, till, on the approach of the mistress, it was restored to the cradle, and renewed its cries. The girl took the first opportunity of telling the adventure to her mistress.

"What'll we do with the wee diel?" said she. "I 'll work it a pirn," replied the lass. At midnight the chimney-top was covered up, and every chink and cranny stopped. The fire was blown till it was glowing hot, and the maid speedily undressed the child, and tossed him on the burning coals. He shrieked and yelled in the most dreadful manner, and in an instant the Fairies were heard moaning on every side, and rattling at the windows, door, and chimney. "In the name of God bring back the bairn," cried the lass. The window flew up, the real child was laid on the mother's lap, and the *wee diel* flew up the chimney laughing.

Departure of the Fairies

On a Sabbath morning, all the inmates of a little hamlet had gone to church, except a herd-boy, and a little girl, his sister, who were lounging beside one of the cottages, when just as the shadow of the garden-dial had fallen on the line of noon, they saw a long cavalcade ascending out of the ravine, through the wooded hollow. It winded among the knolls and bushes, and turning round the northern gable of the cottage, beside which the sole spectators of the scene were stationed, began to ascend the eminence towards the south. The horses were shaggy diminutive things, speckled dun and grey; the riders stunted, misgrown, ugly creatures, attired in antique jerkins of plaid, long grey clokes, and little red caps, from under which their wild uncombed locks shot out over their cheeks and foreheads. The boy and his sister stood gazing in utter dismay and astonishment, as rider after rider, each more uncouth and dwarfish than the other which had preceded it, passed the cottage and disappeared among the brushwood, which at that period covered the hill, until at length the entire rout, except the last rider, who lingered a few yards behind the others, had gone by. "What are you, little manie? and where are ye going?" inquired the boy, his curiosity getting the better of his fears and his prudence. "Not of the race of Adam," said the creature, turning for a moment in its saddle, "the people of peace shall never more be seen in Scotland." [a]

[a] Hugh Miller, The Old Red Sandstone, p. 251. We are happy to have an opportunity of expressing the high feelings of respect and esteem which we entertain for this extraordinary man. Born in the lowest rank of society, and commencing life as a workman in a stone-quarry, he has, by the mere force of natural genius, become not only a most able geologist but an elegant writer, and a sound and discerning critic. Scotland seems to stand alone in producing such men.

The Brownie

The Nis, Kobold, or Goblin, appears in Scotland under the name of Brownie. [a] Brownie is a personage of small stature, wrinkled visage, covered with short curly brown hair, and wearing a brown mantle and hood. His residence is the hollow of the old tree, a ruined castle, or the abode of man, He is attached to particular families, with whom he has been known to reside, even for centuries, threshing the corn, cleaning the house, and doing everything done by his northern and English brethren. He is, to a certain degree, disinterested; like many great personages, he is shocked at anything approaching to the name of a bribe or *douceur*, yet, like them, allows his scruples to be overcome if the thing be done in a genteel, delicate, and secret way. Thus, offer Brownie a piece of bread, a cup of drink, or a new coat and hood, and he flouted at it, and perhaps, in his huff, quitted the place for ever; but leave a nice bowl of cream, and some fresh honeycomb, in a snug private corner, and they soon disappeared, though Brownie, it was to be supposed, never knew anything of them.

A good woman had just made a web of linsey-woolsey, and, prompted by her good nature, had manufactured from it a snug mantle and hood for her little Brownie. Not content with laying the gift in one of his favourite spots, she indiscreetly called to tell him it was there. This was too direct, and Brownie quitted the place, crying,

> A new mantle and a new hood;
> Poor Brownie! ye 'll ne'er do mair gude!

Another version of this legend says, that the gudeman of' a farm-house in the parish of Glendevon having left out some clothes one night for Brownie, he was heard to depart, saying,

Gie Brownie coat, gie Brownie sark,
Ye 'se get nae mair o' Brownie's wark! [b]

At Leithin-hall, in Dumfrieshire, a Brownie had dwelt, as he himself declared, for three hundred years. He used to show himself but once to each master; to other persons he rarely discovered more than his hand. One master was greatly beloved by Brownie, who on his death bemoaned him exceedingly, even abstaining from food for many successive days. The heir returning from foreign parts to take possession of the estate, Brownie appeared to do him homage, but the Laird, offended at his mean, starved appearance, ordered him meat and drink, and new livery. Brownie departed, loudly crying,

Ca', cuttee, ca'!
A' the luck of Leithin Ha'
Gangs wi' me to Bodsbeck Ha'.

In a few years Leithin Ha' was in ruins, and "bonnie Bodsbeck" flourishing beneath the care of Brownie.

Others say that it was the gudeman of Bodsbeck that offended the Brownie by leaving out for him a mess of bread and milk, and that he went away, saying,

Ca, Brownie, ca',
A' the luck of Bodsbeck awa to Leithenha'.

Brownie was not without some roguery in his composition. Two lasses having made a fine bowlful of buttered brose, had taken it into the byre to sup in the dark. In their haste they brought but one spoon, so, placing the bowl between them, they supped by turns. "I hae got but three sups," cried the one, "and it's a' dune."—"It 's a' dune, indeed," cried the other—"Ha, ha, ha!" cried a third voice, "Brownie has got the maist o' it."—And Brownie it was who had placed himself between them, and gotten two sups for their one.

The following story will remind the reader of Hinzelmann. A Brownie once lived with Maxwell, Laird of Dalswinton, and was particularly attached to the Laird's daughter, the comeliest lass in all the holms of Nithadale. In all her bye affairs Brownie was her confidant and assistant; when she was married, it was Brownie who undressed her for the bridal bed; and when a mother's pains first seized her, and a servant, who was ordered to go fetch the *cannie wife*, who lived on the other side of the Nith, was slow in getting himself ready, Brownie, though it was one of dark December's stormy nights, and the wind was howling through the trees, wrapped his lady's fur cloak about him, mounted the servant's horse, and dashed through the waves of the foaming Nith. He went to the cannie wife, got her up behind hint, and, to her terror and dismay, plunged again into the torrent. "Ride nae by the auld pool," said she, "lest we suld meet wi' Brownie." "Fear nae, dame," replied he, "ye 've met a' the Brownies ye will meet." He set her down at the hall steps, and went to the stable. There finding the lad, whose embassy be had discharged, but drawing on his boots, he took off the bridle, and by its vigorous application instilled into the memory of the loitering loon the importance of dispatch. This was just at the time of the Reformation, and a zealous minister advised the Laird to have him baptised. The Laird consented, and the worthy minister hid himself in the barn. When Brownie was beginning his night's work, the man of God flung the holy water in his face, repeating at the same time the form of baptism. The terrified Brownie gave a yell of dismay, and disappeared for ever.

Another name by which the domestic spirit was known in some parts of Scotland was Shellycoat, of which the origin is uncertain. [c]

Scotland has also its water-spirit, called Kelpie, who in some respects corresponds with the Neck of the northern nations. "Every lake," says Graham [d] "has its Kelpie, or Water-horse, often seen by the shepherd, as he sat in a summer's evening upon the brow of a rock, dashing along the surface of the deep, or browsing on the pasture-ground upon its verge. Often did this malignant genius of the waters allure women and children to his subaqueous haunts, there to be immediately devoured. Often did he also swell the torrent or lake beyond its usual limits, to overwhelm the hapless traveller in the flood." [e]

We have now gone through nearly the whole of the Gotho-German race, and everywhere have found their fairy system the same—a proof, we conceive, of the truth of the position of its being deeply founded in the religious system originally common to the whole race. We now proceed to another, and, perhaps, an older European family, the Celts.

NOTES

[a] He is named as we have seen by Gawain Douglas. King James says of him "The spirit called Brownie appeared like a rough man, and haunted divers houses without doing any evil, but doing, as it were, necessarie turns up and down the house; yet some are so blinded as to believe that their house was all the sonsier, as they called It, that such spirits resorted there."

[b] Popular Rhymes of Scotland, p. 33.

[c] Grimm (Deut. Mythol., p. 479) says it is the German Schellenrock, i.e, Bell-coat, from his coat being hung with bells like those of the fools. A Puck be says, once served in a convent in Mecklenburg, for thirty years, in kitchen, and stable, and the only reward he asked was "tunicam de diversis coloribus et *tintinnabulis* plenam."

[d] Sketches of Perthsbire, p. 245.

[e] In what precedes, we have chiefly followed Mr. Cromek. Those anxious for further information will meet it in the Minstrelsy of the Scottish Border, and other works.

CELTS AND CYMRY

There every herd by sad experience knows,
How winged with fate their elf-shot arrows fly;
When the sick ewe her summer-food foregoes,
Or stretched on earth, the heart-smit heifers lie.
—COLLINS.

UNDER THE former of these appellations we include the inhabitants of Ireland, the Highlands of Scotland, and the Isle of Man; under the latter, the people of Wales and Brittany. It is, not, however, by any means meant to be asserted that there is in any of these places to be found a purely Celtic or Cymric population. The more powerful Gotho-German race has, every where that they have encountered them, beaten the Celts and Cymry, and intermingled with them, influencing their manners, language, and religion.

Our knowledge of the original religion of this race is very limited, chiefly confined to what the Roman writers have transmitted to us, and the remaining poems of the Welsh bards. Its character appears to have been massive, simple, and sublime, and less given to personification than those of the more eastern nations. The wild and the plastic powers of nature never seem in it to have assumed the semblance of huge giants and ingenious dwarfs.

Yet in. the popular creed of all these tribes, we meet at the present day beings exactly corresponding to the Dwarfs and Fairies of the Gotho-German nations. Of these beings there is no mention in any works—such as the Welsh Poems, and Mabinogion, the Poems of Ossian, or the different Irish poems and romances—which can by any possibility lay claim to an antiquity anterior to the conquests of the Northmen. Is it not then a reasonable supposition that the Picts, Saxons, and other sons of the North, brought with them their Dwarfs and Kobolds, and communicated the knowledge of, and belief in, them to their Celtic and Cymric subjects and neighbours? Proceeding on this theory, we have placed the Celts and Cymry next to and after the Gotho-German nations, though they are perhaps their precursors in Europe.

IRELAND

Like him, the Sprite,
Whom maids by night
Oft meet In glen that's haunted.
—MOORE.

We commence our survey of the lands of Celts and Cymry with Ireland, as being the first in point of importance, but still more as being
the land of our birth. It is pleasing to us, now in the autumn of our
life, to return in imagination to where we passed its spring—its most
happy spring. As we read and meditate, its mountains and its vales,
its verdant fields and lucid streams, objects on which we probably
never again shall gaze, rise up in their primal freshness and beauty
before us, and we are once more present, buoyant with youth, in
the scenes where we first heard the fairy-legends of which we are
now to treat. Even the forms of the individual peasants who are associated with them in our memory, rise as it were from their humble
resting-places and appear before us, again awaking our sympathies;
for, we will boldly assert it, the Irish peasantry, with all their faults,
gain a faster hold on the affections than the peasantry of any other
country. We speak, however, particularly of them as they were in our
county and in our younger days; for we fear that they are somewhat
changed, and not for the better. But our present business is with the
Irish fairies rather than with the Irish people.

The fairies of Ireland can hardly be said to differ in any respect from those of England and Scotland. Like them they are of
diminutive size, rarely exceeding two feet in height; they live also

in society, their ordinary abode being the interior of the mounds, called in Irish, Raths (*Rahs*), in English, Moats, the construction of which is, by the peasantry, ascribed to the Danes from whom, it might thence perhaps be inferred, the Irish got their fairies direct and not *vid* England. From these abodes they are at times seen to issue mounted on diminutive steeds, in order to take at night the diversion of the chase. Their usual attire is green with red caps. [a] They are fond of music, but we do not in general hear much of their dancing, perhaps because on account of the infrequency of thunder, the fairy-rings are less numerous in Ireland than elsewhere. Though the fairies steal children and strike people with paralysis and other ailments (which is called being *fairy-struck)*, and shoot their elf-ar-rows at the cattle, they are in general kind to those for whom they have contracted a liking, and often render them essential service in time of need. They can make themselves visible and invisible, and assume any forms they please. The pretty tiny conical mushrooms which grow so abundantly in Ireland are called Fairy-mushrooms; a kind of nice regularly-formed grass is named Fairy-flax, and the bells of the foxglove called in some places Fairy-bells, are also said to have some connexion with the Little People.

The popular belief in Ireland also is, that the Fairies are a portion of the fallen angels, who, being less guilty than the rest, were not driven to hell, but were suffered to dwell on earth. They are supposed to be very uneasy respecting their condition after the final judgement.

The only names by which they are known in those parts of Ireland in which the English language is spoken are, Fairies, the Good

People, and the Gentry, these last terms being placatory, like the Greek Eumenides. When, for example, the peasant sees a cloud of dust sweeping along the road, he raises his hat and says, "God speed you, gentlemen!" for it is the popular belief that it is in these cloudy vehicles that the Good People journey from one place to another. The Irish language has several names for the fairies; all however are forms or derivations of the word *Shia,* the meaning of which seems to be Spirit. The most usual name employed by the Minister peasantry is *Shifra;* we are not acquainted with the fairy-belief and terminology of the inhabitants of Connemara and the other wilds of Connaught. [b]

Most of the traits and legends of the Irish fairies are contained in the Fairy Legends and Traditions of the South of Ireland, compiled by Mr. Crofton Croker. As we ourselves aided in that work we must inform the reader that our contributions, both in text and notes, contain only Leinster ideas and traditions, for that was the only province with which we were acquainted. We must make the further confession, that some of the more poetic traits which MM. Grimm, in the Introduction to their translation of this work, give as characteristic of the Irish fairies, owe their origin to the fancy of the writers, who were, in many cases, more anxious to produce amusing tales than to transmit legends faithfully.

The Legend of Knockshegowna *(Hill of the Fairy-calf)* the first given in that work, relates how the fairies used to torment the cattle and herdsmen for intruding on one of their favourite places of resort which was on this hill. The fairy-queen, it says, having failed in her attempts to daunt a drunken piper who had undertaken the charge of the cattle, at last turned herself into a calf and, with the piper on her back, jumped over the Shannon, ten miles off, and back again. Pleased with his courage, she agreed to abandon the hill for the future.

The Legend of Knock-Grafton tells how a little hunchback, while sitting to rest at nightfall at the side of a Rath or Moat, heard the fairies within singing over and over again, *DaLuan, Da Mart!* (i.e.,Monday, Tuesday!) and added, weary with the monotony, *Agus da Cadin! (i.e.,* and Wednesday!) The fairies were so delighted with this addition to their song that they brought him into the Moat, entertained him, and finally freed him from the incumbrance of his hump.

Another hunchback hearing the story went to the Moat to try if he could meet with the same good fortune. He heard the fairies singing the amended version of the song, and, anxious to contribute, without waiting for a pause or attending to the rhythm or melody, he added *Agus da Hena! (i.e.,* and Friday.) His reward was, being carried into the Moat, and having his predecessor's hump placed on his back in addition to his own. [c]

In the story named the Priest's Supper, a fisherman at the request of the fairies, asks a priest who had stopt at his house, whether they would be saved or not at the last day. The priest desired him to tell them to come themselves and put the question to him, but this they declined doing, and the question remained undecided.

The next three stories are of changelings. The Young Piper, one of our own contributions, will be found in the Appendix. The Changeling has nothing peculiar in it; but the Brewery of Eggshells is one which we find in many places, even in Brittany and Auvergne.

In the present version, the mother puts down eggshells to boil, and to the enquiry of the changeling she tells him that she is brewing them, and clapping his hands he says, "Well! I'm fifteen hundred years in the world, and I never saw a brewery of eggshells before!"

In the Capture of Bridget Purcel, a girl is struck with a little switch between the shoulders, by something in the form of a little child that came suddenly behind her, and she pined away and died.

The Legend of Bottle Hill gives the origin of that name, which was as follows. A poor man was driving his only cow to Cork to sell her. As he was going over that hill he was suddenly joined by a strange-looking little old man with a pale withered face and red eyes, to whom he was eventually induced to give his cow in exchange for a bottle, and both cow and purchaser then disappeared. When the poor man came home he followed the directions of the stranger, and spreading a cloth on the table, and placing the bottle on the ground, he said, "Bottle, do your duty!" and immediately two little beings rose out of it, and having covered the table with food in gold and silver dishes, went down again into the bottle and vanished. By selling these he got a good deal of money and became rich for one in his station. The secret of his bottle however transpired, and his landlord induced him to sell it to him. But his prosperity vanished with it, and he was again reduced to one cow, and obliged to drive her to Cork for sale. As he journeyed over the same hill he met the same old man, and sold him the cow for another bottle. Having made the usual preparations, he laid it on the ground and said, "Bottle, do your duty!" but instead of the tiny little lads with their gold and silver dishes, there jumped up out of it two huge fellows with cudgels, who fell to belabouring the whole family. When they had done and were gone back into the bottle, the owner of it, without saying a word, put it under his coat and went to his landlord, who happened to have a great deal of company with him, and sent in word that he was come with another bottle to sell. He was at once admitted, the bottle did its duty, and the men with cudgels laid about them on all present, and never ceased till the original wealth-giving bottle was restored. He now grew richer than ever, and his son married his landlord's daughter, but when the old man and his wife died, the servants, it is recorded, fighting at their wake, broke the two bottles. [d]

The Confessions of Tom Bourke, as it contains a faithful transcript of the words and ideas of that personage, is perhaps the most valuable portion of the work. From this we learn that in Munster the fairies are, like the people themselves, divided into *factions.* Thus we are told that, on the occasion of the death of Bourke's mother, the two parties fought for three continuous nights, to decide whether she should be buried with her own or her husband's *peçple (i. e.* family). Bourke also had sat for hours looking at two parties of the Good People playing at the popular game of hurling, in a meadow at the opposite side of the river, with their coats and waistcoats off, and white handkerchiefs on the heads of one, and red on these of the other party.

A man whom Tom knew was returning one evening from a fair, a little elevated of course, when he met a *berrin (i. e.* funeral), which he joined, as is the custom; but, to his surprise, there was no one there that he knew except one man, and *he* had been dead for some years. When the *berrin* was over, they gathered round a piper, and began to dance in the churchyard. Davy longed to be among them, and the man that he knew came up to him, and bid him take out a partner, but on no account to give her the usual kiss. He accordingly took out the *purtiest girl in the ring,* and danced a jig with her, to the admiration of the whole company; but at the end he forgot the warning, and complied with the custom of kissing one's partner. All at once everything vanished; and when Davy awoke next morning, he found himself lying among the tombstones.

Another man, also a little in liquor, was returning one night from a *berrin.* The moon was shining bright, and from the other side of the river came the sounds of merriment, and the notes of a bag-pipe. Taking off his shoes and stockings, he waded across the river, and there he found a great crowd of people dancing on the Inch [an island, coast, bank of sea or river] on the, other side. He mingled with them without being observed, and he longed to join in the dance; for he had no mean opinion of his own skill. He did so, but found that it was not to be compared to theirs, they were so light and agile. He was going away quite in despair, when a little old man, who was looking on with marks of displeasure in his face, came up to him, and telling him he was his friend, and his father's friend, bade him go into the ring and call for a lilt. He complied, and all were amazed at his dancing; he then got a table and danced on it, and finally he span round and round on a trencher. When he had done, they wanted him to dance again; but he refused with a great oath, and instantly he found himself lying on the Inch with only a white cow grazing beside him. On going home, he got a shivering and a fever. He was for many days out of his mind, and recovered slowly; but ever after he had great skill in fairy matters. The dancers, it turned out, had belonged to a different faction, and the old man who gave him his skill to that to which he himself was attached.

In these genuine confessions it is very remarkable that the Good People are never represented as of a diminutive size; while in every story that we ever heard of them in Leinster, they were of pygmy stature. The following account of their mode of entering houses in Ulster gives them dimensions approaching to those of Titania's 'small elves.'

A Fairy, the most agile, we may suppose, of the party, is selected, who contrives to get up to the keyhole of the door, carrying with him a piece of thread or twine. With this he descends on the inside, where he fastens it firmly to the floor, or some part of the furniture. Those without then 'haul taut and belay,' and when it is fast they prepare to march along this their perilous Es-Sirat, leading to the paradise of pantry or parlour, in this order. First steps up the Fairy-piper, and in measured pace pursues his adventurous route, playing might and main an invigorating elfin-march, or other spirit-stirring air; then one by one the rest of the train mount the cord and follow his steps. Like the old Romans, in their triumphal processions, they pass beneath the lofty arch of the keyhole, and move down along the other side. Lightly, one by one, they then jump down on the floor, to hold their revels or accomplish their thefts.

We have never heard of any being, in the parts of Ireland with which we are acquainted, answering to the Boggart, Brownie, or Nis. A farmer's family still, we believe, living in the county of Wicklow, used to assert that in their grandfather's time they never had any trouble about washing up plates and dishes; for they had only to leave them collected in a certain part of the house for the Good People, who would come in and wash and clean them, and in the morning everything would be clean and in its proper place.

Yet in the county of Cork it would seem that the Cluricaun, of which we shall presently speak, used to enact the part of Nis or Boggart. Mr. Croker tells a story of a little being which he calls a Cluricaun, that haunted the cellar of a Mr. Macarthy, and in a note on this tale he gives the contents of a letter informing him of another ycleped Little Wildbean, that haunted the house of a Quaker gentleman named Harris, and which is precisely the Nis or Boggart. This Wildbean, who kept to the cellar, would, if one of the servants through negligence left the beer-barrel running, wedge himself into the cock and stop it, till some one came to turn it. His dinner used to be left for him in the cellar, and the cook having, one Friday, left him nothing but part of a herring and some cold potatoes, she was at midnight dragged out of her bed, and down the cellar-stairs, and so much bruised that she kept her bed for three weeks. In order at last to get rid of him, Mr. Harris resolved to remove, being told that if he went beyond a running stream the Cluricaun could not follow him. The last cart, filled with empty barrels and such like, was just moving off, when from the bung-hole of one of them Wildbean cried out, "Here, master! here we go all together!" "What!" said Mr. Harris, "dost thou go also?" "Yes, to be sure, master. Here we go, all together!" "In that case, friend," replied Mr. Harris, "let the carts be unloaded; we are just as well where we are." It is added, that "Mr. Harris died soon after, but it is said the Cluricaun still haunts the

Harris family."

In another of these Fairy Legends, Teigue of the Lee, who haunted the house of a Mr. Pratt, in the county of Cork, bears a strong resemblance to the Hinzelmann of Germany. To the story, which is exceedingly well told by a member of the society of Friends, now no more, also the narrator of the Legend of Bottle-hill, Mr. Croker has in his notes added some curious particulars.

A being named the Fear Dearg (i. e. Red Man) is also known in Munster. A tale named The Lucky Guest, which Mr. Croker gives as taken down *verbatim* from the mouth of the narrator by Mr. M'Clise, the artist, gives the fullest account of this being. A girl related that, when she was quite a child, one night, during a storm of wind and rain; a knocking was heard at the door of her father's cabin, and a voice like that of a feeble old man craving admission. On the door's being opened, there came in a little old man, about two feet and a half high, with a red sugar-loaf hat and a long scarlet coat, reaching down nearly to the ground, his hair was long and grey, and his face yellow and wrinkled. He went over to the fire (which the family had quitted in their fear), sat down and dried his clothes, and began smoking a pipe which he found there. The family went to bed, and in the morning he was gone. In about a month after he began to come regularly every night about eleven o'clock. The signal which he gave was thrusting a hairy arm through a hole in the door, which was then opened, and the family retired to bed, leaving him the room to himself. If they did not open the door, some accident was sure to happen next day to themselves or their cattle. On the whole, however, his visits brought good luck, and the family prospered, till the landlord put them out of their farm, and they never saw the Fear Dearg more.

As far as our knowledge extends, there is no being in the Irish rivers answering to the Nix or Kelpie; but on the sea coast the people believe in beings of the same kind as the Mermen and Mermaids. The Irish name is Merrow, and legends are told of them similar to those of other countries. Thus the Lady of Gollerus resembles the Mermaid-wife and others which we have already related. Instead, however, of an entire dress, it is a kind of cap, named *Cohuleen Driuth,* without which she cannot return to her subaqueous abode. Other legends tell of matrimonial unions formed by mortals with these sea—ladies, from which some families in the south claim a descent. The Lord of Dunkerron, so beautifully told in verse by Mr. Croker, relates the unfortunate termination of a marine amour of one of the O'Sullivan family. The Soul-cages alone contains the adventures of a Mermnan.

The Irish Pooka [e] is plainly the English Pouke, Puck, and would seem, like it, to denote an evil spirit. The notions respecting it are very vague. A boy in the mountains near Killarney told Mr. Croker that "old people used to say that the Pookas were very numerous in the times long ago. They were wicked-minded, black-looking, bad things, that would come in *the form of wild colts,* with chains hanging about them. They did great hurt to benighted travellers." Here we plainly have the English Puck; but it is remarkable that the boy should speak of Pookas in the plural number. In Leinster, it was always *the,* not *a* Pooka, that we heard named. When the blackberries begin to decay, and the seeds to appear, the children are told not to eat them any longer, as *the* Pooh has dirtied on them.

The celebrated fall of the Liffey, near Ballymore Eustace, is named Pool-a-Phooka, or The Pooka's Hole. Near Macroom, in the county of Cork, are the ruins of a castle built on a rock, named Carrig-a-Phooka, or The Pooka's Rock. There is an old castle not far from Dublin, called Puck's Castle, and a townland in the county of Kildare is named Puckstown. The common expression *play the Puck* is the same as *play the deuce, play the Devil.*

The most remarkable of the Fairy-tribe in Ireland, and one which is peculiar to the country, is the Leprechaun. [f] This is a being in the form of an old man, dressed as he is described in one of the following tales. He is by profession a maker of brogues; he resorts in general only to secret and retired places, where he is discovered by the sounds which he makes hammering his brogues. He is rich, like curmudgeons of his sort, and it is only by the most violent threats of doing him some bodily harm, that be can be made to show the place where his treasure lies; but if the person who has caught him can be induced (a thing that always happens, by the way) to take his eyes off him, he vanishes and with him the prospect of wealth. The only instance of more than one Leprechaun being seen at a time is that which occurs in one of the following tales, which was related by an old woman, to the writer's sister and early companion, now no more.

Yet the Leprechaun, though, as we said, peculiar to Ireland, seems indebted to England, at least, for his name. In Irish, as we have seen, he is called *Lobaircin,* and it would not be easy to write the English Lubberkin more accurately with Irish letters and Irish sounds. Leprechaun is evidently a corruption of that word. In the time of Elizabeth and James, the word Lubrican was used in England to indicate some kind of spirit. Thus Drayton gives as a part of Nymphidia's invocation of Proserpina:

> By the mandrake's dreadful groans;
> By the Lubrican's sad moans;
> By the noise of dead men's bones
> In charnelhouse rattling.

That this was the Leprechaun is, we think, clear; for in the Honest Whore of Decker and Middleton, the following words are used of an Irish footman:

> As for your Irish Lubrican, that spirit
> Whom by preposterous charms thy lust has raised.
> Part II, i. 1. [8]

We thus have the Leprechaun as a well-known Irish fairy, though his character was not understood, in the sixteenth century.

The two following tales we ourselves beard from the peasantry of Kildare in our boyhood:

NOTES

[a] Mr. Croker says, that according to the Munster peasantry the ordinary attire of the Fairy is a black bat, green coat, white stockings, and red shoes.

[b] We never heard a fairy-legend from any of the Connaught-men with whom we conversed in our boyhood. Their tales were all of Finn-mac-Cool and his heroes.

[c] See *Brittany,* and *Spain,* in both of which the legend is more perfect; but it is impossible to say which is the original. Parnell's pleasing Fairy Tale is probably formed on this Irish version, yet it agrees more with the Breton legend.

[d] This story may remind one of the Wonderful Lamp, and others. There Is something of the same kind in the Pentamerone.

[e] It is a rule of the Irish language, that the initial consonant of an oblique case, or of a word *in regimine,* becomes aspirated; thus *Pooka* (nom.), *na Phooka* (gen.), *mac* son, *a mhic (vic)* my son.

[f] In Irish *lubárkin;* the Ulster name is Logheryman, in Irish *lucharman.* For the Cork term Cluricaun, the Kerry Luricaun and the Tipperary Lurigadaun, we have found no equivalents in the Irish dictionaries. The short *o* in Irish, we may observe, is pronounced as in French and Spanish, *i. e.* as *u* in *but, cut; ai* nearly as *a* in *fall.* It may be added, on account of the following tales, that in Kildare and the adjoining counties the short English *u,* in *but, cut,* etc., is invariably pronounced as in *pull, full,* while this *u* is pronounced as that in *but, cut.*

[f] In the place of the Witch of Edmonton usually quoted with this, Lubrick is plainly the Latin *lubricus.*

[g] It will be observed that these, as well as the Young Piper in the Appendix are related in the character of a peasant. This was in accordance with a frame that was proposed for the Fairy Legends, but which proved too difficult of execution to be adopted.

Clever Tom and the Leprechaun

Oliver Tom Fwich-(i.e. Fitz)pathrick, as people used to call him, was the eldest son o' a comfortable farmer, who lived nigh hand to Morristown-Lattin, not far from the Liftey.

Tom was jist turned o' nine-an'-twinty, whin he met wid the follyin' advinthur, an' he was as cliver, clane, tight, good-lukin' a boy as any in the whole county Kildare. One fine day in harvist (it was a holiday) Tom was takin' a ramble by himsilf thro' the land, an' wint sauntherin' along the sunny side uv a hidge, an' thinkin' in himsilf, whare id be the grate harm if people, instid uv idlin' an' goin' about doin' nothin' at all, war to shake out the hay, an' bind and stook th' oats that was lyin' an the ledge, 'specially as the weather was raither brokm uv late, whin all uv a suddint he h'ard a clackin' sort o' n'ise jist a little way fornint him, in the hidge.

"Dear me," said Tom, "but isn't it now raaly suiprisin' to hear the stonechatters singin' so late in the saison." So Tom stole an, goin' on the tips o' his toes to thry iv he cud git a sight o' what was makin' the n'ise, to see iv he was right in his guess. The n'ise stopt; but as Tom hiked sharp thro' the bushes, what did he see in a neuk o' the hidge but a brown pitcher that might hould about a gallon an' a haff o' liquor; an' bye and bye he seen a little wee deeny dawny bit iv an ould man, wid a little motty iv a cocked hat stuck an the top iv his head, an' a deeshy daushy leather apron hangin' down afore him, an' he pulled out a little wooden stool, an' stud up upon it, and dipped a little piggen into the pitcher, an' tuk out the full av it, an' put it beside the stool, an' thin sot down undher the pitcher, an' begun to work at put' a heelpiece an a bit iv a brogue jist fittin' fur himself.

"Well, by the powers!" said Tom to himsilf, "I aften hard tell o' the Leprechauns, an', to tell God's thruth, I nivir rightly believed in thim, but here 'a won o' thim in right airnest; if I go knowin'ly to work, I 'm a med man. They say a body must nivir take their eyes aff o' thim, or they'll escape."

Tom now stole an a little farther, wid his eye fixed an the little man jist as a cat does wid a mouse, or, as we read in books, the rattlesnake does wid the birds he wants to inchant. So, whin he got up quite close to him, "God bless your work, honest man," sez Tom. The little man raised up his head, an' "Thank you kindly," sez he. "I wundher you 'd be workin' an the holiday," sez Tom. "That's my own business, an' none of your's," was the reply, short enough. "Well, may be, thin, you'd be civil enough to tell us, what you 'ye got in the pitcher there," sez Tom. "Aye, will I, wid pleasure," sez he: "it's good beer." "Beer!" sez Tom: "Blud an' turf man, whare did ye git it?" "Whare did I git it is it? why I med it to be shure; an' what do ye think I med it av?" "Divil a one o' me knows," sea Tom, "but av malt, I 'spose; what ilse?" "'Tis there you 're out; I med it av haith." "Av haith!" sez Tom, burstin' out laughin'. "Shure you don't take me to be sich an omedhaun as to b'lieve that?" "Do as ye plase," sez he, "but what I tell ye is the raal thruth. Did ye nivir hear tell o' the Danes?" "To be shure I did," sea Tom, "warn't thim the chaps we gev such a lickin' whin they thought to take Derry frum huz?" "Hem," sez the little man dhryly, "is that all ye know about the matther?" "Well, but about thim Danes," sea Tom. "Why all th' about thim is," said he, "is that whin they war here they taught huz to make beer out o' the haith, an' the saicret 's in my family ivir sense." "Will ye giv a body a taste o' yer beer to thry?" sez Tom. "I 'll tell ye what it is, young man, it id be fitther fur ye to be lukin' afther yer father's propirty thi'n to be botherin' dacint, quite people wid yer foolish questions. There, now, while you 're idlin' away yer time here, there 's the cows hay' bruk into th' oats, an' are knockin' the corn all about."

Tom was taken so by surprise wid this, that he was jist an the very point o' turnin' round, whin he recollicted himsilf. So, afeard that the like might happin agin, he med a grab at the Leprechaun, an' cotch him up in his hand, but in his hurry he ovirset the pitcher, and spilt all the beer, so that he couldn't git a taste uv it to tell what sort it was. He thin swore what he wouldn't do to him iv he didn't show him whare his money was. Tom luked so wicked, an' so bloody-minded, that the little man was quite frightened. "So," sez he, "come along wid me a couple o' fields aff an' I 'll show ye a crock o' gould." So they wint, an' Tom held the Leprechaun fast in his hand, an' nivir tuk his eyes frum aff uv him, though they had to crass hidges an' ditches, an' a cruked bit uv a bog (fur the Leprechaun seemed, out o' pure mischief, to pick out the hardest and most conthrairy way), till at last they come to a grate field all full o' *balyawn buies,* [a] an' the Leprechaun pointed to a big bolyawn, an' sez he, "Dig undher that bolyawn, an' you 'll git a crock chuck full o' goulden guineas."

Tom, in his hurry, had nivir minded the bringin' a fack [b] wid him, so he thought to run home and fetch one, an' that he might know the place agin, he tuk aff one o' his red garthers, and tied it round the bolyawn. "I s'pose," sez the Leprechaun, very civilly, "ye 've no further occashin fur me?" "No," sez Tom, "ye may go away now, if ye like, and God speed ye, an' may good luck attind ye whareivir ye go." "Well, good bye to ye, Tom Fwichpathrick," sed the Leprechaun, "an' much good may do ye wid what ye 'll git."

So Tom run fur the bare life, till he come home, an' got a fack, an' thin away wid him as hard as he could pilt back to the field o' bolyawns; but whin he got there, lo an' behould, not a bolyawn in the field, but had a red garther, the very idintical model o' his own, tied about it; an' as to diggin' up the whole field, that was all nonsinse, fur there was more nor twinty good Irish acres in it. So Tom come home agin wid his fack an his shouldher, a little cooler nor he wint; and many's the hearty curse he gev the Leprechaun ivry time he thought o' the nate turn he sarved him. [c]

NOTES

[a] Lit. Yellow-stick, the ragwort or ragweed, which grows to a great size in Ireland.

[b] A kind of spade with but one step, used in Leinster.

[c] All that is said in this legend about the beer is a pure fiction, for we never heard of a Leprechaun drinking or smoking. It is, however, a tradition of the peasantry, that the Danes used to make beer of the heath. It was a Protestant farmer in the county of Cavan, that showed such knowledge of the siege of Derry; the Catholic gardener who told us this story, knew far better. It is also the popular belief that the Danes keep up their claim on Ireland, and that a Danish father, when marrying his daughter, gives her a portion in Ireland.

The Leprechaun in the Garden

There's a sort a' people that every body must have met wid sumtime or another. I mane thim people that purtinds not to b'lieve in things that in their hearts they *do* b'lieve in, an' are mortially afeard o' too. Now Failey [a] Mooney was one o' these. Failey (iv any o' yez knew him) was a rollockin', rattlin', divil-may-care sort ov a chap like—but that 'a neither here nor there; he was always talkin' one nonsinse or another; an' among the rest o' his fooleries, he purtinded not to b'lieve in the fairies, the Leprechauns, an' the Poocas, an' he evin sumtimes had the impedince to purtind to doubt o' ghosts, that every body b'lieves in, at any rate. Yit sum people used to wink an' luk knowin' whin Failey was gostherin', fur it was obsarved that he was mighty shy o' crassin' the foord a' Ahnamoe afther nightfall; an' that whin onst he was ridin' past the ould church o' Tipper in the dark, tho' he'd got enough o' pottheen into him to make any man stout, he med the horse trot so that there was no keepin' up wid him, an' iv'ry now an' thin he'd throw a sharp luk-out ovir his lift shouldher.

Well, one night there was a parcel o' the neighbours sittin' dhrinkin' an' talkin' at Larry Rielly's public-house, an' Failey was one o' the party. He was, as usual, gittin' an wid his nonsinse an' baldherdash about the fairies, an' swearin' that he didn't b'lieve there was any live things, barrin' min an' bastes, an' birds and fishes, an' sich like things as a body cud see, and he wint on talkin' in so profane a way o' the good people, that som o' the company grew timid an' begun to crass thimsilves, not knowin' what might happin', whin an ould woman called Mary Hogan wid a long blue cloak about her, that was sittin' in the chimbly corner smokin' her pipe widout takin' the laste share in the conversations tuk the pipe out o' her mouth, an' threw the ashes out o' it, an' spit in the fire, an' turnin' round, luked Failey straight in the face. "An' so you don't b'lieve there 's sich things as Leprechauns, don't ye?" sed she.

Well, Failey luked rayther daunted, but howsumdivir he sed nothin'. "Why, thin, upon my throth, an' it well becomes the likes a' ye, an' that 's nothin' but a bit uv a gossoon, to take upon yer to purtind not to b'lieve what yer father, an' yer father's father, an' his father dare him, nivir med the laste doubt uv. But to make the matther short, seein' 's b'lievin' they say, an' I, that might be yer gran'mother, tell ye there is sich 'things as Leprechauns, an' what 'a more, that I mysilf sedn one o' thim,—there 'a fur ye, now!"

All the people in the room luked quite surprised at this, an' crowded up to the fireplace to listen to her. Failey thried to laugh, but it wouldn't do, nobody minded him.

"I remimber," sed she, "some time afther I married the honest man, that 's now dead and gone, it was by the same token jist a little afore I lay in o' my first child (an' that 'a many a long day ago), I was sittin', as I sed, out in our little bit a' a gardin, wid my knittin' in my hand, watchin' sum bees we had that war goin' to swarm. It was a fine sunshiny day about the middle o' June, an' the bees war hummin' and flyin' backwards an' forwards frum the hives, an' the birds war chirpin' an' hoppin' an the bushes, an' the buttherflies war flyin' about an' sittin' an the flowers, an' ev'ry thing smelt so fresh an' so sweet, an' I felt so happy, that I hardly knew whare I was. Well, all uv a suddint, I heard among sum rows of banes we had in a corner o' the gardin, a n'ise that wint tick tack tick tack, jist fur all the world as iv a brogue-maker was puttin' an the heel uv a pump. 'The Lord presarve us,' sed I to mysilf, 'what in the world can that be?' So I laid down my knittin', an' got up, an' stole ovir to the banes, an' nivir believe me iv I didn't see, sittin' right forenint me, in the very middle of thim, a bit of an ould man, not a quarther so big as a newborn child, wid a little' cocked hat an his head, an' a dudeen in his mouth, smokin' away; an' a plain, ould-fashioned, dhrab-coloured coat, wid big brass buttons upon it, an his back, an' a pair o' massy silver buckles in his shoes, that a'most covered his feet they war so big, an' be workin' away as hard as ivir he could, heelin' a little pair o' pumps. The instant <u>minnit</u> I clapt my two eyes upon him I knew him to be a Leprechaun, an' as I was stout an' foolhardy, sez I to him ' God save ye honist man! that 's hard work ye 're at this hot day.' He luked up in my face quite vexed like; so wid that I med a run at him an' cotch hould o' him in my hand, an' axed him whare was his purse o' money! 'Money?' sed he, 'money *annagh!* an' whare on airth id a poor little ould crathur like myself git money?' 'Come, come,' sed I, 'none o' yer thricks upon thravellers; doesn't every body know that Leprechauns, like ye, are all as rich as the dlvil himsilf.' So I pulled out a knife I'd in my pocket, an' put on as wicked a face as ivir I could (an' in throth, that was no aisy matther fur me thin, fur I was as comely an' good-humoured a lukin' girl as you'd see frum this to Ballitore)—an' swore by this and by that, if 'he didn't instantly gi' me his purse, or show me a pot o' goold, I'd cut the nose aft his face. Well, to be shure, the little man did luk so frightened at hearin' these words, that I a'most found it in my heart to pity the poor little crathur. 'Thin,' sed he, 'come wid me jist a couple o' fields aft, an' I'll show ye whare I keep my money.' So I wint, still houldin' him fast in my hand, an' keepin' my eyes fixed upon him, whin all o' a suddint I h'ard.a whiz-z behind me. 'There! there! cries he, 'there's yer bees all swarmin' an' goin' aff wid thimsilves like blazes.' I, like a fool as I was, turned my head round, an' whin I seen nothin' at all, an' luked back at the Leprechaun, an' found nothin' at all at all in my hand—fur whin I had the ill luck to take my eyes aff him, ye see, he slipped out o' my fingers jist as iv he was med o' fog or smoke, an' the sarra the fut he iver, come nigh my garden again."

NOTE

[a] *i. e.* Felix. On account of the Romish custom of naming after Saints, Felix, Thaddaeus, Terence, Augustine, etc., are common names among the peasantry.

The Three Leprechauns

Mrs. L. having heard that Molly Toole, an old woman who held a few acres of land from Mr. L., had seen Leprechauns, resolved to visit her, and learn the truth from her own lips. Accordingly, one Sunday, after church, she made her appearance at Molly's residence, which was—no very common thing—extremely neat and comfortable. As she entered, every thing looked gay and cheerful. The sun shone bright in through the door on the earthen floor. Molly was seated at the far side of the fire in her arm-chair; her daughter Mary, the prettiest girl on the lands, was looking to the dinner that was boiling; and her son Mickey, a young man of about two-and-twenty, was standing lolling with his back against the dresser.

The arrival of the mistress disturbed the stillness that had hitherto prevailed. Mary, who was a great favourite, hastened to the door to meet her, and shake hands with her. Molly herself had nearly got to the middle of the floor when the mistress met her, and Mickey modestly staid where he was till he should catch her attention. "O then, musha! but isn't it a glad sight for my ould eyes to see your own silf undher my roof? Mary, what ails you, girl? and why don't you go into the room and fetch out a good chair for the misthress to sit down upon and rest herself?" "Deed faith, mother, I 'm so glad I don't know what I 'm doin'. Sure you know I didn't see the misthress since she cum down afore."

Mickey now caught Mrs. L.'s eye, and she asked him how he did. "By Gorra, bravely, ma'am, thank you," said be, giving himself a wriggle, while his two hands and the small of his back rested on the edge of the dresser.

"Now, Mary, stir yourself alanna," said the old woman, "and get out the bread and butther. Sure you know the misthress can't but be hungry afther her walk."—"O, never mind it, Molly; it's too much trouble."—"Throuble, indeed! it 's as nice butther, ma'am, as iver you put a tooth in; and it was Mary herself that med it."—"O, then I must taste it."

A nice half griddle of whole-meal bread and a print of fresh butter were now produced, and Molly helped the mistress with her own hands. As she was eating, Mary kept looking in her face, and at last said, "Ah then, mother, doesn't the misthress luk mighty well? Upon my faikins, ma'am, I never seen you luking half so handsome."—"Well! and why wouldn't she luk well? And niver will she luk betther nor be betther nor I wish her."—"Well, Molly, I think I may return the compliment, for Mary is prettier than ever; and as for yourself, I really believe it 's young again you're growing."—"Why, God be thanked, ma'am, I 'm stout and hearty; and though I say it mysilf, there 'a not an ould woman in the county can stir about betther nor me, and I 'm up ivery mornin' at the peep of day, and rout them all up out of their beds. Don't I?" said she, looking at Mary.—"Faith, and sure you do, mother," replied Mickey; "and before the peep of day, too; for you have no marcy in you at all at all."—"Ah, in my young days," continued the old woman, "people woren't slugabeds; out airly, home late—that was the way wid thim."—"And usedn't people to see Leprechauns in thim days, mother?" said Mickey, laughing.— "Hould your tongue, you saucy cub, you," cried Molly; "what do you know about thim?"—"Leprechauns?'" said Mrs. L., gladly catching at the opportunity; "did people really, Molly, see Leprechauns in your young days?"—"Yes, indeed, ma'am; some people say they did," replied Molly, very composedly.—"O com' now, mother," cried Mickey, "don't think to be goin' it upon us that away; you know you seen thim one time yoursilf, and you hadn't the gumption in you to cotch thim, and git their crocks of gould from thim."—"Now, Molly, is that really true that you saw the Leprechauns?"—"'Deed, and did I, ma'am; but this boy 's always laughin' at me about thim, and that makes me rather shy in talkin' o' thim"—"Well, Molly, I won't laugh at you; so, come, tell me how you saw them."

"Well, ma'am, you see it was whin I was jist about the age of Mary, there. I was comin' home late one Monday evenin' from the market; for my aunt Kitty, God be marciful to her! would keep me to take a cup of tay. It was in the summer time, you see, ma'am, much about the middle of Tune, an' it was through the fields I come. Well, ma'am, as I was sayin', it was late in the evenin', that is, the sun was near goin' down, an' the light was straight in my eyes, an' I come along through the bog-meadow; for it was shortly afther I was married to him that 'a gone, an' we wor livin' in this very house you're in now; an' thin whin I come to the castle-field—the pathway you know, ma'am, goes right through the middle uv it—an' it was thin as fine a field of whate, jist shot out, as you'd wish to luk at; an' it was a purty sight to see it wavin' so beautifully wid every air of wind that was goin' over it, dancin' like to the music of a thrash, that was singin' down below in the hidge. [a] Well, ma'am, I crasst over the style that 'a there yit, and wint along fair and aisy, till I was near about the middle o' the field, whin somethin' med me cast my. eyes to the ground, a little before me; an' thin I saw, as sure as I 'm sittin' here, no less nor three o' the Leprechauns, all bundled together like so miny tailyors, in the middle o' the path before me. They worn't hammerin' their pumps, nor makin' any kind, of n'ise whatever; but there they wor, the three little fellows, wid their cocked hats upon thim, an' their legs gothered up undher thim, workin' away at their thrade as hard as may be. If you wor only to see, ma'am, how fast their little ilbows wint as they pulled out their inds! Well, every one o' thim had his eye cocked upon me, an' their eyes wor as bright as the eye of a frog, an' I cudn't stir one step from the spot for the life o' me.. So I turned my head round, and prayed to the Lord in his marcy to deliver me from thim, and when I wint to luk at thim agin, ma'am, not a sight o' thim was to be seen: they wor gone like a dhrame."—"But, Molly, why did you not catch them?"—"I was afeard, ma'am, that 'a the thruth uv it; but maybe I was as well widout thim. I niver h'ard tell of a Leprechaun yit that wasn't too many for any one that cotch him."—"Well, and Molly, do you think there are any Leprechauns now?"—"It 's my belief, ma'am, they're all gone out of the country, diver and dane, along wid the Fairies; for I niver hear tell o' thim now at all."

Mrs. L. having now attained her object, after a little more talk with the good old woman, took her leave, attended by Mary, who would see her a piece of the way home. And Mary being asked what she thought of the Leprechauns, confessed her inability to give a decided opinion: her mother, she knew, was incapable of telling a lie, and yet she had her doubts if there ever were such things as Leprechauns.

The following tale of a Cluricaun, related by the writer of the Legend of Bottle Hill, is of a peculiar character. We have never heard anything similar of a Leprechaun.

NOTE

[a] In our Tales and Popular Fictions, p. 16, we noticed the coincidence between this and a passage in an Arabic author. We did not then recollect the. following verses of Milton,
The willows and the hazle copses green
Shall now no more be seen
Fanning their joyous leaves to thy soft lays.
Lycidas, 42.
The simile of the moon among the stars in the same place, we have since found in the Nibelungen Lied (st. 285), and in some of our old poets, and Hammer says (Schirin i. note 7), that it occurs even to satiety in Oriental poetry. In like manner Camoens' simile of the mirror, mentioned in the same place, occurs in Poliziano's Stanze i. 64.

The Little Shoe

"Now tell me, Molly," said Mr. Coote to Molly Cogan, as he met her on the road one day, close to one of the old gateways of Kilmallock, "did you ever hear of the Cluricaun?"—"Is it the Cluricaun? Why, thin, to be shure; aften an' aften. Many 'a the time I h'ard my father, rest his sowl! tell about 'em over and over agin."—"But did you ever see one, Molly—did you ever see one yourself?"—"Och! no, I niver seen one m my life; but my gran'father, that 's my father's, father, you know, he seen one, one time, an' cotch him too."—"Caught him! Oh! Molly, tell me how was that."

"'Why, thin, I 'll tell ye. My gran'father, you see, was out there above in the bog, dhrawin' home turf; an' the poor ould mare was tir't afther her day's work, an' the ould man wint out to the stable to look afther her, an' to see if she was aitin' her hay; an' whin he come to the stable door there, my dear, he h'ard sumthin' hammerin', hammerin', hammerin', jist for all the wurld like a shoemaker makin' a shoe, and whis'lin' all the time the purtiest chune he iver h'ard in his whole life afore. Well, my gran'father he thought it was the Cluricaun, an' he sed to himsilf, sez he, 'I'll ketch you, if I can, an' thin I 'll have money enough always.' So he opened the door very quitely, an' didn't make a taste o' n'ise in the wurld, an' luked all about, but the niver a bit o' the little man cud be see anywhare, but he h'ard his hammerin' and 'whis'lin', an' so he luked and luked, till at last he seen the little fellow; an' whare was he, do ye think, but in the girth undher the mare; an' there he was, wid his little bit ov an apron an him, an' his hammer in his hand, an' a little red night-cap an his head, an' be makin' a shoe; an' he was so busy wid us work, an' was hammerin' an' whis'lin' so loud, that he niver minded my gran'father, till be cotch him fast in his hand. 'Faix, I have ye now,' says he, an' I'll niver let ye go till I git yer purse—that 'a what I won't; so give it here at onst to me, now.' 'Stop, stop,' says the Cluricaun; 'stop, stop,' says he, 'till I get it for ye.' So my gran'father, like a fool, ye see, opened his hand a little, an' the little weeny chap jumped away laughin', an' he niver seen him any more, an' the divil a bit o' the purse did he git; only the Cluricaun left his little shoe that he was makin'. An' my gran'father was mad enough wid himself for lettin' him go; but he had the shoe all his life, an' my own mother tould me she aftin seen it, an' had it in her hand; an' 'twas the purtiest little shoe she ivir seen."—"An' did you see it yourself; Molly?"—"Oh! no, my dear, 'twas lost long afore I was born; but my mother tould me aftin an' aftin enough."

SCOTTISH HIGHLANDS

Brownie has got a cowl and coat,
And never more will work a jot.
–STEWART.

Colonies of Gothic Fairies, it would appear, early established themselves in the Highlands, and almost every Lowland, German, and
Scandinavian Fairy or Dwarf-tale will there find its fellow. The Gaelic Fairies are very handsome in their persons; their usual attire is
green. They dance and sing, lend and borrow, and they make cloth
and shoes in an amazingly short space of time. They make their
raids upon the low country, and carry off women and children; they
fetch midwives to assist at the birth of their children, and mortals
have spent a night at the fairy revels, and next morning found that
the night had extended a hundred years. Highland fairies also take
the diversion of the chase. "One Highlander," says Mc.Culloch, [a]
"in passing a mountain, bears the tramp of horses, the music of the
horn, and the cheering of the huntsmen; when suddenly a gallant
crew of thirteen fairy hunters, dressed in green, sweep by him, the
silver bosses of their bridles jingling in the night breeze."

The Gael call the Fairies Daoine Shi', [b] *(Dheenè Shee)* and their
habitations Shians, or Tomhans. These are a sort of turrets, resembling masses of rock or hillocks. By day they are indistinguishable,
but at night they are frequently lit up with great splendour.

Brownie, too, 'shows his honest face' in the Highlands; and
the mischievous water-Kelpie also appears in his equine form, and
seeks to decoy unwary persons to mount him, that he may plunge

with his rider into the neighbouring loch or river.

The Highlanders have nearly the same ideas as their Shetland neighbours, respecting the seals.

The following legends will illustrate what we have stated. [c]

NOTES

[a] Account of the Highlands, etc. iv. 358

[b] *Men of Peace*, perhaps the *Stille-folk*, Still-people, or rather, merely Fairy—or Spirit—people.

[c] See Stewart, The Popular Superstitions of thc Highlanders. Edinburgh, 1823. As Mr. Stewart's mode of narrating is not the very best, we have taken the liberty of re-writing and abridging the legends.

The Fairy's Inquiry

A clergyman was returning home one night after visiting a sick member of his congregation. His way led by a lake, and as he proceeded he was surprised to hear most melodious strains of music. He sat down to listen. The music seemed to approach coming over the lake accompanied by a light. At length he discerned a man walking on the water, attended by a number of little beings, some bearing lights, others musical instruments. At the beach the man dismissed his attendants, and then walking up to the minister saluted him courteously. He was a little grey-headed old man, dressed in rather an unusual garb. The minister having returned his salute begged of him to come and sit beside him. He complied with the request, and on being asked who he was, replied that he was one of the Daoine Shi. He added that he and they had originally been angels, but having been seduced into revolt by Satan, they had been cast down to earth where they were to dwell till the day of doom. His object now was, to ascertain from the minister what would be their condition after that awful day. The minister then questioned him on the articles of faith; but as his answers did not prove satisfactory, and as in repeating the Lord's Prayer, he persisted in saying *wed* instead of *art in heaven,* he did not feel himself justified in holding out any hopes to him. The fairy then gave a cry of despair and flung himself into the loch, and the minister resumed his journey.

The Young Man in the Shian

A farmer named Macgillivray, one time removed from the neighbourhood of Cairngorm in Strathspey to the forest of Glenavon,
in which the fairies are said to reside. Late one night, as two of his
sons, Donald and Bory, were in search of some of his sheep that had
strayed, they saw lights streaming from the crevices of a fairy turret
which in the day time had only the appearance of a rock. They drew
nigh to it, and there they heard jigs and reels played inside in the
most exquisite manner. Rory was so fascinated that he proposed that
they should enter and take part in the dance. Donald did all he could
to dissuade him, but in vain. He jumped into the Shian, and plunged
at once into the whirling movements of its inhabitants. Donald was
in great perplexity, for he feared to enter the Shian. All he could do
therefore was to put his mouth to one of the crevices, and calling,
as the custom was, three times on his brother, entreating him in the
most moving terms, to come away and return home. But his entreaties were unheeded and he was obliged to return alone.

Every means now was resorted to for the recovery of Rory,
but to no purpose. His family gave him up for lost, when a *Duin
Glichd* or Wise man, told Donald to go to the place where he had
lost his brother, a year and a day from the time, and placing in his
garments a rowan-cross, to enter the Shian boldly, and claim him in
the divine name, and if he would not come voluntarily, to seize him
and drag hine out; for the fairies would have no power to prevent
him. After some hesitation Donald assented. At the appointed time
he approached the Shian at midnight. It was full of revelry, and the

merry dance was going on as before. Donald had his terrors no doubt, but they gave way to his fraternal affection. He entered and found Rory in the midst of a Highland Fling, and running up, to him, seized him by the collar, repeating the words dictated by the Wise man. Rory agreed to go provided he would let him finish his dance; for he had not been, he assured him, more than half an hour in the place, but Donald was inexorable, and took him home to his parents. Rory would never have believed that his half-hour had been a twelve-month, "did not the calves grown now into stots, and the new-born babes now toddling about the house, at length convince him that in his single reel he had danced for a twelvemonth and a day."

The Two Fiddlers

Nearly three hundred years ago, there dwelt in Strathspey two fiddlers, greatly renowned in their art. One Christmas they resolved to go try their fortune in Inverness. On arriving in that town they took lodgings, and as was the custom at that time, hired the bellman to go round announcing their arrival, their qualifications, their fame, and their terms. Soon after they were visited by a venerable-looking grey-haired old man, who not only found no fault with, but actually offered to double their terms if they would go with him. They agreed, and he led them out of the town, and brought them to a very strange-looking dwelling which seemed to them to be very like a Shian. The money, however, and the entreaties of their guide induced them to enter it, and their musical talents were instantly put into requisition, and the dancing was such as in their lives they had never witnessed.

When morning came they took their leave highly gratified with the liberal treatment they had received. It surprised them greatly to find that it was out of a hill and not a house that they issued, and when they, came to the town, they could not recognise any place or person, every thing seemed so altered. While they and the townspeople were in mutual amazement, there came up a very old man, who on hearing their story, said: "You are then the two men who lodged with my great-grandfather, and whom Thomas Rimer, it was supposed, decoyed to Tomnafurach. Your friends were greatly grieved on your account, but it is a hundred years ago, and your names are now no longer known." It was the Sabbath day and the bells were tolling; the fiddlers, deeply penetrated with awe at what had occurred, entered the church to join in the offices of religion. They sat in silent meditation while the bell continued ringing, but the moment that the minister commenced the service they crumbled away into dust.

The Fairy-Labour

Many years ago there dwelt in Strathspey a midwife of great repute. One night just as she was going to bed, she heard a loud knocking at the door, and on opening it she saw there a man and a grey horse, *both out of breath.* The rider requested her to jump up behind him and come away to assist a lady who was in great danger. He would not even consent to her stopping to change her dress, as it would cause delay. She mounted and away they went at full speed. On the way she tried to learn from the rider whither she was going, but all she could get from him was, that she would be well paid. At length he let out that it was to a fairy-lady he was taking her. Nothing daunted, however, she went on, and on reaching the Shian, she found that her services were really very much needed. She succeeded in bringing a fine boy to the light, which caused so much joy, that the fairies desired her to ask what she would, and if it was in their power, it should be granted. Her desire was that success might attend herself and her posterity in all similar operations. The gift was conferred and it continued, it was said, with her great-grandson, at the time the collector of these legends wrote.

The Fairy borrowing Oatmeal

A fairy came one day from one of the turrets of Craig-ail-naic to the wife of one of the tenants in Delnabo, and asked her to lend her a firlot of oatmeal for food for her family, promising to repay it soon, as she was every moment expecting an ample supply. The woman complied with this request, and after, as was the custom of the country, having regaled her with bread, cheese, and whiskey, she went, as was usual, to see her a part of the way home. When they had reached the summit of an eminence near the town, the *Béanshi* told her she might take her meal home again as she was now abundantly supplied. The woman did as desired, and as she went along she beheld the corn-kiln of an adjacent farm all in a blaze.

The Fairy-Gift

A farmer in Strathspey was one day engaged in sowing one of his fields and singing at his work. A fairy damsel of great beauty came up to him and requested him to sing for her a favourite old Gaelic song named *NighanDonne na Bual*. He complied, and she then asked him to give her some of his corn. At this he demurred a little and wished to know what she would give him in return. She replied with a significant look that his seed would never fail him. He then gave to her liberally and she departed. He went on sowing, and when he had finished a large field, he found that his bag was as full and as heavy as when he began. He then sowed another field of the same size, with the same result, and satisfied with his day's work, he threw the bag on his shoulder and went home. Just as he was entering the barn-door he was met by his wife, a foolish talkative body with a tongue as long, and a head as empty as the church bell, who, struck with the appearance of the bag after a day's sowing, began to ask him about it. Instantly it became quite empty. "I'll be the death of you, you foolish woman," roared out the farmer; "if it were not for your idle talk, that bag was worth its weight in gold."

The Stolen Ox

The tacksman *(i. e.* tenant) of the farm of Auchriachan in Strathavon, while searching one day for his goats on a hill in Glenlivat, found himself suddenly enveloped in a dense fog. It continued till night came on when he began to give himself up to despair. Suddenly he beheld a light at no great distance. He hastened toward it, and found that it proceeded from a strange-looking edifice. The door was open, and he entered, but great was his surprise to meet there a woman whose funeral he had lately attended. From her he learned that this was an abode of the fairies for whom she kept house, and his only chance of safety, she said, was in being concealed from them; for which purpose she hid him in a corner of the apartment. Presently in came a troop of fairies, and began calling out for food. An old dry-looking fellow then reminded them of the miserly, as he styled him, tacksman of Auchriachan, and how he cheated them out of their lawful share of his property, by using some charms taught him by his old grandmother. "He is now from home," said he, "in search of our allies, [a] his goats, and his family have neglected to use the charm, so come let us have his favourite ox for supper." The speaker was Thomas Rimer, and the plan was adopted with acclamation. "But what are we to do for bread?" cried one. "We'll have Auchriachan's new baked bread," replied Thomas; "his wife forgot to cross the first bannock." So said, so done. The ox was brought in and slaughtered before the eyes of his master, whom, while the fairies were employed about their cooking, his friend gave an opportunity of making his escape.

The mist had now cleared away and the moon was shining.

Auchriachan therefore soon reached his home. His wife instantly produced a basket of new-baked bannocks with milk and urged him to eat. But his mind was running on his ox, and his first question was, who had served the cattle that night. He then asked the son who had done it if he had used the charm, and he owned he had forgotten it. "Alas! alas!" cried he, "my favourite ox is no more." "How can that be?" said one of the sons, "I saw him alive and well not two hours ago." "It was nothing but a fairy stock," cried the father. "Bring him out here." The poor ox was led forth, and the farmer, after abusing it and those that sent it, felled it to the ground. The carcase was flung down the brae at the back of the house, and the bread was sent after it, and there they both lay untouched, for it was observed that neither cat nor dog would put a tooth in either of them.

NOTE

[a] "The goats are supposed to be upon a very good understanding with the fairies, and possessed of more cunning and knowledge than their appearance bespeaks."—Stewart: see *Wales*.

The Stolen Lady

John Roy, who lived in Glenbroun, in the parish of Abernethy, being out one night on the hills in search of his cattle, met a troop of fairies, who seemed to have got a prize of some sort or other. Recollecting that the fairies are obliged to exchange whatever they may have with any one who offers them anything, however low in value, for it, he flung his bonnet to them, crying *Shuis slo slumus sheen* (i. e., mine is yours and yours is mine). The fairies dropped their booty, which proved to be a Sassenach (English) lady whom the dwellers of the Shian of Coir-laggac had carried away from her own country, leaving a stock in her place which, of course, died and was buried. John brought her home, and she lived for many years in his house. "It happened, however, in the course of time," said the Gaelic narrator, "that the *new king*; found it necessary to make the great roads through these countries by means of soldiers, for the purpose of letting coaches and carriages pass to the northern cities; and those soldiers had officers and commanders in the same way as our fighting army have now. Those soldiers were never great favourites m these countries, particularly during the time that our kings were alive; and consequently it was no easy matter for them, either officers or men, to procure for themselves comfortable quarters." But John Roy would not keep up the national animosity to the *cottan dearg* (red-coats),and he offered a residence in his house to a *Saxon* captain and his son. When there they could not take their eyes off the English lady, and the son remarked to his father what a strong likeness she bore to his deceased mother. The father replied that be too had been struck with the resemblance, and said he could almost fancy she *was* his wife. He then mentioned her name and those of some persons connected with them. The lady by these words at once recognised her husband and son, and honest John Roy had the satisfaction of reuniting the long-separated husband and wife, and receiving their most grateful acknowledgments. [a]

NOTE

[a] There is a similar legend in Scandinavia. As a smith was at work in his forge late one evening, he heard great wailing out on the road, and by the light of the red-hot iron that he was hammering, he saw a woman whom a Troll was driving along, bawling at her "A little more! a little more!" He ran out, put the red-hot iron between them, and thus delivered her from the power of the Troll. He led her into his house and that night she was delivered of twins, In the morning he waited on her husband, who lie supposed must be in great affliction at the loss of his wife. But to his surprise he saw there, in bed, a woman the very image of her he had saved from the Troll. Knowing at once what she must be, he raised an axe he had in his band, and cleft her skull. The matter was soon explained to the satisfaction of the husband, who gladly received his real wife and her twins."—. Thiele, i. 88. *Oral.*

The Changeling

A couple of Strathspey lads who dealt in whiskey that never paid duty, which they used to purchase in Glenlivat, and sell at Badenoch and Fort William, were one night laying in stock at Glenlivat when they heard the child in the cradle give a piercing cry, just as if it had been shot. The mother, of course, blessed it, and the Strathspey lads took no further notice, and soon after set out with their goods. They had not gone far when they found a fine healthy child lying all alone on the road-side, which they soon recognised as that of their friend. They saw at once how the thing was. The fairies had taken away the real child and left a stock, but, owing to the pious ejaculation of the mother, they had been forced to drop it. As the urgency of their business did not permit them to return, they took the child with them, and kept it till the next time they had occasion to visit Glenlivat. On their arrival they said nothing about the child, which they kept concealed. In the course of conversation, the mother took occasion to remark that the disease which had attacked the child the last time they were there had never left it, and she had now little hopes of its recovery. As if to confirm her statement, it continued uttering most piteous cries. To end the matter at once, the lads produced the real child healthy and hearty, and told how they had found it. An exchange was at once effected, and they forthwith proceeded to dispose of their new charge. For this purpose they got an old *creel* to put him in and some straw to light under it. Seeing the serious turn matters were likely to take, he resolved not to await the trial, but flew up the *smoke-hole,* and when at the top he cried out that things would

have gone very differently with them had it not been for the arrival
of their guests.

The Wounded Seal

There once dwelt on the northern coast, not far from Taign Jan Crot Callow *(John o' Groat's House), a* man who gained his living by fishing. He was particularly devoted to the killing of the seals, in which he had great success. One evening just as he had returned home from his usual occupation, he was called upon by a man on horseback who was an utter stranger to him, but who said that he was come on the part of a person who wished to make a large purchase of seal-skins from him, and wanted to see him for that purpose that very evening. He therefore desired him to get up behind him and come away without any delay. Urged by the hope of profit he consented, and away they went with such speed that the wind which was in their backs seemed to be in their faces. At length they reached the verge of a stupendous precipice overhanging the sea, where his guide bade him alight, as they were now at the end of their journey. "But where," says he, "is the person you spoke of?" "You 'll see him presently," said the guide, and, catching hold of him, he plunged with him into the sea. They went down and down, till at last they came to a door which led into a range of apartments inhabited by seals, and the man to his amazement now saw that he himself was become one of these animals. They seemed all in low spirits, but they spoke kindly to him, and assured him of his safety. His guide now produced a huge *gully* or *joctaleg,* at sight of which, thinking his life was to be taken away, he began to cry for mercy. "Did you ever see this knife before?" said the guide. He looked at it and saw it was his own, which he had that very day stuck into a seal who had made his escape with it sticking in him. He did not, therefore, attempt to deny that it had been his property. "Well," said. the guide, "that seal was my father. He now lies dangerously ill, and as it is only you that can cure him, l have brought you hither." He then led him into an inner room, where the old seal lay suffering grievously from a cut in his hind quarters. He was then desired to lay his hand on the wound, at which it instantly healed, and the patient arose hale and sound. All now was joy and festivity in the abode of the seals, and the guide, turning to the seal-hunter, said, "l will now take you back to your family, but you must first take a solemn oath never again to kill a seal as long as you live." Hard as the condition was, he cheerfully accepted it. His guide then laid hold on him, and they rose up, up, till they reached the surface of the sea, and landed at the cliff. He breathed on him and they resumed the human form. They then mounted the horse and sped away like lightning till they reached the fisherman's house. At parting his companion left with him such a present as made him think light of giving over his seal-hunting.

The Brownies

Two Brownies, man and woman, were attached to the ancient family of Tullochgorm, in Strathspey. The former was named Brownie-Clod, from a habit he had of flinging clods at passers-by; the latter was called Maug Vuluchd *(i.e.,* Hairy Mag), on account of her great quantity of hair. She was a capital housekeeper, and used invisibly to lay out the table in the neatest and handiest manner. Whatever was called for came as if floating through the air. She kept a very strict hand over the maids, with whom she was no great favourite, as she reported their neglect of duty to their mistress. Brownie-Clod was not so pawky, and he was constantly overreached by the servants, with whom he used to make contracts. He, however, was too able for them on one occasion. He had agreed with two of them to do their whole winter's threshing for them, on condition of getting in return an old coat and a Kilmarnock hood to which he had taken a fancy. He wrought away manfully, and they had nothing to do but lie at their ease on the straw and look on. But before the term was expired they laid the coat and hood for him in the barn. The moment Brownie laid his eyes upon them he struck work, using the words prefixed to this section of our volume.

Martyn describes the Brownie of the Western Isles as a *tall man,* and. he tells a story of his invisibly directing a person, at Sir Norman M'Leod's, who was playing at draughts, where to place his men.

The Urisk

There is also in the Highlands a rough hairy spirit, called the Urisk. The following legend will display his nature and character:

To the very great annoyance of a Highland miller, and to the injury of the machinery, his mill, he found, used to be set to work at night when there was nothing in it to grind. One of his men offered to sit up, and try to discover who it was that did it; 'and, having kindled a good turf-fire, sat by it to watch. Sleep, however, overcame him, and when he awoke about midnight, he saw sitting opposite him a rough shaggy being. Nothing daunted, he demanded his name, and was told that it was Urisk. The stranger, in return, asked the man his name, who replied that it was Myself. The conversation here ended, and Urisk soon fell fast asleep. The man then tossed a panful of hot ashes into his shaggy lap, which set his hair all on fire. In an agony, and screaming with the pain, he ran to the door, and in a loud yelling tone several of his brethren were heard to cry out, "What 's the matter'with you?" "Oh! he set me on fire!" "Who?" "Myself!" "Then put it out yourself" was the reply. [a]

NOTE

[a] Told, without naming his authority, by the late W. S. Rose, in the Quarterly Review for 1825.

ISLE OF MAN

Mona once hid from those that search the main,
Where thousand elfin shapes abide.
−COLLINS.

The Isle of Man, peopled by Celts, and early and frequently visited and colonised by the Northmen, has also its Fairies, which differ little from those of the greater islands between which it lies. An English gentleman, named Waldron, who resided in the island in the early part of the last century, was curious about its Fairy-lore, and he has recorded a number of the legends which he heard. [a] His book, indeed, has been the chief source whence Ritson, Sir Walter Scott, [b] and others, have drawn their illustrations of English Fairy-lore in general, and the subsequent inquiries of Mr. Train have enabled him to add but very little to it. We will here relate some of these legends:

The great peculiarity of the Manks Fairies, according to Mr. Waldron, is their fondness for riding, and this not on little steeds of their own, or on the small breed of the country, but on the large English and Irish horses, which are brought over and kept by the gentry. Nothing, it was said, was more common than to find in the morning horses covered with foam and sweat, and tired to death, which had been shut up at night in the stable. One gentleman assured Mr. Waldron that three or four of his best horses had been killed with these nocturnal exercises.

They called them the Good People, and said that their reason for dwelling in the hills and woods was, their dislike of the vices of towns. Hence the houses which they deigned to visit were thought to be blest. In these houses, a tub or pail of clean water was always left for them to bathe in. Good, however, as they were, they used to change children. Mr. Waldron saw one of these changelings; it was nearly six years old, but was unable to walk or even stand, or move its limbs. Its complexion was delicate, and it had the finest hair in the world. It never cried or spoke, and it ate scarcely anything; it rarely smiled, but if any one called it *Fairy-elf,* it would frown and almost look them through. Its mother, who was poor, was often obliged to go out for whole days a-charing, and leave it by itself, and when the neighbours would look in on it through the window, they always saw it laughing and in great delight, whence they judged that it had agreeable company with it, more especially as let it be left ever so dirty, the mother on her return found it with a clean face, and its hair nicely combed out.

NOTES

[a] Description of the Isle of Man. London, 1731.

[b] In his Essay on Fairies in the Minstrelsy of the Sottish Border, and in the notes on Peveril of the Peak.

The Fairy-Chapman

A man being desirous of disposing of a horse he had at that time no great occasion for, and riding him to market for that purpose, was accosted in passing over the mountains by a little man in a plain dress, who asked him if he would sell his horse. "Tis the design I am going on," replied he: on which the other desired to know the price. "Eight pounds," said he. "No," returned the purchaser, "I will give no more than seven, which if you will take, here is your money." The owner thinking he had bid pretty fair, agreed with him, and the money being told out, the one dismounted and the other got on the back of the horse, which he had no sooner done than both beast and rider sunk into the earth immediately, leaving the person who had made the bargain in the utmost terror and consternation. As soon as he had a little recovered himself he went directly to the parson of the parish, and related what had passed, desiring he would give his opinion whether be ought to make use of the money he had received or not. To which

he replied, that as he had made a fair bargain, and no way circumvented nor endeavoured to circumvent the buyer, he saw no reason to believe, in case it was an evil spirit, it could have any power over him. On this assurance, he went borne well satisfied, and nothing afterwards happened to give him any disquiet concerning this affair. This was told to Waldron by the person to whom it happened.

The Fairy-Banquet

A man one time was led by invisible musicians for several miles together, and not being able to resist the harmony, followed till it conducted him to a large common, where were a great number of little people sitting round a table, and eating and drinking in a very jovial manner. Among them were some faces whom he thought be had formerly seen, but forbore taking any notice, or they of him, till the little people offering him drink, one of them, whose features seemed not unknown to him, plucked him by the coat, and forbade him whatever he did to taste anything he saw before him, "For if you do," added be, "you will be as l am, and return no more to your family." The poor man was much affrighted, but resolved to obey the injunction. Accordingly, a large silver cup, filled with some sort of liquor, being put into his hand, he found an opportunity to throw what it contained on the ground. Soon after, the music ceasing, all the company disappeared, leaving the cup in his hand, and he returned home, though much wearied and fatigued. He went the next day, and communicated to the minister of the parish all that had happened, and asked his advice, how he should dispose of the cup, to which the parson replied, he could not do better than to devote it to the service of the church, and this very cup, they say, is that which is now used for the consecrated wine in Kirk Merlugh.

The Fairies' Christening

A woman related that being great with child, and expecting every moment the good hour, as she lay awake one night in her bed, she saw seven or eight little Women come into her chamber, one of whom had an infant in her arms. They were followed by a man of the same size with themselves, but in the habit of a minister. One of them went to the pail, and finding no water in it, cried out to the others, what *must* they do to christen the child? On which they replied it should be done in beer. With that the seeming parson took the child in his arms, and performed the ceremony of baptism, dipping his head into a great tub of strong beer, which the woman had brewed the day before to be ready for her lying-in. She said they baptised the infant by the name of Joan, which made her know she was pregnant of a girl, as it proved a few days after when she was delivered. She added, that it was common for the fairies to make a mock christening when any person was near her time, and that, according to what child, male or female, they brought, such should the woman bring into the world.

The Fairy-Whipping

A woman who lived about two miles distant from Ballasalli, and used to serve Mr. Waldron's family with butter, made him once very merry with a story she told him of her daughter, a girl of about ten years old, who being sent over the fields to the town for a pennyworth of tobacco for her father, was on the top of a mountain surrounded by a great number of little men, who would not suffer her to pass any farther. Some of them said she should go with them, and accordingly laid hold of her; but one, seeming more pitiful, desired they would let her alone, which they refusing, there ensued a quarrel, and the person who took her part fought bravely in her defence. This so incensed the others, that to be revenged on her for being the cause, two or three of them seized her, and. pulling up her clothes, whipped her heartily; after which, it seems, they had no farther power over her, and she ran home directly telling what had befallen her, and showing her buttocks, on which were the prints of several small hands. Several of the town's-people went with her to the mountain; and she conducting them to the spot, the little antagonists were gone, but had left behind them proofs, as the good woman said, that what the girl had informed them was true, for there was a great deal of blood to be seen on the stones, This did she aver with all the solemnity possible.

The Fairy-Hunt

A young sailor coming off a long voyage, though it was late at night, chose to land rather than lie another night in the vessel. Being permitted to do so, he was set on shore at Douglas. It happened to be a line moonlight night, and very dry, being a small frost; he therefore forbore going into any house to refresh himself, but made the best of his way to the house of a sister he had at Kirk-Merlugh. As he was going over a pretty high mountain, he heard the noise of horses, the halloo of a huntsman, and the finest horn in the world. He was a little surprised that any one pursued those kinds of sports in the night; but he had not time for much reflection before they all passed by him so near, that he was able to count what number there was of them, which he said was thirteen, and that they were all dressed in green, and gallantly mounted. He was so well pleased with the sight, that he would gladly have followed could he have kept pace with them. He crossed the footway, however, that he might see them again, which he did more than once, and lost not the sound of the horn for some miles. At length being arrived at his sister's, he tells her the story, who presently clapped her hands for joy that he was come home safe; "for," said she, "those you saw were *fairies*, and 'tis well they did not take you away with them."

The Fiddler and the Fairy

A fiddler having agreed with a person, who was a stranger, for so much money, to play to some company he should bring him to, all the twelve days of Christmas, and received earnest for it, saw his new master vanish into the earth the moment he had made the bargain. Nothing could be more terrified than was the poor fiddler. He found he had entered himself into the Devil's service, and looked on himself as already damned; but having recourse to a clergyman, he received some hope. He ordered him, however, as he had taken earnest, to go when he should be called, but that whatever tunes should be called for, to play none but psalms. On the day appointed the same person appeared, with whom he went, but with what inward reluctance it is easy to guess; and punctually obeying the minister's directions, the company to whom he played were so angry, that they all vanished at once, leaving him at the top of a high hill, and so bruised and hurt, though he was not sensible when or from what hand be received the blows, that he got not home without the utmost difficulty.

The Phynodderee

The Phynnodderee, or Hairy-one, is a Manks spirit of the same kind with the Brownie or the Kobold. He is said to have been a fairy who was expelled from the fairy society.

The cause was, he courted a pretty Manx maid who lived in a bower beneath *the blue tree* of Glen Aldyn, and therefore was absent from the Fairy court during the *Re-hollys vooar yn ouyr*, or harvest-moon, being engaged dancing in the merry glen of Rushen. He is condemned to remain in the Isle of Man till doomsday, in a wild form, covered with long shaggy hair, whence his name.

He is very kind and obliging to the people, sometimes driving home the sheep, or cutting and gathering the hay, if he sees a storm coming on. On one of these occasions, a farmer having expressed his displeasure with him for not having cut the grass close enough to the ground, he let him cut it himself the next year; but he went after him stubbing up the roots so fast, that it was with difficulty that the farmer could escape having his legs cut off. For several years no one would venture to mow that meadow; at length a soldier undertook it, and by beginning in the centre of the field, and cutting round, as if on the edge of a circle, keeping one eye on the scythe, and looking out for the Phynnodderee with the other, he succeeded in cutting the grass in safety.

A gentleman having resolved to build a large house on his property, at a place called Sholt-e-will, near the foot of Snafield mountain, caused the stones to be quarried on the beach. There was one large block of white stone which he was very anxious to have, but all the men in the parish could not move it. To their surprise, the Phynnodderee in the course of one night conveyed all the stones that bad been quarried, the great white one included, up to the proposed site, and the white stone is there still to be seen. The gentleman, to reward the Phynnodderee, caused some clothes to be left for him in one of his usual haunts. When he saw them, he lifted them up one by one, saying in Mania:

> Bayrm da'n choine, dy doogh da'n choine,
> Cooat da'n dreeym, dy doogh da'n dreeym,
> Breechyn da'n toyn, dy doogh da'n toyn,
> Agh my she lhiat ooiley, shoh cha nee lhiat Glen reagh Rushen.
> Cap for the head, alas, poor head!
> Coat for the back, alas, poor back
> Breeches for the breech, alas, poor breech!
> If these be all thine, thine cannot be the merry glen of Rushen.

And he departed with a melancholy wail, and has never been seen since. The old people say, "There has not been a merry world since he lost his ground." [a]

NOTE
[a] Train. Account of the Isle of Man. ii. p. 148.

WALES

It was the Druid's presage, who had long
In Geirionydd's [a] airy temple marked
The songs that from the Gwyllion [b] rose, of eve
The children, in the bosom of the lakes.
–TALIESIN.

The oldest account we have met with of Welsh Fairies is in the Itinerary of Giraldus Cambrensis, who, in the year 1188, accompanied Archbishop Baldwin in his tour through Wales, undertaken for the purpose of exciting the zeal of the people to take part in the crusade then in contemplation.

Giraldus, who was an attentive observer of nature and of mankind, has in this work given many beautiful descriptions of scenery, and valuable traits of manners. He is liberal of legends of saints, but such was the taste of his age. Among his narratives, however, he gives the two following, which show that there was a belief in South Wales in beings similar to the Fairies and Hobgoblins of England.

NOTES
[a] A lake, on whose banks Taliesin resided.
[b] These Mr. Davies thinks correspond to the Gallicenae of Mela: see, *Brittany.*

Tale of Elidurus

A short time before our days, a circumstance worthy of note occurred in these parts, which Elidurus, a priest, most strenuously affirmed had befallen himself. When he was a youth of twelve years,—
since, as Solomon says, "The root of learning is bitter, although the
fruit is sweet,"—and was following his literary pursuits, in order to
avoid the discipline and frequent stripes inflicted on him by his pre-
ceptor, he ran away, and concealed himself under the hollow bank
of a river; and, after fasting in that situation for two days, two little
men of pygmy stature appeared to him, saying, "If you will come
with us, we will lead you into a country full of delights and sports."
Assenting, and rising up, he followed his guides through a path, at
first subterraneous and dark, into a most beautiful country, adorned
with rivers and meadows, woods and plains, but obscure, and not
illuminated with the full light of the sun. All the days were cloudy, and
the nights extremely dark, on account of the absence of the moon
and stars. The boy was brought before the king, and introduced to
him in the presence of the court; when, having examined him for a
long time, he delivered him to his son, who was then a boy. These
men were of the smallest stature, but very well proportioned for
their size. They were all fair-haired, with luxuriant hair falling over
their shoulders, like that of women. They had horses proportioned
to themselves, of the size of greyhounds. They neither ate flesh nor
fish, but lived on milk diet, made up into messes with saffron. They
never took an oath, for they detested nothing so much as lies. As
often as they returned from our upper hemisphere, they reprobated

our ambition, infidelities, and inconstancies. They had no religious worship, being only, as it seems, strict lovers and reverers of truth.

The boy frequently returned to our hemisphere, sometimes by the way he had first gone, sometimes by another; at first in company with others, and afterwards alone, and confided his secret only to his mother, declaring to her the manners, nature, and state of that people. Being desired by her to bring a present of gold, with which that region abounded, he stole, while at play with the king's son, the golden ball with which he used to divert himself, and brought it to his mother in great haste; and when he reached the door of his father's house, but not unpursued, and was entering it in a great hurry, his foot stumbled on the threshold, and, falling down into the room where his mother was sitting, the two Pygmies seized the ball, which had dropped from his hand, and departed, spitting at and deriding the boy. On recovering from his fall, confounded with shame, and execrating the evil counsel of his mother, he returned by the usual track to the subterraneous road, but found no appearance of any passage, though he searched for it on the banks of the river for nearly the space of a year. Having been brought back by his friends and mother, and restored to his right way of thinking and his literary pursuits, he attained in process of time the rank of priesthood. Whenever David the Second, bishop of St. David's, talked to him in his advanced state of life concerning this event, he could never relate the particulars without shedding tears.

He had also a knowledge of the language of that nation, and used to recite words of it he had readily acquired in his younger days. These words, which the bishop often repeated to me, were very conformable to the Greek idiom. When they asked for water, they said, *Udor udorum,* which signifies "Bring water;" for Udor, in their language, as well as in the Greek, signifies water; and Dwr also, in the British language, signifies water. When they want salt, they say, *Halgein udorum,* "Bring salt." Salt is called άλς in Greek, and Halen in British; for that language, from the length of time which the Britons (then called Trojans, and afterwards Britons from Brito, their leader) remained in Greece after the destruction of Troy, became, in many instances, similar to the Greek. [a]

"If," says the learned archdeacon, "a scrupulous inquirer should ask my opinion of the relation here inserted, I answer, with Augustine, 'admiranda fore divina miracula non disputatione discutienda;' nor do I, by denial, place bounds to the Divine power; nor, by affirming insolently, extend that power which cannot be extended. But on such occasions I always call to mind that saying of Hieronymus: "Multa," says he, 'incredibilia reperies et non verisimilia, quae nihilominus tamen vera sunt.' These, and any such that might occur, I should place, according to Augustine's opinion, among those things which are neither to be strongly affirmed nor denied.

David Powel, who edited this work in 1585, thinks that this legend is written in imitation of the relation of Eros the Armenian, in Plato, or taken from Polo's account of the garden of the Old Man of the Mountain. [b]

Again Giraldus writes,—"In these parts of Penbroch it has happed, in our times, that unclean spirits have conversed with mankind, not indeed visibly, but sensibly; for they manifested their presence at first in the house of one Stephen Wiriet, and some time after of William Not, by throwing dirt and such things as rather indicate an intention of mockery and injury. In the house of William, the spirit used to make rents and holes in both linen and woollen garments, to the frequent loss of both host and guest, from which injury no care and no bolts could protect them. In the house of Stephen, which was still more extraordinary, the spirit used to converse with people; and when they taunted him, which they frequently did out of sport, he used to charge them openly with those actions of theirs, from their birth, which they least wished to be heard or known by others. If you ask the cause and reason of this matter, I do not take on me to assign it; only this, that it, as is said, used to be the sign of a sudden change, either from poverty to riches, or rather from riches to desolation and poverty, as it was found to be a little after with both of these. But this I think worthy of remark, that places cannot be freed from illusions of this kind by the sprinkling of holy water, not merely of the ordinary, but even of the great kind; nor by the aid of any ecclesiastical sacrament. Nay, the priests themselves, when coming in with devotion, and fortified as well with the cross as with holy water, were forthwith among the first deified by the dirt thrown at them. From which it would appear that both sacramentals and sacraments defend from hurtful, not harmless things, and from injury, not from illusion." [c]

NOTES

[a] Giraldus Cambrensis, Itinerarium Cambriae, I, i. c 8, translated by Sir R. C. Hoare.

[b] Very likely indeed that Elidurus, or Giraldus either, should know any thing of Plato or of Marco Polo, especially as the latter was not yet born!

[c] Book i. chap. 12.

The Tylwyth Teg

In the mountains near Brecknock, says Davies, [a] there is a small lake, to which tradition assigns some of the properties of the fabled Avernus. I recollect a Mabinogi, or mythologic tale, respecting this piece of water, which runs thus:-

In ancient times a door in a rock near this lake was found open upon a certain day every year. I think it was May-day. Those who had the curiosity and resolution to enter were conducted by a secret passage, which terminated in a small island in the centre of the lake. Here the visitors were surprised with the prospect of a most enchanting garden stored with the choicest fruits and flowers, and. inhabited by the Tylwyth Teg, or Fair Family, a kind of Fairies, whose beauty could be equalled only by the courtesy and affability which they exhibited to those who pleased them. They gathered fruit and flowers for each of their guests, entertained them with the most exquisite music, disclosed to them many secrets of futurity, and invited them to stay as long as they should find their situation agreeable. But the island was secret, and nothing of its produce must be carried away. The whole of this scene was invisible to those who stood without the margin of the lake. Only an indistinct mass was seen in the middle; and it was observed that no bird would fly over the water, and that a soft strain of music at times breathed with rapturous sweetness in the breeze of the morning.

It happened upon one of these annual visits that a sacrilegious wretch, when he was about to leave the garden, put a flower, with which be had been presented, in. his pocket; but the theft boded him no good. As soon as he had touched unhallowed ground the flower vanished and he lost his senses. Of this injury the Fair Family took no notice at the time. They dismissed their guests with their accustomed courtesy, and the door was closed as usual. But their resentment ran high. For though, as the tale goes, the Tylwyth Teg and their garden undoubtedly occupy the spot to this day, though the birds still keep at a respectful distance from the lake, and some broken strains of music are still heard at times, yet the door which led to the island has never re-opened, and from the date of this sacrilegious act the Cymry have been unfortunate.

Some time after this, an adventurous person attempted to draw off the water, in order to discover its contents, when a terrific form arose from the midst of the lake, commanding him to desist, or otherwise he would drown the country.

These Tylwyth Teg are, as we see, regarded as Fairies, but we think improperly; for diminutive size is an attribute of the Fairies in all parts of the British Isles, and Mr. Owen (in his Welsh Dictionary, *s. v.)* expressly says that such is not the case with these beings.

NOTE
[a] Mythology and Rites of the British Druids.

The Spirit of the Van

Among the mountains of Carmarthen, lies a beautiful and romantic piece of water, named The Van Pools. Tradition relates, that after midnight, on New Year's Eve, there appears on this lake a being named The Spirit of the Van. She is dressed in a white robe, bound by a golden girdle; her hair is long and golden, her face is pale and melancholy; she sits in a golden boat, and manages a golden oar.

Many years ago there lived in the vicinity of this lake a young farmer, who having heard much of the beauty of this spirit, conceived a most ardent desire to behold her, and be satisfied of the truth. On the last night of the year, he therefore went to the edge of the lake, which lay calm and bright beneath the rays of the full moon, and waited anxiously for the first hour of the New Year. It came, and then he beheld the object of his wishes gracefully guiding her golden gondola to and fro over the lake. The moon at length sank behind the mountains, the stars grew dim at the approach of dawn, and the fair spirit was on the point of vanishing, when, unable to restrain himself, he called aloud to her to stay and be his wife; but with a faint cry she faded from his view. Night after night he now might be seen pacing the shores of the lake, but all in vain. His farm was neglected, his person wasted away, and gloom and melancholy were impressed on his features. At length he confided his secret to one of the mountain-sages, whose counsel was—a Welsh one, by the way—to assail the fair spirit with gifts of cheese and bread! The counsel was followed; and on Midsummer Eve the enamoured swain went down to the lake, and let fall into it a large cheese and a loaf of bread. But all was vain; no spirit rose. Still he fancied that the spot where he had last seen her shone with more than wonted brightness, and that a musical sound vibrated among the rocks. Encouraged by these signs, he night after night threw in loaves and cheeses, but still no spirit came. At length New Year's Eve returned. He dressed himself in his best, took his largest cheese and seven of his whitest loaves, and repaired to the lake. At the turn of midnight, he dropped them slowly one by one into the water, and then remained in silent expectation. The moon was hid behind a cloud, but by the faint light she gave, he saw the magic skiff appear, and direct its course for where he stood. Its owner stepped ashore, and hearkened to the young man's vows, and consented to become his wife. She brought with her as her dower flocks and herds, and other rural wealth. One charge she gave him, never to strike her, for the third time he should do so she would vanish.

They married, and were happy. After three or four years they were invited to a christening, and to the surprise of all present, in the midst of the ceremony, the spirit burst into tears. Her husband gave an angry glance, and asked her why she thus made a fool of herself? She replied, "The poor babe is entering in a world of sin and sorrow, and misery lies before it; why should I rejoice?" He gave her a push. She warned him that he had struck her once. Again they were, after some time, invited to attend the funeral of that very child. The spirit now laughed, and danced, and sang. Her husband's wrath was excited, and he asked her why she thus made a fool of herself? "The babe," she said, "has left a world of sin and sorrow, and escaped the misery that was before it, and is gone to be good and happy for ever and ever. Why, then, should I weep?" He gave her a push from him, and again she warned him. Still they lived happily as before. At length they were invited to a wedding, where the bride was young and fair, the husband a withered old miser. In the midst of the festivity, the spirit burst into a copious flood of tears, and to her husband's angry demand of why she thus made a fool of herself, she replied in the hearing of all, "Because summer and winter cannot agree. Youth is wedded to age for paltry gold. I see misery here, and tenfold misery hereafter, to be the lot of both. It is the devil's compact." Forgetful of her warnings, the husband now thrust her from him with real anger. She looked at him tenderly and reproachfully, and said, "You have struck me for the third and last time. Farewell!"

So saying, she left the place. He rushed out after her, and just reached his home in time to see her speeding to the lake, followed by all her flocks and herds. He pursued her, but in vain; his eyes never more beheld her. [a]

As far as we have been able to learn, the belief in Fairies is confined in Wales to the southern counties of Glamorgan, Carmarthen, and Pembroke, the parts into which the Saxons had penetrated farthest, and where they of course had exercised most influence. In these counties the popular belief in these beings is by no means yet extinct, and their attributes in the creed of the Welsh peasant are similar to those of their British and Irish kindred.

The usual name given to the fairies in these parts of Wales, is Y Dynon Bach Têg, i. e. *The Little Fair People.* Ellyll, in the plural Ellyllon, also signifies an Elf, from which word, indeed, it may have been derived. The bells of the Digitalis or fox-glove are called Menyg

Ellylon, or the Elves'-gloves; in Ireland, also, they are connected with the fairies. The toadstools or poisonous mushrooms are named Bwyd Ellyllon, or Elves'-food. Perhaps, however, it is not the large ugly toadstools that are so named, but those pretty small delicate fungi, with their conical heads, which are named Fairy-mushrooms in Ireland, where they grow so plentifully. Finally, there was formerly in the park of Sir Robert Vaughan a celebrated old oak-tree, named Cr-wbenyr-Ellyll, or The Elf's Hollow-tree. The popular belief respecting these Ellyllon is, that they are the souls of the ancient Druids, who, being too good for relegation to Hell, and too evil for re-admittance to Heaven, are permitted to wander among men upon earth till the last day, when they also will enter on a higher state of being. [b]

The legends of which we will now proceed to give a specimen, were collected and published in the latter half of the eighteenth century, by a Welsh clergyman, who seems to have entertained no doubt whatever of the truth of the adventures contained in them. [c]

The two daughters of a respectable farmer in the parish of Bedweilty were one day out hay-making with their man and maid servant and a couple of their neighbours, when on a hill, about quar-ter of a mile distant, they saw a large flock of sheep. Soon after, they saw them going up to a place half a mile off, and then going out of their sight as if they vanished in the air. About half-an-hour before sunset, they saw them again, but not all alike; for some saw them like sheep, some like greyhounds, some like swine, and some like naked infants. They appeared in the shade of the mountain between them and the sun, and the first sight was as if they rose out of the earth. "This was a notable appearance of the fairies, seen by credible witnesses. The sons of infidelity are very unreasonable not to believe the testimonies of so many witnesses of the being of spirits."

E. T. going home by night over Bedwellty Mountains, saw the fairies on each side of him. Some of them were dancing. He also heard the sound of a bugle-horn, as if people were hunting. He began to grow afraid, but recollecting to have heard that if on seeing the fairies, you draw out your knife, they will vanish, he did so, and saw them no more. "This the old gentleman sincerely related to me. He was a sober man, and of the strictest veracity."

A young man having gone early one morning to a barn to feed oxen, when he had done, lay down on the hay to rest. As he lay he heard the sound of music approaching the barn, and presently came in a large company, wearing striped clothes (some more gay than others), and commenced dancing to their music. He lay quite still, thinking to escape their notice; but a woman, better dressed than the others, came up to him with a striped cushion, with a tassel at each corner, and put it under his head. Some time after, a cock was heard to crow, which seemed either to surprise or displease them, and they hastily drew the cushion from under his head, and went away.

P. W., "an honest virtuous woman," related that one time, when she was a little girl on her way to school, she saw the fairies dancing under a crab-tree. As they appeared to be children of her own size, and had small pleasant music, she went and joined in their exercise, and then took them to dance in an empty barn. This she continued to do for three or four years. As she never could hear the sound of their feet, she always took off her shoes, supposing noise to be displeasing to them. They were of small stature, looked rather old, and wore blue and green aprons. Her grandfather, who kept school in the parish-church, used, when going home from it late in the evening, to see the fairies dancing under an oak, within two or three fields of the church.

The learned writer gives finally a letter to himself, from a "pious young gentleman" of Denbighshire, dated March 24, 1772, in which he informs him, that about fifteen years before, as himself, his sister, and two other little girls were playing at noon of a summer's day in a field, they saw a company of dancers, about seventy yards from them. Owing to the rapidity of their whirling motions, they could not count them, but guessed them at fifteen or sixteen. They were in red, like soldiers, with red handkerchiefs spotted with yellow, on their heads. As they were gazing and wondering at them, one of the dancers came running towards them. The children, in a fright, made for an adjacent stile. The girls got over, but the boy was near being caught, and on looking back when over, he saw the red man stretching his arms after him over the stile, which it would seem he had not the power to cross. When they came to the house, which was close at hand, they gave the alarm, and people went out to search the fields, but could see nothing. The little man was very grim-looking, with a topper-coloured face. His running-pace was rather slow, but he took great strides for one of his size.

The following legends were collected in 1827, in the Vale of Neath, in Glamorganshire, by a lady with whom we became acquainted when travelling through North Wales, in the preceding autumn. [d]

An old woman assured our fair friend, that she one time, many years before, saw the fairies to the number of some hundreds. They were very small, were mounted on little white horses, not bigger than dogs, and rode four a-breast. It was almost dusk at the time, and they were not a quarter of a mile from her. Another old woman said that her father had often seen the fairies riding in the air on little white horses, but he never saw them come down on the ground. He also used to hear their music in the air. She had heard, too, of a man who had been five-and-twenty years with the fairies, and thought he had been away only five minutes.

NOTES

[a] Abridged from "A Day at the Van Pools;" MS. of Miss Beale, the author of "Poems" and of "The Vale of the Towey," a most delightful volume. We have since received from our gifted friend the following additional information. "Since writing this letter, I have heard a new version of the last part of the Spirit of the Van. The third offence is said to be, that she and her husband were *ploughing;* he guiding the plough, and she driving the horses. The horses went wrong, and the husband took up something and threw it at them, 'which struck her. She seized the plough and went off, followed by the flocks and herds she had brought with her to Van Pool, where they all vanished, and the *mark of the ploughshare* is shown on the mountain at this present day. She left her children behind her, who became famous as doctors. Jones was their name, and they lived at a place called Muddfi. In them was said to have originated the tradition of the seventh son, or Septimus, being born for the healing art; as for many generations, seven sons were regularly horn in each family, the seventh of whom became the doctor, and wonderful in his profession. It is said even now, that the Jones of Muddfl are, or were, until very recently, clever doctors."—A. B. A somewhat different version of this legend is given by Mr. Croker, iii. 256.

[b] For the chief part of our knowledge respecting the fairy lore of Wales we are indebted to the third or supplemental volume of the Fairy Legends, in which Mr. Croker, with the aid of Dr. Owen Pugh and other Welsh scholars, has given a fuller account of the superstitions of the people of the Principality, than is, we believe, to be found any where else.

[c] A Relation of Apparitions of Spirits in the County of Monmouth and the Principality of Wales, by the Rev. Edward Jones of the Tiarch.—For our extracts from this work we are indebted to Mr. Croker.

[d] The lady's name was Williams. The legends were originally Intended for the present work, but circumstances caused them to appear in the supplemental volume of the Irish Fairy Legends. We have abridged them.

Rhys at the Fairy Dance

Rhys and Llewellyn, two farmer's servants, who bad been all day carrying lime for their master, were driving in the twilight their mountain ponies before them, returning home from their work. On reaching a little plain, Rhys called to his companion to stop and listen to the music, saying it was a tune to which he had danced a hundred times, and must go and have a dance now. He bade him go on with the horses, and he would soon overtake him. Llewellyn could hear nothing, and began to remonstrate; but away sprang Rhys, and he called after him in vain. He went home, put up the ponies, ate his supper, and went to bed, thinking that Rhys had only made a pretext for going to the ale-house. But when morning came, and still no sign of Rhys, he told his master what had occurred. Search was then made everywhere, but no Rhys could be found. Suspicion now fell upon Llewellyn of having murdered him, and he was thrown into prison, though there was no evidence against him. A farmer, however, skilled in fairy-matters, having an idea of how things might have been, proposed that himself and some others should accompany Llewellyn to the place where he parted with Rhys. On coming to it, they found it green as the mountain ash. "Hush!" cried Llewellyn, "I hear music, I hear sweet harps." We all listened, says the narrator, for I was one of them, but could hear nothing. "Put your foot on mine, David," said he to me (his own foot was at the time on the outward edge of the fairy-ring). I did so, and so did we all, one after another, and then we beard the sound of many harps, and saw within a circle, about twenty feet across, great numbers of little people, of the size of children of three or four years old, dancing round and round. Among them we saw Rhys, and Llewellyn catching him by the smock-frock, as he came by him, pulled him out of the circle. "Where are the horses? where are the horses?" cried he. "Horses, indeed!" said Llewellyn. Rhys urged him to go home, and let him finish his dance, in which he averred he had not been engaged more than five minutes. It was by main force they took him from the place. He still asserted he had been only five minutes away, and could give no account of the people he had been with. He became melancholy, took to his bed, and soon after died. "The morning after," says the narrator, "we went to look at the place, and we found the edge of the ring quite red, as if trodden down, and I could see the marks of little heels, about the size of my thumb-nail."

Gitto Bach

Gitto Bach, [a] who was a fine boy, used often to ramble to the top of the mountain to look after his father's sheep. On his return, he would show his brothers and sisters pieces of remarkably white paper, like crown-pieces, with letters stamped upon them, which he said. were given him by the little children with whom he used to play on the mountain. One day he did not return, and during two whole years no account could be got of hint, and the other children were beginning to go up the mountain, and bring back some of those white crown-pieces. At length, one morning, as their mother opened the door, she saw Gitto sitting on the threshold, with a bundle under his arm. He was dressed, and looked exactly as when she last had seen him. To her inquiry of where he had been for so long a time, he replied that it was only the day before he had left her; and he bade her look at the pretty clothes the little children on the mountain had given him for dancing with them to the music of their harps. The dress in the bundle was of very white paper, without seam or sewing. The prudent mother committed it to the flames.

"This," said the narrator, "made me more anxious than ever to see the fairies," and his wish was gratified by a gipsy, who directed him to find a four-leaved clover, and put it with nine grains of wheat on the leaf of a book which she gave him. She then desired him to meet her next night by moonlight on the top of Craig y Dinis. She there washed his eyes with the contents of a phial which she had, and be instantly saw thousands of fairies, all in white, dancing to the sounds of numerous harps. They then placed themselves on the edge of the hill, and sitting down and putting their hands round their knees, they tumbled down one after another, rolling head-over-heels till they disappeared in the valley.

Another old man, who was present at the preceding narration, averred that he had often seen the fairies at waterfalls; particularly at that of Sewyd yr Rhyd in Cwm Pergwm, Vale of Neath, where a road runs between the fall and the rock. As he stood behind the fall, they appeared in all the colours of the rainbow, and their music mingled with the noise of the water. They then retired into a cavern, which they had made in the rock, and, after enjoying themselves there, ascended the rock, and went off through the mountains, the sounds of their harps dying away as they receded.

NOTE
[a] Gitto is the dim. of Griffith: *bach (beg* Ir.) is little.

The Fairies Banished

One of those old farm-houses, where the kitchen and cow-house are on the same floor, with only a low partition between them, was haunted by the fairies. If the family were at their meals in the kitchen, *they* were racketing in the cow-house, and if the people were engaged about the cows, the fairies were making a riot in the kitchen. One day, when a parcel of reapers were at their harvest-dinner in the kitchen, the elves, who were laughing and dancing above, threw down such a quantity of dust and dirt as quite spoiled the dinner. While the mistress of the house was in perplexity about it, there came in an old woman, who, on hearing the case, said she could provide a remedy. She then told her in a whisper to ask six of the reapers to dinner next day in the hearing of the fairies, and only to make as much pudding as could be boiled in an egg-shell. She did as directed, and when the fairies saw that a dinner for six men was put down to boil in an egg-shell, there was great stir and noise in the cow-house, and at length one angry voice was heard to say, "We have lived long in this world; we were born just after the earth was made, and before the acorn was planted, and yet we never saw a harvest-dinner dressed in an egg-shell! There must be something wrong in this house, and we will stop here no longer." They went away and never returned.

The fairies are said to take away children, and leave change-lings. They also give pieces of' money, one of which is found every day in the same place as long as the finder keeps his good fortune a secret. One peculiarity of the Cambrian fairies is, that every Friday night they comb the goats' beards "to make them decent for Sunday? "

We hear not of Brownies or Kobolds in the Welsh houses now, but Puck used to haunt Wales as well as Ireland. His Welsh name, Pwcca, is the same as his Irish one. In Brecon there is Cwm Pwcca, or Puck's Glen, and though an iron-foundry has in a great measure scared him from it, yet he occasionally makes his appearance. As a man was returning one night from his work, he saw a light before him, and thought he discerned some one that carried it. Supposing it to be one of his fellow-workmen with a lanthorn, he quickened his pace to come up with him, wondering all the while how so short a man as he appeared to be could get over the ground so fast. He also fancied he was not going the right way, but still thought that he who had the light must know best. At last, he came up with him, and found himself on the very edge of one of the precipices of Cwm Pwcca, down which another step would have carried him. The Pwcca, for it was he, sprang over the glen, turned round, held the light above his head, and then with a loud laugh put it out and vanished.

BRITTANY

Mut ant este noble Barun
Cil de Bretaine il Bretun.
Marie de France.
Thise oldé gentil Bretons in hir dayes
Of diverse aventurès maden layes.
−CHAUCER

Brittany, the ancient Armorica, retains perhaps as unmixed a population as any part of Western Europe. Its language has been, however, like the Welsh and the Celtic dialects, greatly affected by the Latin and Teutonic. The ancient intercourse kept up with Wales and Cornwall by the Bretons, who were in a great measure colonists from these parts of Britain, caused the traditions and poetry of the latter to be current and familiar in Little Britain, as that country was then called. To poetry and music, indeed, the whole Celto-Cymric race seem to have been strongly addicted; and, independently of the materials which Brittany may have supplied for the history of Geoffrey of Monmouth, many other true or romantic adventures were narrated by the Breton poets in their Lais. Several of these Lais were translated into French verse in the thirteenth century by a poetess named Marie de France, resident at the court of the English monarchs of the house of Plantagenet, to one of whom, probably Henry the Third, her Lais are dedicated. [a] This circumstance may account for the Lais being better known in England than in France. The only manuscript containing any number of them is in the Harleian Library; for those of France contain but five Lais. The Lai du Fresne was translated into English; and from the Lai de Lanval and

Lai de Graelent—which last by the way is not in the Harleian Collection—Chestre made his Launfal Miles, or Sir Launfal Chaucer perhaps took the concluding circumstance of his Dream from the Lai de Eliduc.

In some of these Lais we meet with what may be regarded as Fairy machinery. The word Fée, indeed, occurs only once; but in the Lais de Gugemer, de Lanval, d'Ywenec, and de Graelent, personages are to be met with differing in nothing from the Fays of Romance, and who, like them, appear to be human beings endowed with superior powers.

The origin of the Breton Korrigan, as they are called, has been sought, and not improbably, in the Gallicenae [b] or ancient Gaul, of whom Pomponius Mela thus writes:-

"Sena [c] in the British sea, opposite the Ofismician. coast, is remarkable for an oracle of the Gallic God. Its priestesses, holy in perpetual virginity, are said to be *nine* in number. They are called Gallicenae, and are thought to be endowed with singular powers, so as to raise by their charms the winds and seas, *to turn themselves into what animals they will,* to cure wounds and diseases incurable by others, to know and predict the future; but this they do only to navigators who go thither purposely to consult them." [d]

We have here certainly all the attributes of the Damoiselles of the Lais of Marie de France. The doe whom Gugemer wounds speaks with a human voice. The lady who loved Lanval took him away into an island, and Graelent and his mistress crossed a deep and broad river to arrive at her country, which perhaps was also an island in the original Breton Lai. The part most difficult of explanation is the secret manner in which these dames used to visit their lovers; but perhaps the key is to be found in the Lai d'Ywenec, of which, chiefly on that account, we give an analysis. The hero of that Lai differs not in point of power from these ladies, and as he is a real man, with the power of assuming at will the shape of a bird, so it is likely they were real women, and that it was in the bird-shape they entered the chambers of their lovers. Graelent's mistress says to him, [e]

> I shall love you trewely;
> But one thing I forbid straitly,
> You must not utter a word apérte
> Which might our love make discovérte.
> I will give unto you richly,
> Gold and silver, clothes, and fee.
> Much love shall be between us two—
> Night and day I'll go to you:
> You'll see me come to you always—
> With me laugh and talk you may.
> You shall no comrade have to see,
> Or who shall know my privacy,
>
>   * * *
>
> Take care now that you do not boast
> Of things by which I may be lost.
> The lady says to Lanval,
> When you would speak to me of ought—
> You must in no place form the thought
> Where no one could meet his amie
> Without reproach and villainie—
> I will be presently with you,
> All your commands ready to do;
> No one but you will me see,
> Or hear the words that come from me.

She also bad previously imposed on the knight the obligation of secresy.

As a further proof of the identity of the Korrigan and the Gal-licenae, it may be remarked, that in the evidently very ancient Breton poem, Ar-Rannou, or The Series, we meet the following passage:—"There are *nine* Korrigen, who dance, with flowers in their hair, and robes of white wool, around the fountain, by the light of the full moon." [f]

NOTES

[a] Poésies de Marie de France, par De Roquefort. Paris, 1820. If any one should suspect that these are not genuine translations from the Breton, his doubts will be dispelled by reading the original of the Lai du Laustic in the Barzan-Breiz (i. 24) presently to be noticed.

[b] The Bas-Breton *Korrigan* or *Korrigwen* differs, as we may see, but little from *Gallican*. Strabo (i. p .304) says that Denieter and *Kora* were worshipped in an island in these parts.

[c] Sena is supposed to be L'Isle des Saints, nearly opposite Brest.

[d] Pomp. Mela, iii. 6.

[e] It might seem hardly necessary to inform the reader that these verses and those that follow, are our own translations, from Marie de France. Yet some have taken them for old English verses.

[f] E korole nao c'horrigan,
Bleunvek ho bleo, gwisket gloan,
Kelc'h ar feunteun, d'al loar-gann.
Villemarqué, *Barzan-Breiz*, i. 8,
The *c'h* expresses the guttural.

Lai D'Ywenec

I HAVE in thought and purpose too,
Of Ywenec to tellon you—
Of whom he born was, his sire's fame,
How first he to his mother came.
He who did beget Ywenec
Y-clepod was Eudemarec.

There formerly lived in Britain a man who was rich and old. He was Avoez or governor of Caerwent on the Doglas, and lord of the surrounding country. Desirous of having an heir to his estates, he espoused a maiden "courteous and sage, and passing fair." She was given to him because he was rich, and loved by him for her beauty. Why should I say more, but that her match was not to be found between Lincoln and Ireland? "Great sin did they who gave her him," adds the poet.

On account of her rare beauty, the jealous husband now turned all his thoughts to keeping her safe. To this end he shut her up in his tower, in a large room, to which no one had access but himself and his sister, an old widow, without whose permission the young wife was forbidden to speak to any even of her female attendants. In this tower the suspicious husband immured his lovely bride for seven years, during which time they had no children, nor did she ever leave her confinement on any account. She had neither chamberlain nor huissier to light the tapers in her chamber when she would retire, and the poor lady passed her time weeping, sighing, and lamenting; and from grief and neglect of herself losing all her beauty.

The month of April was entering,
When every bird begins to sing;
Her lord arose at early day,
And to the wood he takes his way.

Before he set out he called up the old dame to fasten the door after him. This done, she took her psalter and retired to another room to chant it. The imprisoned lady awoke in tears, seeing the brightness of the sun, and thus began her moan:

Alas! said she, why born was I?
Right grievous is my destiny:
In this towére imprisoned,
I ne'er shall leave it till I'm dead.

She marvels at the unreasonable jealousy of her old husband, curses her parents, and all concerned in giving her to a man not only so unamiable, but who was of so tough a constitution that the chance of his dying seemed infinitely remote.

When baptised he was to be,
In hell's rivere deep dipt was he;
Hard are his sinews, hard each vein,
And lively blood they all contain.
Oft have I heard the people tell,
That in this country there befell
Adventures in the days of yore,
That did to joy grieved hearts restore;
Knights met with damsels, fair and gent,
In all things unto their talent;
And dames met lovers courteous,
Handsome, and brave, and generous;
So that they never blamed were,
For save themselves none saw them e'er. [a]
If this may be, or ever was,

Or any it befallen has,
May God, who hath all might and power,
My wish perform for me this hour.

Scarcely had she uttered this pious wish, when she perceived the shadow of a large bird at a narrow window. The bird now flew into the room. He had jesses on his legs, and appeared to be a goss-hawk. [b] He placed himself before the lady, and in a few minutes after became a handsome gentle knight. The lady was terrified at the sight, and covered her head; but the knight was courteous, and addressed her,

> Lady, said he, be not thus stirred;
> A goss-hawk is a gentle bird.
> If my secréte should be obscure,
> Attend, and I will you assure;
> Maketh now of me your lovére,
> For that it is I am come here.
> Long have I loved you and admired,
> And in my heart have much desired;
> I ne'er have loved save you alone,
> And save you never shall love none;
> But I could never come to you,
> Nor from own countrie issue,
> If you had not required me:
> Your lover now I may well be.

The lady was now re-assured: she uncovered her head, and told the knight she would accept him as her *Dru*, if she were satisfied that he believed in God. On this head, he assures her,

> I in the Créator believe,
> Who did from misery us relieve,
> In which us Adam our sire put,

> By eating of that bitter fruit:
> He is, and was, and ever he
> To sinners life and light will be.

And to put the matter out of all doubt, he directs her to feign sickness, and send for the chaplain, when he undertakes to assume her form, and receive the holy Sacrament. The dame does accordingly; and the old woman, after many objections, at length sends for the chaplain.

> And he with all due speed did hie,
> And brought the Corpus Domini.
> The knight received the holy sign,
> And from the chalice drank the wine [c]
> The chaplain then his way is gone—
> The old dame shut the doors anon.

The scruples of the lady being now entirely removed, she grants *le don d'amoureuse merci*, and the bliss of the lovers is complete. At length the knight takes his leave, and in reply to the lady's question, of when she should see him again, he tells her that she has only to wish for him, and the wish will be fulfilled by his appearance; [d] but he warns her to beware of the old woman, who will closely watch her, assuring her at the same time that a discovery will be his certain death.

The lady now bids adieu to all sadness and melancholy, and gradually regains all her former beauty. She desires no longer to leave her tower; for, night or day, she has only to express a wish, and her knight is with her. The old lord marvels greatly at this sudden change, and begins to distrust the fidelity of his sister. On revealing his suspicions, her replies fully satisfy him on that head, and they concert between them how to watch the young wife, and to discover her secret. After an interval of three days, the old lord tells his wife that the king has sent for him, and that he must attend him, but will soon return. He sets out, and the old woman having closed the door as usual after him, gets behind a curtain to watch. The lady now wishes for her lover, and instantly he is with her, and they continue together till it is time to rise. He then departs, leaving the spy, who had seen how he came and went, terrified at the strange metamorphosis.

When the husband, who was at no great distance, came home, his spy informed him of the strange affair. Greatly grieved and incensed at this, he began to meditate the destruction of his rival. He accordingly got four pikes made, with steel-heads so sharp that

> No razor under heaven's sheen
> Was ever yet so sharp and keen.

These he set at the window through which the knight was used to enter. Next day he feigns to go to the chase, the old woman returns to her bed to sleep, and the lady anxiously expects "him whom she loveth loyally,"

> And says that he may come safely,
> And with her at all leisure be.

So said, so done: the bird was at the window; but alas! too eager for caution, he overlooked the pikes, and, flying against them, was mortally wounded. Still he entered the chamber and threw himself on the bed, which his blood soon filled, and thus addressed his distracted mistress:

He said unto her— " My sweet friend,
For you my life comes to an end;
I often told you 't would be so,
That your fair cheer would work us woe."
When she heard this she swooned away,
And long time there for dead she lay;
Her gently to herself he brought,
And said, that grief availeth nought;
That she by him a son would bear,
Valiant and wise, and debonair;
He would dispel her sorrows all.
Ywenec she should him call.
He wouldè vengeance for their sake
Upon their trait'rous enemy take. [e]

Exhausted with loss of blood, he can stay no longer. He departs; and the lady, uttering loud cries of woe, leaps after him, unapparelled as she is, out of the window, which was twenty feet from the ground, and pursues him by the traces of his blood.

Along his path strayed the dame,
Until unto a hill she came. [f]
Into this hill one entrance led;
It with the blood was all sprinkled.
Before her she can nothing see;
Whereat she thinketh full surely
Her lover thither is gone in.
She entereth with mickle teen;
Within it light ne found she none;
Thorow it still she goeth on,
Until she from the hill issued
In a fair meadow, rich and good.
With blood she stained found the grass,
At which she much dismayed was;
The trace lay of it on the ground.
Quite near she there a city found;

With walls it was enclosed all—
There was not house, nor tower, nor hall,
That did not seem of silver fair:
The Mandevent [8] right wealthy are.
Before the town lay marshes rude,
The forest, and wild solitude.
On the other side, toward the donjón,
The water all around did run;
And here the shippès did enter,
More thannè three hundréd they were.
The lower gate wide open lay;
Therein the lady took her way,
Stil following the blood, that fell
The townè thorow to the castél.
Unto her spake there no one,
Ne man nor woman found she none.
She to the palace came; with blood
The steps she found were all embrued;
She entered then a low chambére;
A knight she found fast sleeping there;
She knew him not—she passed on—
To a larger chamber came anon;
A bed, and nothing more, there found,
A knight was on it sleeping sound.
Still farther passed on the dame;
Unto the third chambére she came,
Where she gan find her lover's bed.
The posts were gold enamelled;
I could not price the clothes aright:
The chandeliers and tapers bright,
Which night and day burned constantly,
Were worth the gold of a citee.
She finds her lover at the point of death.

At seeing his wretched state the unhappy lady swoons again.
The expiring knight endeavours to console her; and, foretelling his
own death on that day, directs her to depart, lest his people in their
grief should ill treat her as the cause of his death. She, however,

protests that she will stay and die with him, as, if she returns, her husband will put her to death. The knight repeats his consolations, and gives her a ring, which, while she wears, her husband will retain no remembrance of what relates to her. At the same time he gives her his sword, which she is to keep safely and to give to her son when grown up and become a valiant knight. He says, she then

> Unto a festival will go;
> Her lord will thither wend also;
> Unto an abbey they will come,
> Where they will see a stately tomb,
> Will learn the story of the dead,
> And how he was there buried.
> There thou the sword shalt to him reach,
> And all the adventure then teach,
> How he was born, who was his sire;
> His deeds enough will then admire.

He then gave her a dress of fine silk, and insisted on her departure. She is with difficulty induced to leave him, and is hardly half a league from the place when she hears the bells tolling, and the cries of grief of the people for the death of their lord. She faints four times, but at length recovering retraces her steps, and returns to her tower. Her husband makes no inquiry, and gives her no farther uneasiness. She bare a son, as Eudemarec had foretold, and named him Ywenec. As he grew up, there was not his peer in the kingdom for beauty, valour, and generosity.

After Ywenec had been dubbed a knight, his supposed father was summoned to attend the feast of St. Aaron at Carlion. He went, accompanied by his wife and Ywenec. On their way, they stopped at a rich abbey, where they were received with the utmost hospitality.

Next day, when they asked to depart, the abbot entreated them to stay a little longer till he should show them the rest of the abbey. They consented, and after dinner,

> On entering the chapter-room,
> They found a large and stately tomb,
> Covered with rich tapestry,
> Bordered with gold embroidery.
> At head and feet and sides there were
> Twenty tapers burning clear;
> Of fine gold were the chandeliers;
> Of amethyst were the censéres,
> With which they incensed alwáy,
> For great honour, this tomb each day.

The curiosity of the visitors was excited by the sight of this magnificent tomb, and they learned, on inquiry, that therein lay one of the noblest and most valiant knights that had ever lived. He had been king of that country, and had been slain at Caerwent for the love of a lady, leaving a vacancy in the throne which had never been since filled, it being reserved, according to his last commands, for his son by that lady.

When the Dame heard this, she called aloud to her son,

> "Fair son, you now have heard," she said,
> "That God hath us to this place led.
> It is your father here doth lie,
> Whom this old man slew wrongfully."

She then gave him the sword she had kept so long, relating the whole story to him. At the conclusion she fainted on the tomb, and expired. Filled with rage and grief, Ywenec at one blow struck off the head of the old man, and avenged both his father and mother.

The lady was buried in the coffin with him whom she had loved, and the people joyfully acknowledged Ywenec as king of the country.

> Long time after maden they,
> Who heard this adventure, a Lay
> Of the grief and the dolour
> That for love these did endure.

There are still to be seen in Brittany the rock, the cavern, the fountain, the hole, the valley, etc., of the Fées.

The forest of Brezeliande, near Quintin, was, in the twelfth and thirteenth centuries, regarded as the chief seat of Breton wonders. It contained the tomb of Merlin. Robert de Ware, hearing of the wonders of this forest, visited it; but, by his own account, to little purpose.

> La allai je merveilles querre (*chercher*),
> Vis lit forêt et via la terre;
> Merveilles quis (*cherchai*) main ne troval,
> Fol m'en revins, fol y allai;
> Fol y allai, fol men revins,
> Folie quis, por fol me tins. [h]

There were also the Fountain of Berenton and the Perron (*block*, or *steps*) Merveilleux.

> En Bretagne ce treuve-on
> Une Fontaine et un Perron;
> Quant on gette l'iaue (*eau*) dessus
> Si vente et tonne et repluit jus (*à bas*).

Huon do Méry was more fortunate than Ware. He sprinkled the Perron from the golden basin which hung from the oak that shaded it, and beheld all the marvels. [i]

Such is the result of our inquiries respecting the Fairy system of the "oldè gentil Bretons." Owing to the praiseworthy labours of a Breton gentleman of the present day, [i] we are enabled to give the following account of it as it actually prevails in Brittany.

Our author divides the Breton fairies into two classes,—the Fays (*Fées*) and the Dwarfs (*Nains*); of which the Breton name seems to be Korrig or Korrigan, and Korr or Korred. [k] The former he identifies, as we have seen, very plausibly, with the Gallicenae of Mela; for he says that the ancient Welsh bards declare that they reverenced a being of the female sex named Korid-gwen, *i. e.* Korid-woman, to whom they assigned nine virgins as attendants. To this being Taliesin gives a magic vase, the edges of which are adorned with pearl, and it contains the wondrous water of bardic genius and of universal knowledge.

The Korrigan, our authority further states, can predict the future, assume any form they please, move from place to place with the rapidity of thought, cure maladies by the aid of charms which they communicate to their favourites. Their size is said not to exceed two feet, but their proportions are most exact; and they have long flowing hair, which they comb out with great care. Their only dress is a long white veil, which they wind round their body. Seen at night, or in the dusk of the evening, their beauty is great; but in the daylight their eyes appear red, their hair white, and their faces wrinkled; hence they rarely let themselves be seen by day. They are fond of music, and have fine voices, but are not much given to dancing. Their favourite haunts are the springs, by which they sit and comb their hair. They are said to celebrate there every returning spring a great nocturnal festival. On the sod at its brink is spread a table-cloth white as the driven snow, covered with the most delicious viands. In the centre is a crystal cup, which emits such light that there is no need of lamps. At the end of the banquet a cup goes round filled with a liquor, one drop of which would make one as wise as God himself. At the approach of a mortal the whole vanishes.

Like fairies in general the Korrigan steal children, against which the remedy usually employed is, to place the child under the protection of the Virgin, by putting a rosary or a scapulary about its neck. They are also fond of uniting themselves with handsome young men to regenerate, as the peasants say, their accursed race. The general belief respecting them is, that they were great princesses who, having refused. to embrace Christianity when it was preached in Armorica by the Apostles, were struck by the curse of God. Hence it is that they are said to be animated by a violent hatred of religion and the clergy. The sight of a *soutane*, or the sound of a bell, puts them to flight; but the object of greatest abhorrence to them is the Holy Virgin. The last trait to be noticed. of these beings is, that, like simiilar beings in other countries, their breath is deadly.

The reader must have observed. the strong resemblance which the Korrigan bear to the Elle-maids of Scandinavia. In like manner the Korred are very similar to the Trolls. [1] These are usually represented as short and stumpy with shaggy hair, dark wrinkled faces, little deep-set eyes, but bright as carbuncles. Their voice is cracked and hollow:

their hands have claws like a cat's; their feet are horny like those of a goat. They are expert smiths and coiners; the are said to have great treasures in the *dolmen* [m] in which they dwell, and of which they are regarded as the builders. They dance around them by night, and wo to the belated peasant who, passing by, is forced to join in their roundel; he usually dies of exhaustion. Wednesday is their holiday; the first Wednesday in May their annual festival, which they celebrate with dancing, singing, and music. They have the same aversion to holy things as the Korrigan; like them, too, they can fortell events to come. The Korrid is always furnished with a large leathern purse, which is said to be full of gold; but if any one succeeds in getting it from him, he finds nothing in it but hair and a pair of scissors.

The Bretons also believe in Mermaids; they name them Morgan (*sea-women*) and Morverc'h (*sea-daughters*), and say that they draw down to their palaces of gold and crystal at the bottom of the sea or of ponds, those who venture imprudently too neat the edge of the water. Like the mermaids they sing and comb their golden hair. In one of the ballads we read, "Fisher, hast thou seen the mermaid combing her hair, yellow as gold, by the noontide sun, at the edge of the water?" "I have seen the fair mermaid. I have also heard her singing; her, songs were plaintive as the waves." [n]

In M. Villemarqué's collection there are three ballads relating to the Korrigan and Korred. The following is a faithful translation of the first of them in the exact measure of the original. All the Breton poetry is rimed, very frequently in triads or tercets.

NOTES

[a] This manifestly alludes to Laval or Graeleat, or similar stories.

[b] It follows, in M. de Roquefort's edition,

"Deci ne muez fu ou déeis"

Of which we can make no sense, and the French translation gives no aid. In the Harleian MS. it is

"De cinc muez fu ou de sis,"

which is more intelligible.

[c] This tends to prove that this is a translation from the Breton; for Innocent III., in whose pontificate the cup was first refused to the laity, died in 1216, when Henry III., to whom Marie is supposed to have dedicated her Lais, was a child.

[d] The same was the case with the Wünschelweib (*Wish-woman*) of German romance.

Swenne du einêst wünachest nach mir,

So bin ich endelichen bi dir,

says the lady to the Staufenberger. She adds,

War ich wil da bin ich,

Den Wunsch hat mir Got gegeben.

He finds it to be true,

Er wünschte nach der frouwen sin,

Bi im so war diu schiune sin.

GRIMM, *Deut. Mythol*, p. 391.

[e] In the Shah-nameh, Siyawush, when he foresees his own death by the treachery of Afrasiab, tells his wife Ferengis, the daughter of that monarch, that she will bear a son whom she is to name Ky Khosroo, and who will avenge the death of his father: see Görres, Heldenbuch von Iran, ii. 32.

[f] Desi k'a une hoge vint:

En cele hoge ot une entree.

M. de Roquefort, in his Glossaire de la Langue Romaine, correctly renders *hoge* by *colline*. In his translation of this Lai he renders it by *cabane*, not, perhaps, understanding how a hill could be pervious. The story, however, of Prince Ahmed, and the romance of Orfeo and Heurodis, are good authority on this point.

[g] In the Harleian MS. Mandement. M. Ce Roquefort confesses his total ignorance of this people; we follow his example. May it not, however, be connected with *manant*, and merely signify people, inhabitants?

[h] Roman de Roux, *v*. ii. 234.

[i] See Roquefort, Supplément au Glossaire de la Langue Romaine *s. v.* Perron.

[j] Barzan-Breiz, Chants Populaires de la Bretagne, recueilles et publiés par Th. Hersart de la Villemarqué. Paris, 1846. This is a most valuable work and deserving to take its place with the Ballads of Scotland, Scandinavia, and Servia, to none of which is it inferior. To the credit of France the edition which we use is the fourth. How different would the fate of such a work be in this country!

[k] We make this distinction, because in the ballads in which the personage is a Fay, the word used is Korrigan or Korrig, while in that in which the Dwarfs are actors, the words are Korr and Korred. But the truth is, they are all but different forms of Korr. They are all the same, singular and plural. The Breton changes its first consonant like the Irish. We also meet with Crion, Goric, Couril, as names of these beings, but they are only forms of those given above.

[l] Hence we may infer that they came originally from Scandinavia, communicated most probably by the Normans.

[m] Stone-tables. They are called by the same name in Devon and Cornwall; is Irish their appellation is Cromleach.

[n] Barzan-Breiz., l. xlix. 69.

Lord Nann and the Korrigan

The Lord Nann and his bride so fair
In early youth united were,
In early youth divided were.
The lady lay-in yesternight
Of twins, their skin as snow was white,
A boy and girl, that glad his sight.
"What doth thy heart desire, loved one,
For giving me so fair a son?
Say, and at once it shall be done.
"A woodcock from the pool of the glyn,
Or roebuck from the forest green?
"The roebuck's flesh is savoury,
But for it thou to the wood should'st hie."
Lord Nann when he these words did hear,
He forthwith grasped his oaken spear,
And vaulting on his coal-black steed
Unto the green-wood hied with speed.
When he unto the wood drew nigh,
A fair white doe he there did spy,
And after her such chase he made,
The ground it shook beneath their tread.
And after her such chase made he,
From his brows the water copiously
And from his horse's sides ran down.
The evening had now come on,
And he came where a streamlet flowed
Fast by a Korrigan's abode;
And grassy turf spread all around.
To quench his thirst he sprang to ground.
The Korrig at her fount sat there
A-combing of her long fair hair.
She combed it with a comb of gold—
These ladies ne'er are poor, we 're told.
"Rash man," cried she, "how dost thou dare
To come disturb my waters fair!
"Thou shalt unto me plight thy fay,

Or seven years thou shalt waste away,
Or thou shalt die ere the third day."
"To thee my faith plight will I ne'er,
For I am married now a year.
"I shall not surely waste away,
Nor shall I die ere the third day;
"I shall not die within three days,
But when it unto God shall please."—
"Good mother, mine, if you love me,
See that my bed made ready be,
For I have ta'en a malady.
"Let not one word to my wife be told;
In three days I shall lie in the mould,
A Korrigan has thus foretold."
And when three days were past and gone,
The young wife asked this question,—
"My mother-in-law, now tell me why
The bells all ring thus constantly?
"And why the priests a low mass sing,
All clad in white, as the bells ring?"
"Last night a poor man died whom we
A lodging gave through charity."
"My mother-in-law, tell me, I pray,
My Lord Nann whither is he gone away?"
"My daughter, to the town he 'a gone,
To see thee he will come anon."
"Good mother-in-law, to church to fare,
Shall I my red or blue gown wear?"
"The custom now is, daughter dear,
At church always in black to appear."
As they crossed o'er the churchyard-wall,
On her husband's grave her eye did fall.
"Who is now dead of our family,
That thus fresh dug our ground I see?"
"Alas! my child, the truth can I
Not hide: thy husband there doth lie."
On her two knees herself she cast
And rose no more, she breathed her last.
It was a marvel to see, men say,

The night that followed the *day*,
The lady in earth by her lord lay,
To see two oak-trees themselves rear
From the new-made grave into the air;
And on their branches two doves white,
Who there were hopping gay and light;
Which sang when rose the morning-ray
And then toward heaven sped away.

This ballad is very remarkable. Its similarity to that of Sir Olaf, so celebrated in Scandinavia, and of which we have already given two variations out of fifteen, must strike every one; in its concluding stanzas also it resembles other Scandinavian and English ballads. On the other hand, the White Doe and the Korrigan at the fount remind us of the Lais of Marie de France. Our opinion on the whole is, that the ballad belongs to Scandinavia, whence it was brought at an early period—by the Normans, we might say only for its Christian air in both countries—and naturalised in the usual manner. It is rather strange that there is neither an English nor a Scottish version of it.

The next lay, which is entirely composed in tercets, is the story of a changeling. In order to recover her own child the mother is advised by the Virgin, to whom she has prayed, to prepare a meal for ten farm-servants in an eggshell, which will make the Korrid speak, and she is then to whip him well till he cries, and when he does so he will be taken away. The woman does as directed: the Korr asks what she is about: she tells him: "For ten, dear mother, in an eggshell! I have seen the egg before I saw the white hen: I have seen the acorn before I saw the tree: I have seen the acorn and I have seen the shoot: I have seen the oak in the wood of Brézal, but never saw

I such a thing as this." "Thou hast seen too many things, my son," replied she, and began to whip him, when one came crying, "Don't beat him, give him back to me; I have not done yours any injury. He is king in our country." When the woman went home she found her own child sleeping sweetly in the cradle. He opened his eyes and said, "Ah! mother, I have been a long time asleep!"

Among the Welsh legends above related, that of the Fairies Banished has some resemblance to this; but M. Villemarqué says that he was told a changeling-story by the Glamorgan peasantry, precisely the same as the Breton legend. In it the changeling is heard muttering to himself in a cracked voice, "I have seen the acorn before I saw the oak: I have seen the egg before I saw the white hen: I have never seen the like of this." It is remarkable that these words form a rimed triad or tercet nearly the same with that in the Breton ballad, [a] whence M. Villemarqué is led to suspect that the legend is anterior to the seventh century, the epoch of the separation of the Britons of Wales and Armorica. But as changelings seem to have come from the North, we cannot consent to receive this theory. He also quotes from Geoffrey of Monmouth's Life of Merlin, "There is in this forest," said Merlin the Wild, "an oak laden with years: I saw it when it was beginning to grow... I saw the acorn whence it rose, germinate and become a twig... I have then lived a long time." This would, in our opinion, tend to show that this was an ordinary formula in the British language.

The third, and last of those ballads tells, and not without humour, how Paskou-Hir, *i. e.*, Long-Paskou, the tailor, one Friday evening, entered the abode of the Korred, and there dug up and carried, home a concealed treasure. They pursued him, and came into the court-yard dancing with might and main, and singing,—

Dilun, dimeurs, dimerc'her
Ha diriaou, ha digwoner.
Monday, Tuesday, Wednesday,
And Thursday, and Friday.

Funding the door secured [b] they mount the roof and break a hole through which they get in, and resume their dance on the floor, still singing, Monday, Tuesday, etc., and calling on the tailor to come and. join them and they would teach him a dance that would crack his back-bone, and they end by telling him that the money of the Korr is good for nothing.

Another version says, that it was a baker who stole the treasure, and, more cunning than the tailor, be strewed the floor of his house with hot ashes and cinders on which the Korred burned their feet. This made them scamper off, but before they went they smashed all his crockery and earthenware. Their words were, "In lannik-ann-Trevou's house we burnt our horny feet and made a fine mess of his crockery."

The following legend will explain the song of the Korred.

NOTES

[a] Welsh

    Gweliz mez ken gwelet derven,
    Gweliz vi ken gwelet iar wenn,
    Erioez ne williz evelhenn.

Breton

    Gweliz vi ken guelot iar wenn,
    Gweliz mez ken gwelet gwezen.
    Gweliz mez ha gweliz gwial,
    Gweliz derven e Koat Brezal,
    Biskoaz na weliz kemend all.

[b] The tailor cries "Shut the door! Here are the little *Duz* of the night" *(Setu ann Duizigou nouz)*, and St. Augustine (De Civ. Dei, c. xxiii.) speaks of "Daemones quos *Duscios* Galli nuncupant." It may remind us of our own word *Deuce*.

The Dance and Song of the Korred

The valley of Goel was a celebrated haunt of the Korred. [a] It was thought dangerous to pass through it at night lest one should be forced to join in their dances, and thus perhaps lose his life. One evening, however, a peasant and his wife thoughtlessly did so, and they soon found themselves enveloped by the dancing sprites, who kept singing—

> Lez y, Lez hon,
> Bas an arer zo gant hon;
> Lez on, Lez y,
> Bas an arer zo gant y.
> Let him go, let him go,
> For he has the wand of the plough;
> Let her go, let her go,
> For she has the wand of the plough.

It seems the man had in his band the *fourche,* or short stick, which is used. as a plough-paddle in Brittany, and this was a protection, for the dancers made way for them to go out of the ring.

When this became known, many persons having fortified themselves with a *fourche,* gratified their curiosity by witnessing the dance of the Korred. Among the rest were two tailors, Peric and Jean, who, being merry fellows, dared each other to join in the dance. They drew lots, and the lot fell upon Peric, a humpbacked red-haired, but bold stout little fellow. He went up to the Korred and asked permission to take share in their dance. They granted it, and all went whirling round and round, singing

Dilun, Dimeurs, Dimerc'her.
Monday, Tuesday, Wednesday.

Perle, weary of the monotony, when there was a slight pause at the last word, added

Ha Diriaou, ha Digwener.
And Thursday and Friday.

Mat!,mat! (good! good!) cried they, and gathering round him, they offered him his choice of beauty, rank, or riches. He laughed, and only asked them to remove his hump and change the colour of his hair. They forthwith took hold of him and tossed him up into the air, throwing him from hand to hand till at last he lighted on his feet with a flat back and fine long black hair.

When Jean saw and heard of the change he resolved to try what *he* could get from the potent Korred, so a few evenings after he went and was admitted to the dance, which now went to the words as enlarged by Peric. To make his addition he shouted out,

Ha Disadarn, ha Disul
And Saturday and Sunday.

"What more? what more?" cried the Korred, but he only went on repeating the words. They then asked him what he would have, and he replied riches. They tossed him up, and kept bandying him about till he cried for mercy, and on coming to the ground, he found he had got Peric's hump and red hair.

It seems that the Korred were condemned to this continual dancing, which was never to cease till a mortal should join in their dance, and after naming all the days of the week, should add, *Ha cetu chu er sizun,* "And now the week is ended." They punished Jean for coming so near the end and then disappointing them. [b]

We add the following circumstances from other authorities:

At Carnac, near Quiberon, says M. de Cambry, in the department of Morbihan, on the sea-shore, is the Temple of Carnac, called in Breton "Ti Goriquet" *(House of the Gorics),* one of the most remarkable Celtic monuments extant. It is composed of more than four thousand large stones, standing erect in an arid plain, where neither tree nor shrub is to be seen, and not even a pebble is to be found in the soil on which they stand. If the inhabitants are asked concerning, this wonderful monument, they say it is an old camp of Caesar's, an army turned into stone, or that it is the work of the Crions or Gorics. These they describe as little men between two and three feet high, who carried these enormous masses on their hands; for, though little, they are stronger than giants. Every night they dance around the stones; and woe betide the traveller who approaches within their reach! he is forced to join in the dance, where he is whirled about till, breathless and exhausted, he falls down, amidst the peals of laughter of the Crions. All vanish with the break of day. [c]

In the ruins of Tresmaiouen dwell the Courils. [d] They are of a malignant disposition, but great lovers of dancing. At night they sport around the Druidical monuments. The unfortunate shepherd that approaches them must dance their rounds with them till cock-crow; and the instances are not few of persons thus ensnared who have been found next morning dead with exhaustion and fatigue. Woe also to the ill-fated maiden who draws near the Couril dance! nine months after, the family counts one member more. Yet so great

---

is the power and cunning of these Dwarfs, that the young stranger bears no resemblance to them, but they impart to it the features of some lad of the village.

A number of little men, not more than a foot high, dwell under the castle of Morlaix. They live in holes in the ground, whither they may often be seen going, and beating on basins. They possess great treasures, which they sometimes bring out; and if any one pass by at the time, allow him to take one handful, but no more. Should any one attempt to fill his pockets, the money vanishes, and he is instantly assailed by a shower of boxes in the ear from invisible hands.

The Bretons also say that there are spirits who silently skim the milk-pans in the dairies. They likewise speak of Sand Yan y Tad (*St. John and Father*), who carry five lights at their finger-ends, which they make spin round and round like a wheel. [e]

There is a species of malignant beings, called Night-washers (*Eur cunnerez noz*), who appear on the banks of streams, and call on the passers-by to aid them to wash the linen of the dead. If any one refuses, they drag him into the water and break his arms.

About Morlaix the people are afraid of evil beings they call Teurst. One of these, called Teursapouliet, appears in the likeness of some domestic animal. [f] In the district of Vannes is a colossal spirit called Teus, or Bugelnoz, who appears clothed in white between midnight and two in the morning. His office is to rescue victims from the Devil. He spreads his mantle over them, and they are secure. The Devil comes over the ocean; but, unable to endure the look of the good spirit, he sinks down again, and, the object of the spirit accomplished, he vanishes.

_____

NOTES

[a] In the original the word is Korrigan.

[b] From an article signed H—Y in a cheap publication called Tracts for the People. The writer says he heard it in the neighbourhood of the Vale of Goel, and it has every appearance of being genuine. Villemarqué (i. 61) mentions the last circumstance as to the end of the penance of the Korred.

[c] Monumens Celtiques, p. 2. An old sailor told M. de Cambry, that one of these stones covers an immense treasure, and that these thousands of them have been set up the better to conceal it. He added that a calculation, the key to which was to be found in the Tower of London, would alone indicate the spot where the treasure lies.

[d] For what follows we are indebted to the MS. communication of Dr. W. Grimm. He quotes as his authority the *Zeitung der Gesellschafter* for 1826.

[e] The former seems to be a house spirit, the *Goblin, Follet,* or *Lutin* of the, north of France; the latter is apparently the *Ignis Fatuus.*

[f] So the Yorkshire Bar-guest,

SOUTHERN EUROPE

O faretrate Ninfe, o agresti Pani,
O Satiri e Silvani, o Fauni e Driadi,
Najadi ed Amadriadi, e Semidee
Oreadi, e Napee, or siete sole.
−SANAZZARO.

UNDER THE title of Southern Europe, we comprise Greece and those nations whose languages are derived from the Latin; Italy, Spain, and France. Of the Fairy-system, if there ever was one, of Portugal we have met with nothing, at least in the works of Camoens, Bernardes, and Lobo.

The reader will, in this part of our work, find little corresponding to the Gothic Dwarfs who have hitherto been our companions. The only one of our former acquaintances that will attend us is honest Hob-goblin, Brownie, Kobold, Nis, or however else he may style himself. And it is very remarkable that we shall meet with him only in those places where the Northmen, the Visigoths or other Scandinavian tribes settled. Whence perhaps it might be concluded that they brought him with them to the South of Europe.

GREECE

Like a tender Nymph
Within the dewy caves.
–EURIPIDES

The Grecian mythology, like its kindred systems, abounded in personifications. [a] Modified by scenery so beautiful, rich, and various as Hellas presented, it in general assigned the supposed intelligences who presided over the various parts of external nature more pleasing attributes than they elsewhere enjoyed. They were mostly conceived to be of the female sex, and were denominated Nymphs, a word originally signifying a new-married woman.

Whether it be owing to soil, climate, or to an original disposition of mind and its organ, the Greeks have above all other people possessed a perception of beauty of form, and a fondness for representing it. The Nymphs of various kinds were therefore always presented to the imagination, in the perfection of female youth and beauty. Under the various appellations of Oreades, Dryades, Naides, Limniades, Nereides, they dwelt in mountains, trees, springs, lakes, the seas where, in caverns and grottos, they passed a life whose occupations resembled those of females of human rare. The Wood-nymphs were the companions and attendants of the huntress goddess Artemis; the Sea-nymphs averted shipwreck from pious navigators; and the Spring- and River-nymphs poured forth fruitfulness on the earth. All of them were honoured with prayer and sacrifice; and all of them occasionally 'mingled in love' with favoured mortals.

In the Homeric poems, the most ancient portion of Grecian

literature, we meet the various classes of Nymphs. In the Odyssey, they are the attendants of Calypso, herself a goddess and a nymph. Of the female attendants of Circe, the potent daughter of Helios, also designated as a goddess and a nymph, it is said,

> They spring from fountains and from sacred groves,
> And holy streams that flow into the sea.

Yet these nymphs are of divine nature, and when Zeus, the father of the gods, calls together his council,

> None of the streams, save Ocean, stayed away,
> Nor of the Nymphs, who dwell in beauteous groves,
> And springs of streams, and verdant grassy slades.

The good Eumaeus prays to the Nymphs to speed the return of his master, reminding them of the numerous sacrifices Ulysses had offered to them. In another part of the poem, their sacred cave is thus described:—

> But at the harbour's head a long-leafed olive
> Grows, and near to it lies a lovely cave,
> Dusky and sacred to the Nymphs, whom men
> Call Naides. In it large craters lie,
> And two-eared pitchers, all of stone, and there
> Bees build their combs. In it, too, are long looms
> Of stone, and there the Nymphs do weave their robes
> Sea-purple, wondrous to behold. Aye-flowing
> Waters are there; two entrances it hath;
> That to the north is pervious unto men;
> That to the south more sacred is, and there
> Men enter not, but 'tis the Immortals' path.

Yet though thus exalted in rank, the Homeric Nymphs frequently 'blessed the bed' of heroes; and many a warrior who fought before Troy could boast descent from a Nais or a Nereis.

The sweet, gentle, pious, Ocean-nymphs, who in the Prometheus of Aeschylus appear as the consolers and advisers of its dignified hero, seem to hold a nearly similar relation with man to the supernal gods. Beholding the misery inflicted on Prometheus by the power of Zeus, they cry,—

> May never the all-ruling
> Zeus set his rival power
> Against my thoughts;
> Nor may I ever fail
> The gods, with holy feasts
> Of sacrifices, drawing near,
> Beside the ceaseless stream

Of father Ocean:

> Nor may I err in words;
> But this abide with me
> And never fade away.

One of the most interesting species of Nymphs is the Dryads, or Hamadryads, those personifications of the vegetable life of plants. In the Homeric hymn to Aphrodite, we find the following full and accurate description of them. Aphrodite, when she informs Anchises of her pregnancy, and her shame to have it known among the gods, says of the child;—

> But him, when first he sees the sun's clear light,
> The Nymphs shall rear, the mountain-haunting Nymphs,
> Deep-bosomed, who on this mountain great
> And holy dwell, who neither goddesses
> Nor women are. Their life is long; they eat
> Ambrosial food, and with the deathless frame

The beauteous dance. With them, in the recess
Of lovely caves, well-spying Argos-slayer
And the Sileni mix in lova Straight pines
Or oaks high headed spring with them upon
The earth man-feeding, soon as they are born;
This fair and flourishing; on the high hills
Lofty they stand; the Deathless' sacred grove
Men call them, and with iron never cut.
But when the fate of death is drawing near,
First wither on the earth the beauteous trees,
The bark around them wastes, the branches fall,
And the Nymph's soul at the same moment leaves
The sun's fair light.

They possessed power to reward and punish these who pro-
longed or abridged the existence of theft associate-tree. In the Ar-
gonautics of Apollonius Rhodius, Phineus thus explains to the heroes
the cause of the poverty of Peraebius

But he was paring the penalty laid on
His fathers crime; for one time, cutting trees
Alone among the hills, he spurned the prayer
Of the Hamadryas Nymph, who, weeping sore,
With earnest words besought him not to cut
The trunk of an oak tree, which, with herself
Coeval, had endured for many a year.
But, in the pride of youth, he foolishly
Cut it; and to him and to his race the Nymph
Gave ever after a lot profitless.

The Scholiast gives on this passage the following tale from
Charon of Lampsacus:

A man, named Rhoecus, happening to see an oak just ready
to fall to the ground, ordered his slaves to prop it. The Nymph, who

had been on the point of perishing with the tree, came to him and expressed her gratitude to him for having saved her life, and at the same time desired him to ask what reward he would. Rhoecus then requested her to permit him to be her lover, and the Nymph acceded to his wishes. She at the same time charged him strictly to avoid the society of every other woman, and told him that a bee should be her messenger. One time the bee happened to come to Rhoecus as he was playing at draughts, and he made a rough reply. This so incensed the Nymph that she deprived him of sight.

Similar was the fate of the Sicilian Daphnis. [b] A Nais loved him and forbade him to hold intercourse with any other woman under pain of loss of sight. Long he abstained, though tempted by the fairest maids of Sicily. At length a princess contrived to intoxicate him: he broke his vow, and the threatened penalty was inflicted.

NOTES

[a] See our Mythology of Ancient Greece and Italy, where (p. 237) most of what follows will be found, with notes.
[b] Parthenius, Erotica, chap. xxix

ITALY

Faune Nympharum fuglentum amator,
Per meos fines at aprica rura
Lenis incedas, abeasque parvis
Aequus alumnis.
    –HORATIUS.

Unfortunately for our knowledge of the ancient Italian mytholo-gy, the ballad-poetry of Rome is irrecoverably lost. A similar fate has befallen the literature of Etruria, Umbria, and other parts of the peninsula. The powerful influence exercised by Grecian genius over the conquerors of the Grecian states utterly annihilated all that was national and domestic in literature. Not but that Latin poetry abounds in mythologic matter; but it is the mythology of Greece, not of Italy; and the reader of Virgil and Ovid will observe with surprise how little of what he meets in their works is Italian.

So much however of the population of ancient Italy, particu-larly of Latium, was Pelasgian, that it is natural to suppose a great similarity between the religious systems of Latium and Hellas. The Latins do not, however, appear to have believed in choirs of Nymphs. Those we read of, such as Egeria, Anna Perenna, Juturna, are all solitary, all dwellers of fountains, streams, and lakes The Italian Diana did not, like the Grecian Artemis, speed over the mountains attended by a train of buskined nymphs. No Dryads sought to avert the fate of their kindred trees—no Nereides sported on the waves.

Dwarfish deities they had none. We are indeed told of the Lars, particularly the rural Lars, as answering to the Gothic Dwarfs; but no proofs are offered except the diminutive size of their statues. This we hold to amount to nothing. Are we to suppose the following lines of Plautus to have been delivered by an "eyas?"

> Lest any marvel who I am, I shall
> Briefly declare it. I am the family Lar
> Of this home whence you see me coming out.
> 'Tis many years now that I keep and guard
> This family; both father and grandsire
> Of him that has it now, I aye protected.
> Now his grandsire intrusted me a treasure
> Of gold, that I, unknown to all, should keep it.
>
> * * *
>
> He has one daughter, who, each day with wine
> Or incense, or with something, worships me.
> She gives me crowns, and I in recompense
> Have now made Euclio find the treasure out,
> That if he will, he may more readily
> Get her a match. [a]

The Lars were a portion of the Etrurian religion. The Etruscan word Lar signifies Lord, with which it has a curious but casual resemblance. [b] The Lars were regarded, like the Grecian heroes, as being the souls of men who, after death, still hovered about their former abodes, averting dangers from, and bestowing blessings on, the inhabitants.

They differed from the Penates, who were, properly speaking Gods, beings of a higher nature, personifications of natural powers, the givers of abundance and wealth.

The old Italians, it appears, believed in a being, we know not of what size, called an Incubo, that watched over treasure. "But what they say I know not," says Petronius, [c] but I have heard how he snatched the cap of an Incubo and found a treasure."

Respecting the Fairy mythology of the modern Italians, what we have been able to collect is very little.

The people of Naples, we are told, [d] believe in a being very much resembling the Incubo, whom they call the Monaciello, or Little Monk. They describe him as a short, thick kind of little man, dressed in the long garments of a monk, with a broad-brimmed hat. He appears to people in the dead of the night, and beckons to them to follow him. If they have courage to do so, he leads them to some place where treasure is concealed. Several are said to have made sudden fortunes through him. In the Neapolitan story-book, named the Pentamerone, of which we shall presently give an account, we meet with a Monaciello of a very different character from this guardian of hidden treasure.

In the second tale of the first day of that work, when the prince in the night heard the noise made by the Fairy in his room, "he thought it was some chamber-boy coming to lighten his purse for him, or some Monaciello to pull the clothes off him." And in the seventh tale of the third day of the same collection, when Corvetto had hidden himself under the Ogre's [e] bed to steal his quilt, "he began to pull quite gently, when the Ogre awoke, and bid his wife not to pull the clothes that way, or she'd strip him, and he would. get his death of cold." "Why, it's you that are stripping me," replied the Ogress, "and you have not left a stitch on me." "Where the devil is the quilt?" says the Ogre; and putting his hand to the ground, he happened to touch the face of Corvetto, and immediately began to shout out, "The Monaciello, the Monaciello, hola! candles! run, run!" Corvetto, meanwhile, got off with his prize through the window. [f]

It is quite clear that the Monaciello is the same kind of being as the House-spirit of the Gotho-German nations. He seems to belong peculiarly to Naples, for we have not heard of him in any other part of Italy. Now we are to recollect that this was the very place in which the Normans settled, and so he may be their Nis or Kobold; [g] or, as he is so very like the Spanish Duende, he may be that being introduced by the Aragonese, who seem to have exercised so much influence over the language and manners of the people of Naples.

The belief in Mermaids also prevailed in modern Italy. In the reign of Roger, king of Sicily, a young man happening to be bathing in the sea late in the evening, perceived that something was following him. Supposing it to be one of his companions, he caught it by the hair, and dragged it on shore. But finding it to be a maiden of great beauty and of most perfect form, he threw his cloak about her, and took her home, where she continued with him till they had a son. There was one thing however which greatly grieved him, which was the reflection that so beautiful a form should be dumb, for he had never heard her speak. One day he was reproached by one of his companions, who said that it was a spectre, and not a real woman, that he had at home: being both angry and terrified, he laid his hand on the hilt of his sword, and urged her with vehemence to tell him who or what she was, threatening if she did not do so, to kill the child before her eyes. The spirit only saying, that he had lost a good wife by forcing her to speak, instantly vanished, leaving her son behind. A few years after, as the boy was playing on the sea-shore with his companions, the spirit his mother dragged him into the seas where he was drowned. [h]

We now come to the Fate of romance and tale.

The earliest notice that we can recollect to have seen of these potent ladies is in the Orlando Innamorato, where we meet the celebrated Fata Morgana, who would at first appear to be, as a personification of Fortune, a being of a higher order.

> Ivi è una fata nomata Morgana,
> Che a le genti diverse dona l'oro;
> Quanto e per tutto il mondo or se ne spande
> Convien che ad essa prima si dimande.
> L. l. c. xxv. st. 5. ed. 1831.

But we afterwards find her in her proper station, subject, with the Fate and Witches, to the redoubtable Demogorgon. [i] When Orlando, on delivering Zilante from. her, makes her swear by that awful power, the poet says:

> Sopra ogni fata è quel Demogorgone
> (Non so se mal l'odiste raccontare)
> E giudica tra loro e fa ragione,
> E quel che piace a lui puo di lor fare.
> La notte si cavalca ad un montone,
> Travarca le montague e passa il mare,
> E *strigie*, e *fate,* e fantasime vane
> Batte con serpi vive ogni dimane.
> Se le ritrova la dimane al mondo,
> Perchè non ponno al giorno comparire,
> Tanto le batte al colpo furibondo
> Che volentier vorrien poter morire.
> Or le incatena giu nel mar profondo,
> Or sopra il vento scalze le fa gire,
> Or per il fuoco dietro a se le mena;

A cui dà questa, a cui quell' altra pena.
L. ll. c. xiii. at. 27, 28.

According to Ariosto, [i] Demogorgon has a splendid temple palace in the Himalaya mountains, whither every fifth year the Fate are all summoned to appear before him, and give an account of their actions. They travel through the air in various strange conveyances, and it is no easy matter to distinguish between their convention and a Sabbat of the Witches.

We meet with another Fata in Bojardo, [k] the beautiful Silvanella, who raised a tomb over Narcissus, and then dissolved away into a fountain.

When Brandamarte opens the magnificent tomb and kisses the hideous serpent that thrusts out its head, it gradually becomes a beautiful maiden.

Questa era Febosilla quella fata,
Che edificato avea l'alto palaccio
E 'l bel giardino e quella sepoltura,
Ove un gran tempo è stata in pena dura.
Perchè una fata non può morir mai,
Sin che non giunge il giorno del giudizio,
Ma ben ne la sua forma dura assai,
Mill' anni o piu, si come io aggio indizio.
Poi (siccome di questa io vi contai
Qual fabbricato avea il bell' edifizio)
In serpe si tramuta e stavvi tanto
Che di baciarla alcun si doni il vanto.
L. ll. c. xxvi. st. 14, 15.

The other Fate who appear in this poem are Le Fate Nera and Bianca, the protectresses of Guidone and Aquilante; the Fata della Fonte, from whom Mandricardo obtains the arms of Hector, and finally Alcina, the sister of Morgana, who carries off Astolfo. Drag-ontina and Falerina, the owners of such splendid gardens, may also have been Fate, though they are not called so by the poet.

Alcina re-appears in great splendour in the Orlando Furioso, where she is given a sister named Logistilla, and both, like Morgana in the preceding poem, are in a great measure allegorical. We also obtain there a glimpse of the White and Black Fate. The Maga Man-to of Dante becomes here a Fata, and we meet her in the form of a serpent; to account for which she says,

> Nascemmo ad un punto che d' ogni altro male
> Siamo capaci fuor che della morte.
> Ma giunta è con questo essere immortale
> Condizion non men del morir forte;
> Ch' ogni settimo giorno ognuna è certa
> Che la ma forma in biscia si converta.
> C. xliii. st. 98.
> Elsewhere (x. 52) the poet tells us that
> Morir non puote alcuna fata mai
> Fin che il Sol gira, o il ciel non muta stilo.

In the Amadigi of Bernardo Tasso the Fate appear for the last time in Italian poetry; [l] but in greater number, and, we may say, greater splendour than elsewhere. There are two classes of them, the beneficent and protective, and the seductive and injurious. The terms Maga and Incantatrice, as well as Fata, are applied to them all indif-ferently. The good Fairy-ladies are Urganda, termed *La savia* and *La sconosciuta,* [m] the guardian of Amadigi, and the fair Oriana; Silvana or Silvanella who stands in a similar relation to Alidoro; Lucina, also named La Donna del Lago, another protectress of Alidoro and of his lady-love, the fair warrior Mirinda, sister of Amadigi; Eufrosina, the sister of Lucina; Argea, called La Reina della Fate, the protectress of Floridante, to whom, after making him undergo various trials, she gives her daughter Filidora in marriage; finally, Argea's sister Filidea. The Fate whose character resembles that of Alcina are Morganetta, Nivetta, and Carvilia, the three daughters of Morgana. Beside these then are two Fate of neutral character, Dragontina, who formed a palace, temple and gardens, in which, at the desire of her father, she enchanted a young prince and his wife; and Montana, who, to avenge the fate of her lover, slain by Alidoro, enchanted that warrior in a temple which she had raised to the memory of the fallen. [n]

> Ma veggiam ch' io non stessi troppo a bada
> Con queste Alcine e Morgane.

The earliest collections of European Fairy-tales in prose belong to Italy. In 1550, Straparola, a native of Caravaggio, in the Milanese, published at Venice his Notti Piacevoli, a collection of tales, jokes, and riddles, of which several, and those the best, are Fairy-tales. These were translated into French in 1560—76, and seem to have been the origin of the so well known Contes des Feés. Perrault's Puss in Boots *(Le Chat Botté,)* and the Princess Fairstar *(Belle Etoile,)* and many others of Madame D'Aulnoy's, who borrowed largely from the Notti Piacevoli, are to be found in Straparola. In 1637, eighty-seven years after the Notti Piacevoli appeared at Naples, and in the Neapolitan dialect, the Péntamerone, the best collection of Fairy-tales ever written. [o] The author, Giambattista Basile, [p] had spent his youth in Candia, and then passed several years rambling through Italy. He seems to have carefully treasured up all the tales he heard, and he wrote and published them, under the feigned name of Gian Alesio Abbatutis, in his native dialect, not long before his death.

In the Tales and Popular Fictions we gave some translations from the Notti Piacevoli, the only ones in English, and they will probably remain such, as the work is not one likely ever to be translated. In the same work we gave two from the Pentamerone, and. three (the Dragon, Gagliuso, and the Goatface) in the former edition of the present work. Most certainly we were the first to render any of these curious tales into English, and we look back with a mixture of pleasure and surprise at our success in the unaided struggle with an idiom so different from the classic Italian. [q] We fancied that we had been the first to make translations from it into any language, but we afterwards learned that of the two tales in our other work, the one, Peruonto, had been translated into French (probably by the Abbé Galiani) for the Cabinet des Feés, the other, the Serpent into German, by M. Grimm. [r] Of late, this most original work has been brought within the reach of ordinary readers by two translations, the one in German by Felix Liebrecht, who has given the work complete with few omissions; the other in English by Mr. J. E. Taylor, who has made a selection of thirty tales, and these most carefully expurgated, in order that agreeably to its second title, it might form a book of amusement even for children—a most difficult task, and in which his success has been far greater than might have been anticipated. All our own translations have been incorporated in it, and we can safely refer to it those who wish to know the real character and nature of the Pentamerone.

Whatever name Basile might give his book it is quite plain that he never could have meant it merely for children. The language alone is proof enough on that head. It is, besides, full of learned allusions and of keen satire, so that it could only be understood and relished by grown persons, for whose amusement it was apparently designed; and its tales are surely not much more extravagant than some of those in Ariosto and the other romantic poets. It in fact never was a child's book like the Contes de ma Mère l' Oie. It has now become very scarce; we could not at Naples meet with a copy of it, or even with any one who had read it.

NOTES

[a] Anlularia, Prologue.

[b] See our Mythology of Greece and Italy, p. 543; and our Ovid's Fasti, Excursus iv.

[c] Satyricon, ch. 38. *Sunt qui eundem* (Hercules) *Incubonem esse velint.* Schol. Hor. Sat. ii. 6, 13.

[d] Viessieux, Italy and the Italians, vol. i. pp. 161, 162.

[e] *L'huorco*, the Orco of Bojardo and Ariosto, probably derived from the Latin Orcus: see Mythol. of Greece and Italy, p. 527. In this derivation we find that we had been anticipated by Minucci in his notes on the Malmantile Racquistato, c. ii. St. 50.

In a work, from which we have derived some information (Lettres sur lea Contes des Fées, Paris, 1826), considerable pains are taken, we think to little purpose, to deduce the French Ogre from the Oigours, a Tartar tribe, who with the other tribes of that people invaded Europe in the twelfth century. In the Glossaire de la Langue Romaine, Ogre is explained by Hongrois. Any one, however that reads the Pentamerone will see that the ugly, cruel, man-eating Huorco is plainly an Ogre; and those expert at the *tours de passe passe* of etymology will be at no loss to deduce Ogre from Orco. See Tales and Popular Fictions, p. 223.

[f] In another of these tales, it is said of a young man, who, on breaking open a cask, found a beautiful maiden in it, that he stood for a while *comme o chillo che ha visto lo Monaciello*.

[g] See Tales and Popular Fictions, chap. ix. p. 269; see also *Spain and France*.

[h] Vincentius apud Kornmann, *de Miraculis Vivorum*.

[i] This being, unknown to classic mythology, is first mentioned by Lactantius. It was probably from Boccaccio's Genealogia Deorum that Bojardo got his knowledge of him.

[j] Cinque Canti, c. i. st. I. *seq.*

[k] Lib. ii. xvii. 56, *seq.*

[l] There is, however, a Maga or Fata named Falsirena in the Adone of Marini.

[m] La Sabia and La Desconocida of the original romance, which Tasso follows very closely in everything relating to Amadis and Oriana.

[n] Few of our readers, we presume, are acquainted with this poem, and they will perhaps be surprised to learn that it is, after the Furioso, the most beautiful romantic poem in the Italian language, graceful and sweet almost to excess. It. is strange that it should be neglected in Italy also. One cause may. be its length (One Hundred Cantos), another the constant and inartificial breaking off of the stories, and perhaps the chief one, its serious moral tone so different from that of Ariosto. It might be styled The Legend of Constancy, for the love of its heroes and heroines is proof against all temptations. Mr. Panizzi's charge of abounding in scandalous stories, is not correct, for it is in reality more delicate than even the Faerie Queene. Ginguené, who admired it, appreciates it far more justly.

[o] See Tales and Popular Fictions, p. 183. The Pentamerone we may observe, was not a title given to it by the author; in like manner the only title Fielding gave his great work was The History of a Foundling.

[p] He was brother to Adriana and uncle to Leonora Baroni, the ladies wbo~ musical talents Milton celebrates.

[q] Ex. gr. Fiume is *shiume;* Fiore, *shiure;* Piaggia, *chiaja;* Piombo, *chiummo;* Biondo, *ghiunno*. There are likewise numelous Hispanicisms. Thus *gaiola* in Gagliuso which we all rendered *coffin,*is the Spanish *jaula*, cage, and the meaning apparently is that he would have the cat stuffed and put in a glass-case; in like manner calling the eyes suns (as in *na bellezza a doje*) occurs in the plays of Calderon.

[r] In the Tascheubuch für altdeutscher Zeit und Kunst, 1816.

SPAIN

Duendecillo, duendecillo,
Quien quiera quo seas o fueras,
El dinero que tu das
En lo que mandares vuelve.
Calderon, *La Dama Duende.*

When we inquired, after the fairy-system of Spain, we were told that there was no such thing, for that the Inquisition had long since eradicated all such ideas. Most certainly we would not willingly be regarded as partisans of the Holy Office, yet still we must express our doubt of the truth of this charge. In Señor Llorente's work, as far as we can recollect, there is no account of prosecutions for Duende-heresy; and even to the Holy Office we should give its due. Still, with all our diligence, our collection of Iberian fairy-lore is extremely scanty.

Our earliest authority for Spain, as for other countries, is the celebrated marshall of Champagne, Gervase of Tilbury, who thus relates -

The Daughter of Peter de Cabinam

In the bishoprick of Gerunda (*i.e.* Gerona), and the province of Cat-alonia, stands a mountain which the natives call Convagum. It is very steep, and on its summit is a lake of dark water, so deep that it cannot be fathomed. The abode of the Demons is in this lake; and if a stone, or anything else, be thrown into it, there rises from it an awful tempest.

Not far from this mountain, in a village named Junchera, lived a man named Peter de Cabinam, who being one day annoyed by the crying of his little girl, wished in his anger that the Demons might fetch her away. The child instantly vanished—snatched away by invisible hands—and was seen no more. Time passed on; and it was seven years after this event, when a man belonging to the village, as he was one day rambling about the foot of the mountain, met a man weeping bitterly, and bewailing his hard fate. On inquiry, he said that he had now been seven years in the mountain under the power of the Demons, who employed him as a beast of burden. He added, that there was also a girl in the mountain, the daughter of Peter de Cabinam of Junchera, a servant like himself; but that they were tired of her, and would restore her to her father if he came to claim her. When this information came to Peter de Cabinam, he forthwith ascended the mountain, and going to the edge of the lake, he besought the Demons to give him back his child. Like a sudden gust of wind she came, tall in stature, but wasted and dirty, her eyes rolling wildly, and her speech inarticulate. The father, not knowing what to do with her, applied to the Bishop of Gerunda, who took this opportunity of edifying his people by exhibiting the girl to them, and warning them against the danger of wishing that the Demons had their children. Some time after the man also was released, and from him the people learned that at the bottom of the lake there was a large palace, with a wide gate, to which palace the Demons repaired from all parts of the world, and which no one could enter but themselves, and those they brought thither. [a]

NOTE

[a] Otis Imperialia, p. 982. The Demons must have been some kind of fairies.

Origin of the House of Haro

As Don Diego Lopez, lord of Biscay, was one day lying in wait for the wild boar, he heard the voice of a woman who was singing. On looking around, he beheld on the summit of a rock a damsel, exceedingly beautiful, and richly attired. Smitten with her charms, he proffered her his hand. In reply, she assured him that she was of high descent, but frankly accepted his proffered hand; making, however, one condition—he was never to pronounce a holy name. Tradition says that the fair bride had only one defect, which was, that one of her feet was like that of a goat. Diego Lopez, however, loved her well, and she bore him two children, a daughter, and a son named Iniguez Guerra.

Now it happened one day, as they were sitting at dinner, that the lord of Biscay threw a bone to the dogs, and a mastiff and a spaniel quarrelled about it, and the spaniel griped the mastiff by the throat, and throttled him. "Holy Mary!" exclaimed Don Diego, "who ever saw the like?" Instantly the lady caught hold of the hands of her children; Diego seized and held the boy, but the mother glided through the air with the daughter, and sought again the mountains whence she had come. Diego remained alone with his son; and some years after, when he invaded the lands of the Moors, he was made captive by them, and led to Toledo. Iniguez Guerra, who was now grown up, was greatly grieved at the captivity of his father, and the men of the land told him that his only hope was to find his mother, and obtain her aid. Iniguez made no delay; he rode alone to the well-known mountains, and when he reached them, behold! his fairy-mother stood there before him on the summit of a rock. "Come unto me," said she, "for well do I know thy errand." And she called to her Pardalo, the horse that ran without a rider in the mountains, and she put a bridle into his mouth, and bade Iniguez mount him, and told him that he must not

give him either food or water, or unsaddle or unbridle him, or put shoes upon his feet, and that in one day the demon. steed would carry him to Toledo. And Iniguez obeyed the injunctions of Ins mother, and succeeded in liberating his father; but his mother never returned. [a]

In the large collection of Spanish ballads named El Romancero Castellano, the only one that treats of fairy-lore is the following, which tells of the enchantment of the King of Castille's daughter by seven fairies, [b] for a period of seven years. It is of the same character as the fairy-tales of France and Italy.

NOTES

[a] Related by Sir Francis Palgrave, but without giving any authority, in the Quarterly Review, vol. xxii. See *France*.

[b] In Don Quixote (part i. chap. 50) we read of "los siete castillos de las siete Fadas" beneath the lake of boiling pitch, and of the fair princess who was enchanted in one of them.

La Infantina

A CAZAR va el caballero,
A cazar como solia.—
Los perros lleva cansados,
El falcon perdido at.
Arrimarase á un roble,
Alto es a maravilla,
En un ramo mas alto
Viera estar una Infantina.
Cabellos de su cabeza
Todo aquel roble cobrian;
"No te espantes, caballero.
Ni tengas tamana grima.
"Hija soy del buen rey
Y de la reina de Castilla;
Siete fadas me fadaron [a]
En brazos de una ama mia,
„Que andase los siete anos
Sola en esta montina. [b]
Hoy se cumplan los años
O mañana, en aquel dia.
"Por Dios te ruego, caballero,
Llevesine en tu compania,
Si quisieres por muger,
Si no sea por amiga."
"Espereis me vos, señora,
Esta mañana, aquel dia;
Iré yo tomar consejo
De una madre que tenia."
La nina le respondiera,
Y estas palabras, decia:
"O mal haya el caballero
Que sola deja la nina!"
El se va á tomar consejo,
Y ella queda en la montina.
Aconsejóle su madre
Que la tomase por amiga.

Quando volvio el caballero
No la hallara en la montina.
Vio la que la llevaban,
Com muy grande caballeria.
El caballero, que lo ha visto,
En el suelo se caia.
Desque en si hubo tornado
Estas palabras decia:
"Caballero que tal pierde
Muy grandes penas merecia.
Yo mismo seré el alcalde,
To me seré la justicia,
Que me cortan pies y manos,
Y me arrastran por la villa." [c]

NOTES

[a] *Fada* is certainly the elided part of this verb, for which Latin mode of elision was retained in Spanish as well as Italian. Thus *quedo, junto, harto, marchito, vacio, enjuto, violento*, &c., come from *quedar, juntar, hartar*, &c. As the Spanish, following the Latin, also frequently uses the past as a present participle, as *Un hombre atrevido*, "a daring man;" and the same appears to take place in Italian, as *un huomo accorto, saputo, avveduto, dispietato;* and even in French, as usa *homme réflechi, désespéré;* may we not say that fada, *fata, fée*, is enchanting rather than enchanted?

[b] *Montina* is a small wood.

[c] Romancero Castellano por Depping, ii. p 198, 2nd edit. A translation of this romance will be found in Thoms's Lays and Legends of Spain.

Pepito el Corcovado

Pepito el Corcovado, [a] a gay lively little hunchback, used to gain his living by his voice and his guitar; for he was a general favourite, and was in constant request at weddings and other festivities. He was going home one night from one of these festive occasions, being under engagement for another in the morning, and, as it was in the celebrated Sierra Morena, he contrived to lose his way. After trying in vain to find it, he wrapped his cloak about him, and lay down for the night at the foot of a cork-tree. He had hardly, however, gone to sleep, when be was awakened by the sound of a number of little voices singing to an old air with which he was well acquainted,

Lunes y Martes y Miercoles tres

over and over again. Deeming this to be imperfect, he struck in, adding,

Jueves y Viernes y Sabado seis.

The little folk were quite delighted, and for hours the mountain rang with

Lunes y Martes y Miercoles tres,
Jueves y Viemes y Sabado sies.
Monday and Tueaday and Wednesday three,
Thursday and Friday and Saturday, six.

They finally crowded round Pepito, and bade him ask what he would for having completed their song so beautifully. After a little consideration, he begged to have his hump removed. So said so done, he was in an instant one of the straightest men in all Spain. On his return home, every one was amazed at the transformation. The story soon got wind, and another hunchback, named Cirillo, but unlike Pepito, as crooked in temper as in person, having learned from him where the scene of his adventure lay, resolved to proceed thither and try his luck. He accordingly reached the spot,. sat under the cork-tree, and saw and heard all that Pepito had heard and seen. He resolved also to add to the song, and he struck in with "Y Domingo siete" *(and Sunday seven);* but whether it was the breach of rhythm, or the mention of the Lord's Day that gave offence, he was instantly assailed with a shower of blows or pinches, and to make his calamity the greater, Pepito's hump was added to his own. [b]

We thus may see that there are beings in Spain also answering to the various classes of Fairies. But none of these have obtained the same degree of reputation as the House-spirit, whose Spanish name is Duende or Trasgo. In Torquemada's Spanish Mandeville, as the old English version of it is named, there is a section devoted to the Duende, in which some of his feats, such as pelting people with stones, clay, and such like, are noticed, and in the last century the learned Father Feijoo wrote an essay on Duendes, [c] *i.e.* on House-spirits; for he says little of the proper Spanish Duende, and his examples are Hodiken and the Kobolds, of which he had read in Agricola and other writers. On the whole, perhaps, the best account of the Duende will be found in Calderon's spritely comedy, named La Dama Duende.

In this piece, when Cosme, who pretends that he had seen the Duende when he put out his candle, is asked by ins master what he was like, he replies:

> Era un fraile
> Tamañito, y tenia puesto
> Un cucurucho tamano;
> Que por estas senas creo
> Que era duende capuchino.

This *cucurucho* was a long conical hat without a brim. worn by the clergy in general, nd not by the Capuchins alone. A little before, Cosme, when seeking to avert the appearance *of* the Duende, recites the following lines, which have the appearance of being formed from some popular charm against the House-spirit:

> Señora dama duende,
> Duelase de mi;
> Que soy nino y solo,
> Y nunca en tal me vi.

In De Solis' very amusing comedy of *Un Bobo hace Ciento,* Dona Ana makes the following extremely pretty application of the popular idea of the Duende:

> Yo soy, don Luis, una dama
> Que no conozco este duende
> Del amor, si no es por fama.

In another of his plays *(El Amor al Uso), a* lady says:

> Amor es duende importuno
> Que al mundo asombrando trae;
> Todos dicen que le ay,
> Y no le ha visto ninguno.

The lines from Calderon prefixed to this section of our Work, show that money given by the Duende was as unsubstantial as fairy-money in general. This is confirmed by Don Quixote, who tells his rather covetous squire, that "los tesoros de los caballeros andantes son, como los de los Duendes, aparentes y falsos."

The Spaniards seem also to agree with the people of other countries in regarding the Fairies as being fallen angels. One of their most celebrated poets thus expresses himself:

Disputase por bombres entendidos
Si fue de *los caidos* este duende.

Some Spanish etymologists say that Duende is a contraction of *Duéno de casa;* others, that it comes from the Arabic *Duar,* (dwelling) the term used for the Arab camps on the north-coast of Africa. To us it appears more probable that the Visigoths brought their ancient popular creed with them to Spain [d] also, and that as Duerg became Drac in Provence, it was converted into Duende in Spain. [e] It is further not quite impossible that Duerg may be also the original of Trasgo, a word for which we believe no etymon has been proposed.

NOTES

[a] *i.e.* Joey the Hunchback. Pepito is the dim. of Pepe, *i.e.* José, Joseph.

[b] See Thoms's Lays and Legends of Spain, p.83. It was related, he says, to a friend of his by the late Sir John Malcolm, who had heard it in Spain. It is also briefly related (probably on the same authority) in the Quarterly Review, vol. xxii. (see above pp. 364, 438). Redi, in his Letters, gives another form of it, in which the scene is at Benevento, the agents are witches, and the hump is taken off, *senza verun suo dolor,* with a saw of butter. *Y Domingo .siete* is, we are told, a common phrase when any thing is said or done *mal à propos.*

[c] Teatro Critico, tom. ii. His object is to disprove their existence, and he very justly says that the Duende was usually a knavish servant who had his own reasons for making a noise and disturbing the family. This theory will also explain the Duende-tales of Torquemada.

[d] See Tales and Popular Fictions, p. 269.

[e] The change of *r* and *n* is not without examples. Thus we have ἄργυρον and *argentum; water,* English; *vand,* Danish; *vatn,* Swedish.*Cristofero* is *Cristofano* in Tuscan; *homine, nomine, sanguine,* are *hombre, nombre, sangre,* Spanish. In *Duerg* when *r* became a, euphony changed g to *d,* or *vice versa.* The changes words undergo when the derivation is certain, are often curious.*Alguacil,* Spanish, is *El-wezeer* Arab, as *Azucena* Spanish, *Cecem* Portuguese (white-lily) is *Susan* Arab; *Guancia* (cheek) Italian, is *Wange* German. It might not be safe to assert that the Persian*gurk* and our wolf are the same, and yet the letters in them taken in order are all commutable. Our *God be with you* has shrunk to *Goodbye,* and the Spanish *Vuestra merced* to *Usted,* pr. *Usté.*There must, by the way, some time or other, have been an intimate connexion between Spain and England, so many of our familiar words seem to have a Spanish origin. Thus *ninny* is from *niño: booby* from *bobo; pucker from puchero; launch* (a boat) from *lancha;* and perhaps *monkey* (if not from *mannikin*) from *mono, monico.* We pronounce our *colonel* like the Spanish *coronel.*

FRANCE

Porquol faut-il s'dmerveiller
Que la raison la mteux sensée,
Lasse souvent do veiller,
Par des contes d'ogre et de fée
Ingenieusement bercée,
Prenne plaisir à sommelier?
–PERRAULT.

The Fairy mythology of France may be divided, as respects its locality, into two parts, that of Northern and that of Southern France, the Langue d'Oil and the Langue d'Oc. We will commence with the latter, as adjacent to Spain. Of its mythology, Gervase of Tilbury, who resided in the kingdom of Arles, has left us some interesting particulars, and other authorities enable us to trace it down to the present day. Speaking of the inhabitants of Arles, Gervase thus expresses himself:

"They also commonly assert, that the Dracs assume the human form, and come early into the public market-place without any one being thereby disturbed. These, they say, have their abode in the caverns of rivers, and occasionally, floating along the stream in the form of gold rings or cups, entice women or boys who are bathing on the banks of the river; for, while they endeavour to grasp what they see, they are suddenly seized and dragged down to the bottom: and this, they say, happens to none more than to suckling women, who are taken by the Dracs to rear their unlucky offspring; and sometimes, after they have spent seven years there, they return to our hemisphere. These women say that they lived with the Dracs and their wives in ample palaces, in the caverns and banks of riven. We have ourselves seen one of these women, who was taken away while washing clothes on the banks of the Rhone. A wooden bowl floated along by her, and, in endeavouring to catch it, having got out into the deep water, she was carried down by a Drac, and made nurse to his son below the water She returned uninjured, and wäs hardly recognised by her husband and friends after seven years' absence.

"After her return she related very wonderful things, such as that the Dracs lived on people they had carried off, and turned themselves into human forms; and she said that one day, when the Drac gave her an eel-pasty to eat, she happened to put her fingers, that were greasy with the fat, to one of her eyes and one side of her face, and she immediately l became endowed with most clear and distinct vision under the water. When the third year of her time was expired, and she had returned to her family, she very early one morning met the Drac in the market-place of Beaucaire. She knew him at once, and saluting him, inquired about the health of her mistress and the child. To this the Drac replied: 'Harkye,' said he, 'with which eye do you see me?' She, pointed to the eye she had touched with the fat: the Drac, immediately thrust his finger into it, and he was no longer visible to any one." [a]

Respecting the Dracs, Gervase farther adds:
"There is also on the banks of the Rhone, under a house, at the North-gate of the city of Arles, a great pool of the river . . . . In these deep places, they say that the Dracs are often seen of bright nights, in the shape of men. A few years ago there was, for three successive

days, openly heard the following words in the place outside the gate of the city, which I have mentioned, while the figure as it were of a man ran along the bank: 'The hour is passed, and the man does not come.' On the third day, about the ninth hour, while that figure of a man raised his voice higher than usual, a young man ran simply to the bank, plunged in, and was swallowed up; and the voice was heard no more."

The word Drac is apparently derived from Draco; but we are inclined to see its origin in the Northern *Duerg*. We must recollect that the Visigoths long occupied Provence and Languedoc. It is, we apprehend, still in use. *Fa le.Drac,* in Provençal, signifies *Fairre le diable.*[b] Goudelin, a provençal poet of the seventeenth century, begins his Castel en l'Ayre with these lines:

> Belomen qu' yeu *faré le Drac*
> Se jamay trobi dins un sac
> Cinc o siés milante pistolos
> Espessos como de redolos.

The following curious narrative also occurs in Gervase's work, and might seem to belong to Provence:

"Seamen tell that one time as a ship was sailing in the Mediterranean sea, which sea we call ours, she was surrounded by an immense number of porpoises *(delphinos),* and that when an active young man, one of the crew, had wounded one of them with a weapon, and all the rest of them had rapidly sought the bottom, a sudden and awful tempest enveloped the ship. While the sailors were in doubt of their lives, lo! one in the form of a knight came borne on a steed on the sea, and demanded that, for the salvation ef all the rest, the person who had wounded the porpoise should be delivered up to him. The sailors were in an agony between their own danger and their aversion to expose their comrade to death, which seemed to them to be most cruel, and they thought it infamous to consult their own safety at the expense of the life of another. At last the man himself, deeming it better that all should be saved at the cost of one, as they were guiltless, than that such a number of people should run the risk of destruction on account of his folly, and lest by defending him they should become guilty, devoted himself to the death he merited, and voluntarily mounted the horse behind the rider, who went over the firm water, taking his road along it as if it had been the solid land. In a short time he reached a distant region, where he found lying in a magnificent bed the knight whom he had wounded the day before as a porpoise. He was directed by his guide to pull out the weapon which was sticking in the wound, and when he had done so, *the,guilty right hand gave aid to the wound.* This being done, the sailor was speedily brought back to the ship, and restored to his companions. Hence it is, that from that tune forth sailors have ceased to hunt the porpoises." [c]

Gervase also describes the Kobold, or House-spirit, the Esprit Follet, or Goblin of the North of France.

"There are," says he, "other demons, commonly called Follets, who inhabit the houses of simple country people, and can be kept away neither by water nor exorcisms; and as they are not seen, they pelt people as they are going in at the door with stones, sticks, and domestic utensils. Their words are heard like those of men, but their form does not appear. I remember to have met several wonderful stories of them in the Vita Abbreviata, et Miraculis beatissimi Antonii." [d]

Elsewhere [e] he speaks of the beings which he says are called Lamiae, who, he relates, are used to enter houses suddenly, ransack the jars and tubs, pots and pitchers, take the children out of the cradles, light lamps or candles, and sometimes oppress those who are sleeping.

Either Gervase mistook, or the Fadas of the south of France were regarded as beings different from mankind. The former is, perhaps, the more likely supposition. He thus speaks of them: "This, indeed, we know to be proved every day by men who are beyond all exception; that we have heard of some who were lovers of phantoms of this kind which they call Fadas; [f] and when they married other women, they died before consummating the marriage. We have seen most of them live in great temporal felicity, who when they withdrew themselves from the embraces of these Fadas, or discovered the secret, lost not only their temporal prosperity, but even the comfort of wretched life." [g]

"In the legend of St. Armentaire, composed about 1800, by Raymond, a gentleman of Provence, we read of the Fée Esterelle, and of the sacrifices to her, who used to give barren women beverages to drink, to make them fruitful; and of a stone called *La Lauza de la Fuda;* that is the Fairy-stone on which they used to sacrifice to her." [h]

Even at the present day the belief in the Fadas seems to linger in Provence and the adjoining districts.

"On the night of the 31st of December," says Du Mege, [i] the "Fées *(Hadas)* enter the dwellings of their worshipers. They bear good-luck in their right, ill-luck in their left-hand. Care has been taken to prepare for them in a clean retired. room, such a repast as is suited to them. The doors and windows are left open; a white cloth is laid on a table with a loaf, a knife, a vessel full of water or wine, and a cup. A lighted candle or wax taper is set in the centre of the table. It is the general belief that those who present them with the best food may expect all kinds of prosperity for their property and their family; while those who acquit themselves grudgingly of their duty toward the Fées, or who neglect to make preparations worthy of these divinities, may expect the greatest misfortunes."

From the following passage of the Roman de Guillaume au Court-Nez it would appear that three was the number of the Hadas.

> Coustume avoient lee gens, par véritez,
> Et *en Provence* et en autres regnez.
> Tables métoient et siéges ordenez,
> Et sur la table iij blans pains bulétez,
> Iij poz do vine et iij hénez de lès
> Et par encoste iert li enfès posez. [1]

Some years ago a lady, named Marie Aycard, published a volume named "Ballades et Chants populaires de la Provence," two of which seem to be founded on popular legends. She names the one La Fée aux Cheveux Verts, and in it relates the story of a young mariner of Marseilles who was in the habit of rowing out to sea by himself in the evening. On one of these occasions he felt himself drawn down by an invisible power, and on reaching the bottom found himself at the gate of a splendid palace, where he was received by a most beautiful fairy, only her hair was green. She at once told him her love, to which he responded as she wished, and after detaining him some time she dismissed him, giving him two fishes, that he might account for his absence by saying that he had been fishing The same invisible power brought him back to his boat, and he reached home at sunrise. The size and form of his fishes, such as had never been seen, excited general wonder; but he feared the fairy too much to reveal his secret. An invincible attraction still drew him to the sub-marine palace, but at last he saw a maiden whose charms, in his eyes, eclipsed those of the fairy. He now fled the sea shore, but every time he approached his mistress he received an invisible blow, and he continually was haunted by threatening voices. At length he felt an irresistible desire to go out again to sea. When there he was drawn down as before to the palace, but the fairy now was changed, and saying, "You have betrayed me—you shall die," she caused him to be devoured by the sea-monsters. But other accounts say that she kept him with her till age had furrowed his brow with wrinkles, and then sent him back to poverty on earth.

The other legend named Le Lutin tells how seven little boys, regardless of the warnings of their old grandmother, would go out at night on various affairs. As they went along a pretty little black horse came up to them, and they all were induced to mount on his back. When they met any of their playmates they invited them also to mount, and the back of the little horse, stretched so that at last he had on him not less than thirty little boys. He then made with all speed for the sea, and plunging into it with them they were all drowned. [k]

Passing to Auvergne we find Gregory of Tours in the sixth

century thus relating an event which happened in his youth. A man was going one morning to the forest, and he took the precaution to have his breakfast, which he was taking with him, blessed before he set out. Coming to the river, before it was yet day, he drove his bullock-cart into the ferry-boat *(in ponte qui super navem est)*, and when he was about half-way over he heard a voice saying, "Down with him! down with him! be quick!" *(Merge, merge, ne moreris!)* to which another replied, "I should have done it without your telling me if something holy did not prevent me; for I would have you to know that he is fortified with the priest's blessing, so that I cannot hurt him." [1]

Miss Costello [m] heard in Auvergne a story of a changeling, which the mother, by the direction of the Curé, took to the market-place, where she whipped it well, till its mother, La Fée du Grand Cascade, brought her back her own child. She also relates at great length a legend which she styles La Blonde de in Roche, in which a young lady, instructed by her nurse, learns to change her form, and thus become a companion of the Fées, who are beings of tiny dimensions. Afterwards, when she is married, they take away her children, but she manages to recover them.

"La Tioul de las Fadas is within five and a half leagues of St. Flour, at Pirols, a village of Haute Auvergne. It is composed of six large rude stones, covered by a seventh, larger and more massive than the rest; it is twelve feet long, and eight and a half wide. The tradition relates that a Fée who was fond of keeping her sheep on the spot occupied by this monument, resolved to shelter herself from the wind and ram. For this purpose she went far, very far, *(bien loin, bien loin)* in search of such masses of granite, as six yoke of oxen could not move, and she gave them the form of a little house. She carried, it is said, the largest and heaviest of them on the top of her spindle, and so little was she incommoded by the weight of it, that she continued to spin all the way." [n]

The following legend is traditional in Périgord:

Embosomed in the forest of the canton of La Double, near the road leading from Périgueux to Ribérac, is a monument named Roque Brun. It consists of four enormous rocks placed two and two, so as to form an alley ten feet long and six wide. A fifth rock, higher and thicker than the others, closes this space on the west. The whole is covered by a huge mass of rock, at least twelve feet by seven, and from three to four feet thick. There can be no doubt of its being the work of man, and it is remarkable that the stone composing it is different from that of the soil on which it stands. [o] The tradition of the canton, however, is, that many thousand years ago there was a Fée who was the sovereign of the whole country, and having lost her husband in a battle fought in this very place she resolved to bury him on the spot. She therefore called six of her pages, and ordered them to fetch, each one of these stones, and to place them in the order which they still maintain. They instantly obeyed, and they carried and arranged the huge masses as easily as if they had been only rose-leaves. When the tomb was completed, the Fairy ascended it, and turning to the east, she thrice cursed, in a voice of thunder, whoever, should henceforth dare even to touch this monument of her royal spouse. Many an instance is still recorded by the peasantry of those who dared and were puxiished. [p]

The Fairy-lore of the North of France, at least of Normandy, is, as was to be expected, similar to that of the other portions of the Gotho-G-erman race. We meet it in the *fées* or fairies, and the *lutins* or *gobelins,* which answer to the Kobolds, Nisses, and such like of those nations [q]

The Fees are small and handsome in person; they are fond of dancing in the night-time, and in their dances which are circular they form the *Cercles des Fées,* or fairy-rings. If any one approaches their dance, he is irresistibly impelled to take part in it. He is admitted with the greatest courtesy; but as the whirling movement increases, and goes faster and faster, his head becomes giddy, and he falls to the ground utterly exhausted. Sometimes the *fées* amuse themselves by flinging him up to a great height in the air, and, if not killed by the fall, he is found next morning full of bruises. These little beings, it is also said, haunt solitary springs, where they wash their linen, which they then dry by way of preference on the Druidic stones, if at hand, and lay up in the hollows of rocks or barrows, thence named *Chambres* or *Grottes des.Fées.* But, further, it is said of them, like the *Lutins,* they select particular farms to which they resort at night, and there making use of horses, harness and utensils of all kinds, they employ themselves at various kinds of work, of which, however, no traces remain in the morning. They are fond of mounting and galloping the horses; their seat is on the neck, and they tie together locks of the mane to form stirrups. Their presence, however, always brings luck, the cattle thrive where they are, the utensils of which they have made use, if broken are mended and made as good as new. They are altogether most kind and obliging, and have been known to give cakes to those to whom they have taken a fancy.

The Fées of Normandy are, like others, guilty of child-changing. A countrywoman as she was one day carrying her child on her arm met a Fée similarly engaged, who proposed an exchange. But she would not consent, even though, she said, the Fée's babe were *nine times finer than her own.* A few days after, having left her child in the house when she went to work in the fields, it appeared to her on her return that it had been changed. She immediately consulted a neighbour, who to put the matter to the proof, broke a dozen eggs and ranged the shells before the child, who instantly began to cry out, *Oh! what a number of cream-pots! Oh! what a number of cream-pots!* The matter was now beyond doubt, and the neighbour next advised to make it cry lustily in order to bring its real mother to it. This also succeeded; the Fee came imploring them to spare her child, and the real one should be restored.

There is another kind of Fées known in Normandy by the name of *Dames Blanches,* or White Ladies, who are of a less benevolent character. These lurk in narrow places, such as ravines, fords and bridges, where passengers cannot well avoid them, and there seek to attract their attention. The Dame Blanche sometimes requires him whom she thus meets to join her in a dance, or to hand her over a plank. If he does so she makes him many courtesies, and then vanishes. One of these ladies named La Dame d' Aprigny, used to appear in a winding narrow ravine which occupied the place of the present Rue Saint Quentin at Bayeux, where, by her involved dances, she prevented any one from passing. She meantime held out her hand, inviting him to join her, and if he did so she dismissed him after a round or two; but if he drew back, she seized him and flung him into one of the ditches which were full of briars and thorns. Another Dame Blanche took her station on a narrow wooden bridge over the Dive, in the district of Falaise, named the Pont d' Angot. She sat on it and would not allow any one to pass unless he went on his knees to her; if he refused, the Fee gave him over to the *lutins,* the cats, owls, and other beings which, under her sway, haunt the place, by whom he was cruelly tormented.

Near the village of Puys, half a league to the north-east of Dieppe, there is a high plateau, surrounded on all sides by large entrencbments, except that over the sea, where the cliffs render it inaccessible. It is named *La Cité de Limes* or *La Camp de César* or simply *Le Catel* or *Castel.* Tradition tells that the Fées used to hold a fair there, at which all sorts of magic articles from their secret stores were offered for sale, and the most courteous entreaties and blandishments were employed to induce those who frequented it to become purchasers. But the moment any one did so, and stretched forth his hand to take the article he had selected, the perfidious Fées seized him and hurled him down the cliffs.

Such are the accounts of the Fées stifi current in Normandy. To these we may add that of Dame Abonde or lTabonde, current in the middle ages. William of Auvergne, bishop of Paris, who died in the year 1248, thus writes:

"Sunt et aliae ludificationes malignorum spiritorum quas faciunt interdum in nemoribus et locis amoenis, et frondosis arboribus, ubi apparent in similtudine *puellarum* aut *matronarum*ornatu muliebri et *candido;* interdum etiam *in stabulis, cum luminaribus cereis, ex quibus apparent distillationes in comis et collis equorum et comae ipsorum diligenter tricatae;* et audies eos, qui talia se vidisse fatentur, dicentes veram ceram esse quae de luminaribus hujusmodi stillaverat. De illis vero substantiis quae apparent in domibus quas *dominas nocturnas* et *principem* earum vocant *Dominam Abundiam* pro eo quod domibus, quas frequentant, abundantiam bonorum temporalium praestare putantur non aliter tibi sentiendum est neque aliter quam quemadmodum de illis audivisti. Quapropter eo usque invaluit stultitia hominum et insania vetularum ut vasa vini et receptacula ciborum discooperta relinquant, et omnino nec obstruent neque claudant eis noctibus quibus ad domos suos eas credunt adventuras; ea de causa videlicet ut cibos et potus quasi paratos inveniant, et eos absque difilcultate apparitionis pro beneplacito sumant." [r]

Dame Abonde is also mentioned in the same century in the celebrated Roman de la Rose as follows:—

Qui les cinc sens ainsine decoit
Par les fantosmes qu'il recoit,
Dont maintes gens par br folie
Cuident estre par nuit estries *(allés)*
Errans avecques *Dame Habonde.*
Et dient que par tout le monde
Si tiers enfant de nacion *(naisaance)*
Sunt de ceste condicion,
Qu'ils vont trois fois en la semaine,
Li cum destinée lea maine *(mène),*
Et par tous ces ostex *(hotels)* se boutent,

Ne cles ne barres ne redoutent.
Ains sen entrent par lea fendaces *(fentes)*
Par chatieres et par crevaces.
Et se partent des cors les ames
Et vont avec lea *bonnes dames*
Par leur forains et par maisons.
Et le prcuvent par tiex *(ces)* raisons:
Que les diversités veues
Ne sont pas en lor liz *(lits)* venues,
Ains *(anzi* lt.) sunt lor ames que laborent
Et par le monde ainsinc sen corent. [s]

In these places we find that Abundia is a queen or ruler over a band of what we may call fairies, who enter houses at night, feast there, twist the horses' manes, etc. This may remind us at once of Shakespeare's Queen Mab, whom, though only acquainted with Habundia through a passage in Heywood, [t] we conjectured to have derived her name from that of this French dame. [u] Chaucer, by the way, always spells *habundance* with an *h,* which may have become *m* as it does *n* in Numps from Humphrey; so Edward makes Ned, Oliver Noll, etc.

The Lutin or Gobelin [v] of Normandy hardly differs in any respect from the domestic spirit of Scandinavia and Germany. He is fond of children and horses; and if the proverb

Ou il y *a* belle fille et bon yin
Là aussi hante le lutin

lie not, of young maidens also. He caresses the children, and gives them nice things to eat, but he also whips and. pinches them if naughty. [w] He takes great care of the horses, gallops them at times, and *lutines* their manes, *i.e., elfs* or plaits and twists them in an inexplicable manner. So fond, indeed, is he of this amusement, that it is related that when one time two young girls fell asleep in a stable, he *lutined* their hair in such a way that they had to cut it all off. Sometimes the Lutin takes the form of a young villager, and struts about with great complacency. On such occasions it is necessary to call him Bon Garçon, a thing the Norman peasant never neglects to do. At other times he appears under the form of a horse ready bridled and saddled. If any peasant, weary after his day's work, is induced to mount him in order to ride home, he begins to kick and fling and. rear and bound, and ends by jerking him into a marsh or a ditch full of water. When he takes this form he is called Le Cheval Bayard, probably after the famous steed of the Paladin Rinaldo.

The following tradition of *"Le Lutin, ou le Fé amoureux,"* is related in the neighbourhood of Argentan:

A Fé was fond of a pretty young *paysanne,* and used to come every evening when she was spinning at her fireside, and take his seat on a stool opposite to her, and. keep gazing on her fair face. The ungrateful object of this respectful attention, however, told her husband the whole story, and in his jealous mood. he resolved to have his revenge of the amorous Lutin. Accordingly, he heated the girdel *(galetiere)* red-hot, and placed it on the seat which he used to occupy, and then dressing himself in his wife's clothes, he sat in her place, and began to spin as well as he could. The Fé came as usual, and instantly perceived the change. "Where," said he, "is La-belle belle of yesterday evening, who draws, draws, and keeps always twirling, while you, you turn, turn, and never twirl?" He, however, went and took his usual seat, but immediately jumped up, screaming with pain. His companions, who were at hand, inquired the cause. "I am burnt," cried he. "Who burned you?" cried they. "Myself," replied he; for this the woman had told him was her husband's name. At this they mocked at him and went away.[x]

The best way, it is said, to banish a Lutin who haunts a house, is to scatter flax-seed in the room that he most frequents. His love of neatness and regularity will not allow him to let it lie there, and he soon gets tired of picking it up, and so be goes away.

A Lutin, named the Nain Rouge, haunts the coast of Normandy. He is kind in his way to the fishermen, and often gives them valuable aid; but be punishes those who do not treat him with proper respect. Two fishermen who lived near Dieppe, were going one day to Pollet. On their way they found a little boy sitting on the road-side; they asked him what he was doing there. "I am resting myself" said he, "for I am going to Berneville" (a village within a league of Pollet.) They invited him to join company; he agreed, and amused them greatly with his tricks as they went alone. At last, when they came to a pond near Berneville, the malicious urchin caught up one of them, and flung him, like a shuttlecock, up into the air over it; but, to his great disappointment, he saw him land safe and sound at the other side. "Thank your patron-Saint," cried he, with his cracked voice, "for putting it into your mind to take some holy water when you were getting up this morning. But for that you 'd have got a nice dip."

A parcel of children were playing on the strand at Pollet, when Le Petit Homme Rouge came by. They began to make game of him, and he instantly commenced pelting them with stones at such a rate that they found it necessary to seek refuge in a fishing-boat, where, for the space of an hour, as they crouched under the hatches, they heard the shower of stones falling so that they were sure the boat must be buried under them. At length the noise ceased, and when they ventured to peep out, not a stone was to be seen.

There is also in Normandy a kind of spirits called Lubins, which take the form of wolves, and enter the churchyards under the guidance of a chief who is quite black. They are very timorous, and at the least noise they fly, crying *".Robert eat mort! .Robert est mort!"* People say of a timorous man, *"Il a peur de Lubin .!"* [y]

A belief in Fées, similar to those which we nave denominated Fairies of Romance, seems to have prevailed all over France during the middle ages.

The great Bertrand Duguesclin married a lady named Tiphaine, "extraite do noble lignée," says his old biographer; "laqueile avoit environ vingt-quatre ans, ne onques n'avoit été mariée et éstoit bonne et sage, et moult experte aux arts d'astronomie; aucuns disoient qu'elle éstoit *faée* mais non éstoit, mais éstoit sinsi inspirée et de la Grace de Dieu."

One of the chief articles of accusation against the heroic and unfortunate Maid. of Orleans, was "Que souvent alloit à une belle fontaine au pais de Lorraine, laquelle elle nommoit*bonne fontaine aux Fées* nostre Seigneur, et en icelui lieu tous ceulx de pays quand ils avoient fiebvre ils alloient pour recouvrer garison, et la alloit souvent la dite Jehanne la Pucelle, sous un grand arbre qui la fontaine ombroit, et s'apparurent à elle St. Katerine et St. Marguerite." [z] She was also asked "Si elle sçait rien de *ceux qui vont avecq les* Fées?"

Of these Fées the most celebrated is Melusina, who was maz-rried to the Count of Lusignan. Toward the end of the fourteenth century, Jean d'Arras collected the traditions relating to her, and composed what he called her "Chronicle." Stephen, a Dominican of the house of Lusignan, took up the history written *by* Jean D'Arras, gave it consistency, and cast such splendour about his heroine, that several noble houses were ambitious of showing a descent from her. Those of Luxembourg and Rohan even falsified their genealogies for that purpose; and the house of Sassenage, though it might claim its descent from a monarch, preferred Melusina, and to gratify them it was feigned that when she quitted Lusignan she retired to the grot of Sassenage, in Dauphiny.

The following is a slight sketch of the story of the fair Melu-sina. [aa]

Ange par la figure, et serpent par le reste.
De Lille

NOTES

[a] *Otia Imperialia*, p. 987

[b] Like the Irish *Play me Puck*

[c] *Otia limper.* p 981: It does not appear that the abode ot these porpoise-knights was beneath the water.

[d] *Otia Imper.* p. 897. Orthone, the House-spirit, who, according to Froissart, attended the Lord of Corasse, in Gascony, resembled HInzelmann in many points.

[e] Ibid.

[f] *Hujusmodi larvarum.* He classes the Fadas 'with Sylvans and Pans.

[g] Page 989. Speaking of the wonderful horse of Giraldus de Cabreriis; Gervase says, *Si Fadus e'rat, i. e.* says Leibnitz, incantatus, ut *Fadae, Fatae*, Fées

[h] Cambry, Monumens Celtiques, p. 342. The author says, that Esterelle, as well as all the Fairies, was the moon. This we very much doubt. He derives her name from the Breton *Escler*,Brightness, Lauza, from *Lac'h* (Irish *Clock)*, a flat stone.

[i] Monuments religieux des Voices Tectosages, *ap.* Mile. Bosquet, Normandie, etc., p. 92

[j] See Leroux de Lincy, *ap.* Mile. Bosquet, p. 93, who adds "In Lower Normandy, in the arrondissement of Bayeux, they never neglect laying a table for the protecting genius of the babe about to be born;" see our note on Virg. Buc. iv. 63. In a collection of decrees of Councils made by Burchard of Worms, who died in 1024, we read as follows: "Fecisti, ut quaedam mulieres in quibusdam temporibus anni facere solent, ut in domo tua *rnensam praepares* et tuos cibos et potum cum *tribus cultelluis* supra mensam poneres, ut si venissent *tres illae sorores* quas antiqua posteritas et antiqua stultitia. Parcas nominavit, ibi reficirentur ... ut credens illas quas tu dicis esse sorores tibi posse aut hic aut in futuro prodesse?" Grimm. *Deut. Mythol. Anhang*, p. xxxviii, where we are also told that these Pares could give a man at his birth the power of becoming a Werwolf. All this, however, does not prove that they wore the Origin of the *Fées*.

[k] This may remind us of the Neck or Kelpie above. It seems confirmatory of our theory respecting the Visigoths.

[l] Greg. Tur. De Glor. Confess. ch. xxxi., *ap.* Grimm. p. 466.

[m] Pilgrimage to Auvergne, ii. p. 294, *seq.*

[n] Cambry, Monuments Celtiques, p. 232.

[o] It is evidently a *cromleach*. What is said of the nature of the stones is also true of Stonehenge.

[p] Lettres de Madame S. à sa Fille. Périgueux, 1830: by M. Jouannet of Bordeaux.

[q] See Mile. Bosquet, La Normandie Romanesque et Merveilleuse, and the works there quoted by this learned and ingenious lady. What follows is so extremely like what we have seen above of the Korrigan of the adjacent Brittany, that we hope she has been careful not to transfer any of their traits to her Fees.

[r] Opera i. 1036; Paris, 1674, *ap.* Grimm, Deut. Mythol. p. 263.

[s] *Ap.* Grimm, *ut sup.* Douce (III, of Shak. i. 382) was, we believe, the first who directed attention to Abundia. He quotes from an old *fabliau:*
Ceste richesse nus abonde,
Nos l'avons de par Dame Abonde.

[t] One kind of these the Italians Fate name;
Fée the French; we Sybils; and the same
Others White Nymphs;
and those that have them seen,

278

Night Ladies some, of which Habundia queen.
Hierarchie, viii. p.507.

[u] Mr. Thoms prefers a derivation from the Cymric, *Mab,* boy, child.

[v] There is no satisfactory derivation of *Lutin,* for we cannot regard as such Grimm's à *luctu.*
Gobelin, Goblin, or *Goubelin,* is evidently the same as *Kobold. Follet* (from *fol, fou)* and
*Farfadet,*are other names. Both *Gobelin* and *Lutin* were in use in the 11th century. Orderic
Vitalis, speaking of the demon whom St. Taurin drove out of the temple of Diana, says,
Hunc vulgus Gobelinum appellat, and Wace (Roman de Rou, *v.* 9715) says of the familiar of
bishop Manger who excommunicated the Conqueror
Ne sei s'esteit lutin ou non.

[w] Mothers also threaten their children with him. *Le gobelin vous mangera, le gobelin vous
emportera.* Père~ L'ABBE, *Etymologie,* i. p. 262.

[x] In another French tale a man to deceive a Fée, put on his wife's clothes and was minding
the child, but she said as she came in, "Non, tu ne point la belle d'hier au soir, tu ne files,
ni ne vogues, ni ton fuseau ne t'enveloppes," and to punish him she turned some apples
that were roasting on the hearth into peas. Schreiber *ap.* GRIMM, p. 385.

[y] Lubin may be only another form of Lutin, and connected with the English Lob. Its likeness
to *loup* may have given occasion to the fiction of their taking the lupine form.

[z] Chattier.

[aa] Histoire de Mélusine, tirée des Chroniques do Poftou. Paris, l698 Dobenek, des
Deutschen Mittelalter und Volksglauben.

Legend of Melusina

Elinas, king of Albania, to divert his grief for the death of his wife, amused himself with hunting. One day, at the chase, he went to a fountain to quench his thirst: as he approached it he heard the voice of a woman singing, and on coming to it he found there the beautiful Fay Pressina.

After some time the Fay bestowed her hand upon him, on the condition that he should never visit her at the time of her lying-in. She had three daughters at a birth: Melusina, Melior, and Palatina. Nathas, the king's son by a former wife, hastened to convey the joyful tidings to his father, who, without reflection, flew to the chamber of the queen, and entered as she was bathing her daughters. Pressina, on seeing him, cried out that he had broken his word, and she must depart; and taking up her three daughters, she disappeared.

She retired to the Lost Island; [a] so called because it was only by chance any, even those who had repeatedly visited it, could find it. Here she reared her children, taking them every morning to a high mountain, whence Albania might be seen, and telling them that but for their father's breach of promise they might have lived happily in the distant land which they beheld. When they were fifteen years of age, Melusina asked her mother particularly of what their father had been guilty. On being informed of it, she conceived the design of being revenged on him. Engaging her sisters to join in her plans, they set out for Albania: arrived there, they took the king and all his wealth, and, by a charm, inclosed him in a high mountain, called Brandelois. On telling their mother what they had clone, she, to punish them for the unnatural action, condemned Melusina to become every Saturday a serpent, from the waist downwards, till she should meet a man who would marry her under the condition of never seeing her on a Saturday, and should keep his promise. She inflicted other judgements on her two sisters, less severe in proportion to their guilt. Melusina now went roaming through the world in search of the man who was to deliver her. She passed through the Black Forest, and that of Ardennes, and at last she arrived in the forest of Colombiers, in Poitou, where all the Fays of the neighbourhood came before her, telling her they had been waiting for her to reign in that place.

Raymond having accidentally killed the count, his uncle, by the glancing aside of his boar-spear, was wandering by night in the forest of Colombiers. he arrived at a fountain that rose at the foot of a high rock. This fountain was called by the people the Fountain of Thirst, or the Fountain of the Fays, [b] on account of the many marvellous things which had happened at it. At the time, when Raymond arrived at the fountain, three lathes were diverting themselves there by the light of the moon, the principal of whom was Melusina. Her beauty and her amiable manners quickly won his love: she soothed him, concealed the deed he had done, and married him, he promising on his oath never to desire to see her on a Saturday. She assured him that a breach of his oath would for ever deprive him of her whom he so much loved, and be followed by the unhappiness of both .for life. Out of her great wealth, she built for him, in the neighbourhood of the Fountain of Thirst, where he first saw her, the castle of Lusignan. She also built La Rochelle, Cloitre Malliers, Mersent, and other places.

But destiny, that would have Melusina single, was incensed against her. The marriage was made unhappy by the deformity of the children born of one that was enchanted; but still Raymond's love for the beauty that ravished both heart and eyes remained unshaken. Destiny now renewed her attacks. Raymond's cousin had excited him to jealousy and to secret concealment, by malicious suggestions of the purport of the Saturday retirement of the countess. He hid himself; and then saw how the lovely form of Melusina ended below in a snake, gray and sky-blue, mixed with white. But it was not horror that seized him at the sight, it was infinite anguish at the reflection that through his breach of faith he might lose his lovely wife for ever. Yet this misfortune had not speedily come on him, were it not that his son, Geoffroi with the tooth, [c] had burned his brother Freimund, who would stay in the abbey of Malliers, with the abbot and a hundred monks. At which the afflicted father, count Raymond, when his wife Melusina was entering his closet to comfort him, broke out into these words against her, before all the courtiers who attended her:—"Out of my sight, thou pernicious snake and odious serpent! thou contaminator of my race!"

Melusina's former anxiety was now verified, and the evil that had lain so long in ambush had now fearfully sprung on him and her. At these reproaches she fainted away; and when at length she revived, full of the profoundest grief, she declared to him that she must now depart from him, and, in obedience to a decree of destiny, fleet about the earth in pain and suffering, as a spectre, until the day of doom; and that only when one of her race was to die at Lusignan would she become visible.

Her words at parting were these:

"But one thing will I say unto thee before I part, that thou, and those who for more than a hundred years shall succeed thee, shall know that whenever I am seen to hover over the fair castle of Lusignan, then will it be certain that in that very year the castle will get a new lord; and though people may not perceive me in the air, yet they will see me by the Fountain of Thirst; and thus shall it be so long as the castle stands in honour and flourishing—especially on the Friday before the lord of the castle shall die." Immediately, with wailing and loud lamentation, she left the castle of Lusignan, [d] and has ever since existed as a spectre of the night. Raymond died as a hermit on Monserrat.

The president de Boissieu says, [e] that she chose for her retreat one of the mountains of Sassenage, near Grenoble, on account of certain vats that are there, and to which she communicated a virtue which makes them, at this day, one of the seven wonders of Dauphiné. They are two in number, of great beauty, and so admirably cut in the rock, that it is easy to see they are not the work of unaided nature, The virtue which Melusina communicated to them was, that of announcing, by the water they contain, the abundance or scantiness of the crops. When there is to be an abundant harvest, it rises over the edges, and overflows; in middling years, the vats are but half full; and when the crops are to fail, they are quite dry. One of these vats is consecrated to corn, the other to wine.

The popular belief was strong in France that she used to appear on what was called the tower of Melusina as often as any of the lords of the race of Lusignan was to die; and that when the family was extinct, and the castle had fallen to the crown,, she was seen whenever a king of France was to depart this life. Mézeray informs us that he was assured of the truth of the appearance of Melusina on this tower previous to the death of a Lusignan, or a king of France, by people of reputation, and who were not by any means credulous. She appeared in a mourning dress, and continued for a long time to utter the most heart-piercing lamentation.

The following passage occurs in Brantôme's Eloge of the Duke of Montpensier, who in 1574 destroyed Lusignan, and several other retreats of the Huguenots:

"I heard, more than forty years ago, an old veteran say, that when the Emperor Charles V came to France, they brought him by Lusignan for the sake of the recreation of hunting the deer, which were there in great abundance in fine old parks of France; that he was never tired admiring and praising the beauty, the size, and the chef d'ceuvre of that house, built, which is more, by such a lady, of whom he made them tell him several fabulous tales, which are there quite common, even to the good old women who washed their linen at the fountain, whom Queen Catherine of Medicis, mother to the king, would also question and listen to. Some told her that they used sometimes to see her come to the fountain to bathe in it, in the form of a most beautiful woman, and in the dress of a widow. Others said that they used to see her, but very rarely, and that on Saturday evening, (for in that state she did not let herself be seen,) bathing, half her body being that of a very beautiful lady, the other half ending in a snake: others, that she used to appear a-top of the great tower in a very beautiful form, and as a snake. Some said, that when any great disaster was to come on the kingdom, or a change of reign, or a death, or misfortune among her relatives, who were the greatest people of France, and were kings, that three days before she was heard to cry, with a cry most shrill and terrible, three times.

"This is held to be perfectly true. Several persons of that place, who have heard it, are positive of it, and hand it from father to son; and say that, even when the siege came on, many soldiers and men of honour who were there affirmed it. But it was when the order was given to throw down and destroy her castles that she uttered her loudest cries and wails. This is perfectly true, according to the saying of people of honour. Since then she has not been heard. Some old wives, however, say she has appeared to them, but very rarely."

Jean d'Arras declares that Servile, who defended the castle of Lusignan for the English against the Duke of Bern, swore to that prince, upon his faith and honour, "that, three days before the surrender of the fortress, there entered into his chamber, though the doors were shut, a large serpent, enamelled with white and blue, which came and struck its tail several times against the feet of the bed where he was lying with his wife, who was not at all frightened at it, though he was very much so; and that when he seized his sword, the serpent changed all at once into a woman, arid said to him, *How, Serville, you who have been at so many sieges and battles, are you afraid! Know that I am the mistress of this castle, which I have built, and that you must surrender it very soon.* When she had ended these words she resumed her serpent-shape, and glided away so swiftly that he could not perceive her." The author adds, that the prince told him that other credible people had sworn to him that they too had seen her at the same time in other places in the neighbourhood, and in the same form.

The old castle of Pirou, on the coast of the Cotentin, in Lower Normandy, likewise owes its origin to the Fées. [f] These were the daughters of a great lord of the country, who was a celebrated magician. They built the castle long before the time of the invasions of the Northmen, and dwelt there in peace and unity. But when these pirates began to make their descents on the coast, the Fees, fearing their violence, changed themselves into wild geese, and thus set them at defiance. They did not, however, altogether abandon their castle; for the elders of the place assert that every year, on the first of March, a flock of wild geese returns to take possession of the nests they had hollowed out for themselves in its walls. It was also said that when a male child was born to the illustrious house of Pirou, the males of these geese, displaying their finest grey plumage, strutted about on the pavement in the courts of the castle; while, if it was a girl, the females, in plumage whiter than snow, took precedence then over the males. If the new-born maiden was to be a nun, it was remarked that one of them did not join with the rest, but kept alone in a corner, eating little, and deeply sighing.

The following traditions are attached to the castles of Argouges and Rânes, in Normandy:—[8]

One of the lords of Argouges, when out hunting one day, met a bevy of twenty ladies of rare beauty, all mounted on palfreys white as the driven snow. One of them appeared to be their queen, and the lord of Argouges became all at once so deeply enamoured of her, that he offered on the spot to marry her. This lady was *fée;* she had for a long time past secretly protected the Sire d'Argouges, and even caused him to come off victorious in a combat with a terrible giant. As she loved the object of her care, she willingly accepted his troth, but under the express condition that he should never pronounce in her presence the name of Death. So light a condition caused no difficulty; the marriage took place under the happiest auspices, and lovely children crowned their union. The fatal word was never heard, and their happiness seemed without alloy. It came to pass, however, one day at length, that the wedded pair were preparing to give their presence at a tournament. The lady was long at her toilet, and her husband waited for her with impatience. At length she made her appearance. "Fair dame," said he, when he saw her, "you would be a good person to send to fetch Death; for you take long enough to perform what you are about." [h] Hardly had he pronounced the fatal word when, uttering a piercing cry, as if actually struck by death, the Fée lady disappeared, leaving the mark of her hand on the gate. She comes every night clad in a white robe, and wanders round and round the castle, uttering deep and continuous groans, amid which may be heard, in funereal notes, *Death! Death!*

The same legend, as we have said, adheres to the castle of Ranes, where, however, it was on the top of a tower that the Fee vanished, leaving, like Melusina, the mark of her foot on the battlements, where it is still to be seen.

In explication of the former legend, M. Pluque observes, that at the siege of Bayeux by Henry I., in 1106, Robert d'Argouges vanquished in single combat a German of huge stature; and that the crest of the house of Argouges is Faith, under the form of a woman naked to the waist, seated in a bark, with the motto, or war-cry, *A la Fé! (i. e. à la foi!)* which the people pronounce *A la Fée!*

So far the genuine French Fees. On the revival of learning they appear to have fallen into neglect, till the memory of them was awakened by the appearance of the translation of the Italian tales of Straparola, many of which seem to have become current among the people; and in the end of the seventeenth century, the Contes des Fées of Perrault, Madame d'Aulnoy, and their imitators and successors, gave them vogue throughout Europe. These tales are too well known to our readers to require us to make any observations on them.

NOTES

[a] i. *e.* Cephalonia, see above, p. 41.

[b] It is at this day (1698) corruptly called La Font de Sée; and every year in the month of May a fair is held in the neighbouring mead, where the pastry-cooks sell figures of women, *bien coiffées,*called Merlusines.—*French Author's Note*

[c] A boar's tusk projected from his mouth. According to Brantôme, a figure of him, cut in stone, stood at the portal of the Mélusine tower, which was destroyed in 1574.

[d] At her departure she left the mark of her foot on the stone of one of the windows, where it remained till the castle was destroyed.

[e] In his poem of Melusina, dedicated to Christina of Sweden.

[f] Mlle Bosquet, *ut sup.* p. 100.

[g] Mlle. Bosquet, *ut sup.* p. 98. The castle of Argouges is near Bayeux, that of Rànes is in the arrondissement of Argentan.

[h] This proverbial expression is to be met with in various languages: see Grimm, Deut. Mythol. p. 802.

EASTERN EUROPE

Up the hill I went, and gazed round.
Hoping golden maids to see;
Trooping lovely maidens came, who
Round the hill danced merrily.
All the sweetest ditties singing,
Sweetest ditties that might be;
Bearing fragrant apple-blossoms,
These fair maidens came to me.
—Lettish Song.

EUROPE IS inhabited on the east and north-east, from the Frozen Ocean to the Adriatic, by two extensive races named the Finns and the Slaves. The former dwell round the northern edge of Scandinavia by the Icy Ocean, and on the east and south-east of the Baltic. The Majjars, or the dominant portion of the people of Hungary, are also of Finnish origin. The Slaves who are akin to the Gotho-German race are also widely spread. This stem numbers among its branches the Russians, Poles, Bohemians, Servians, and the nations dwelling north-east of the Adriatic. Our knowledge of the popular mythology of both races is very limited.

FINNS

Bee! thou little mundane bird!
Fly away to where I bid thee;
O'er the moon, beneath the sun,
Behind the lofty heaven's stars,
Close by the Wain's axle—fly
To the great Creator's court.
—Finnish Rune.

Of the mythology of the Finnish race, the first possibly that appeared in Europe, and. one of the most widely spread in the world, our knowledge, as we have just stated, is very slight. It appears, however, either to have influenced that of the Gothic race, or to have been affected by it.

The Finlanders, Laplanders, and other nations of this race, who are neighbours of the Scandinavians and Germans, believe, like them, in Dwarfs and Kobolds. The former they describe as having a magnificent region under the ground, to which mortals are sometimes admitted and are there sumptuously entertained, getting plenty of tobacco and brandy, and other things esteemed by them delicious.

It is an article of faith with the Finns that there dwell under the altar in every church little misshapen beings which they call *Kirkonwaki, i. e.,* Church-folk. When the wives of these little people have a difficult labour they are relieved if a Christian woman visits them and lays her hand upon them. Such service is always rewarded by a gift of gold and silver. [a]

The Kobold of Finland is called Para (from the Swedish Bjära);

he steals the milk from other people's cows, carries and coagulates it in his stomach, and then disgorges it into the churn of his mistress. There is a species of mushroom, which if it be fried with tar, salt and sulphur, and then beaten with a rod, the woman who owns the Kobold will quickly appear, and entreat to spare him.

The Alp, or nightmare, is called Painajainen, *i. e.,* Presser. It resembles a white maid, and its brightness illumines the whole room. It causes people to scream out wofully; it also hurts young children, and' makes them squint. The remedy against it is *steel* or a broom placed under the pillow. The House-spirit named Touttu (the Swedish Tomtegubbe) is also common in Finland. [b] The Esthonians believe that the Neck has fish's teeth.

An Esthonian legend relates that one time a girl was stopt by a pretty boy that had on him a handsome peasant's belt and forced to scratch his head a little. She did so, and while she was so engaged she was, without her knowledge, fastened to him by his belt, but the rubbing of her hand set him to sleep. Meanwhile a woman passed by, who came up and asked the girl what she was doing there. She told her the whole matter, and as she was speaking she freed herself from the belt. The boy, however, slept sounder than ever and his mouth was wide open. The woman who had come nearer cried at once, Ha! that's a *Näkki* (Neck,) see his *fish's teeth!* The Neck instantly vanished. [c]

The following Esthonian legend, though the Devil is the subject, strongly resembles some of those of France and Great Britain:

A man who had charge of the granary of a farm-house was

sitting one day moulding buttons in lead. The Devil came by, saluted him, and said, "What are you doing there?" "I am moulding eyes." "Eyes! could you make me new ones?" "To be sure I could; but I have none by me at present." "Will you then do it another time?" "That will I." "When shall I come again?" "Whenever you please." Next day the Devil came to get his new eyes. "Will you have them large or small?" said the man. "Very large." The man then put a large quantity of lead down to melt, and said, "I cannot make them for you, unless you first let me tie you fast." He then made him lie on his back on a bench and tied him down with good strong thick ropes. When the Devil was thus fast bound he asked the man what his name was. "My name is Myself *(Issi),*" replied he. "That's a good name, I know none better." The lead was now melted; the Devil opened his eyes as wide as he could, expecting to get the new ones. "Now, I'm going to pour it out," said the. man, and he poured the melting lead into the eyes of the Devil, who jumped up with the bench on his back, and ran away. As he passed by some people who were ploughing, they asked him "Who did that to you?" "Myself did it *(Issi teggi),*" replied the Devil. The people laughed and said, "If you did it yourself; keep it yourself." The Devil died of his new eyes, and since then no one has seen the Devil any more. [d]

The Hungarians or Madyars (Magyars) as they call them-selves, are, as we have seen, a portion of the Finnish race, Two collections of their popular tales have been published of late years. The editor of one of them which we have read, [e] assures us that he took them from the lips of an old Hungarian soldier, who knew no language but his own, We therefore cannot but regard the tales as genuine, though the mode and tone in which they are narrated by the editor are not always the best. They contain no traits of popular mythology,—a circumstance not a little remarkable, rather resembling the French and Italian Fairy tales. Several of them, however, are very pleasing. We regret that we have not seen the other collection, which is apparently of greater value. [f]

NOTES

[a] Mnemosyne, Abo 1821, *ap*. Giimm, Deut. Mytbo]. p. 426.

[b] Ruhs, Finlund und seine Bewohner.

[c] Grimm, Deut. Mythol. p. *459*.

[d] Grimm, Deut. Mythol. p. *979*. This is the fourth place where we have met this story. Could they have all come from the Odyssey, the hero of which tells the Cyclops, whom he blinds, that his name is Nobody?

[e] Gaal, Märchen der Magyaren. Wien, 1822.

[f] Mailath, Magyarische Sagen Mährchen, etc., 2 vols, 8vo. Stutg. 1837.

SLAVES

Whatsoe'er at eve had raised the workmen,
Did the Vila raze ere dawn of morning.
—Bowring, *Servian Popular Poetry.*

A demon, in the attire of a mourning widow, used, in the Eastern Russia, to go through the fields at noon in harvest-time, and break the legs and arms of the workmen, who failed, when they saw her, to fall on their faces. There was a remedy, however, against this. Trees, long venerated, grew in the adjacent wood, the bark of which being laid on the wound, removed the pain and healed it. [a]

The Vends believe in a similar being; but a Vend knows that when be converses with her for an hour together about flax and the preparation of it, if he always contradicts her, or says the paternoster backwards without stopping, he is secure. [b]

The Russians also believe in a species of water and wood-maids, called Rusalki. They are of a beautiful form, with long green hair; they swing and balance themselves on the branches of trees—bathe in lakes and rivers—play on the surface of the water—and wring their locks on the green meads at the water's-edge. It is chiefly at Whitsuntide that they appear, and the people then singing and dancing, weave garlands for them, which they cast into the stream.[c]

The following is the Polish form of a legend which we have already met with in several places: [d]

There came to a nobleman an unknown man, who called himself Iskrzycki *(spark or firestone),* and offered to engage in his service. The contract was drawn up and signed, when the master perceived that Iskrzycki had horse's hoofs, and he accordingly wanted to break off the agreement; but the servant stood on his right, and declared that he would enter on his duties, even against his master's will. From this time forwards he took up his abode invisibly in the stove, and performed all the tasks set him. People gradually grew accustomed to him, but at last the lady prevailed on her lord to remove, and he hired another estate. His people left the castle, and they had already gone the greater part of the way, when on a bad part of the road the carriage was near turning over, and the lady gave a loud cry of terror. Immediately a voice answered from behind the carriage—"Never fear! Iskrzycki is with you!" The lord and his lady now saw that there was no way of getting rid of him, so they went back to the old house, and lived there on good terms with their servant till the term of the engagement had arrived.

The Servian ballads, that have lately appeared [e] have made us acquainted with an interesting species of beings called Vilas. These are represented as mountain-nymphs, young and beautiful, clad in white, with long flying hair. Their voice is said to resemble that of the woodpecker. They shoot, according to popular belief, deadly arrows at men, and sometimes carry off children, whom their mothers in their anger have consigned to them or the devil: yet the general character of the Vilas is to injure none but those who intrude upon their *kolos,* or roundels.

The Vilas sometimes appear gaily dancing their kolos beneath the branches of the Vishnia or Vistula cherry; sometimes a Vila is introduced comforting the sorrows of an enarnoured deer; at other times collecting storms in the heavens; [f] now foretelling to a hero his impending death; [g] now ruthlessly casting down each night the walls of a rising fortress, till a young and. lovely female is immured. within them. [h] She usually rides a seven-year old hart, with a bridle made of snakes.

The following are specimens of these Servian ballads:

NOTES

[a] Delrio, Lib. ii. Sect. 2. Boxhorn Resp. Moscov. Para I.
[b] Grimm, Deut. Mythol. p. 447.
[c] Mone, vol. i. p. 144.   Grimm, Deut. Mythol. p. 460.
[d] Grimm, *ut sup*. p. 480.
[e] Published by Wuk and translated by Talvi and others into German, by Bowring into English.
[f] Bowring, p. 175. *Sabejam oblake,* Cloud-gatherer, is an epithet of the Vila, answering to the Grecian Zeus.
[g] Death of Kralwich Mèrko. Bowring, p. 97.
[h] The building of Skadra. Ibid. p. 64.

Vilas

CHERRY! dearest Cherry!
Higher lift thy branches,
Under which the Vilas
Dance their magic roundels.
Them before Radisha
Dew from flowers, lashes,
Leadeth on two Vilas,
To the third he sayeth—
"Be thou mine, O Vila!
Thou shalt, with my mother,
In the cool shade seat thee;
Soft silk deftly spinning
From the golden distaff." [a]

NOTE

[a] We have made this translation from a German version in the Wiener Jahrbucher, vol. xxx.
which is evidently more faithful than Bowring's.

Deer and Vila

A YOUNG deer track'd his way through the lone forest
One lonely day—another came in sadness—
And the third dawn'd, and brought him sighs and sorrow;
Then he address'd him to the forest Vila:
"Young deer" she said, "thou wild one of the forest!
Now tell me what great sorrow has oppress'd thee;
Why wanderest thou thus in the forest lonely:
Lonely one day—another day in sadness—
And the third day with sighs and anguish groaning?"
And thus the young deer to the Vila answered:
"O thou sweet sister! Vila of the forest!
Me has indeed a heavy grief befallen;
For I once had a fawn, mine own beloved,
And one sad day she sought the running water;
She enter'd it, but came not back to bless me.
Then, tell me, has she lost her way and. wander'd?
Was she pursued and captured by the huntsman?
Or has she left me?—has she wholly left me—
Loving some other deer—and I forgotten?
Oh, if she has but lost her way, and wanders,
Teach her to find it—bring her back to love me!
Oh, if she has been captured by the huntsman,
Then may a fate as sad as mine await him!
But if she has forsaken me—if, faithless,
She loves another deer and I forgotten—
Then may the huntsman speedily o' ertake her." [a]

We have already observed how almost all nations compare female beauty to that of the beings of their legendary creed. With the Servians the object of comparison is the lovely Vila. "She is fairer than the mountain-Vila," is the highest praise of woman's beauty. In the ballad of The Sister of the Kapitan Leka, it is said of the heroine Rossandra, that in no country, either Turkey, or the land of the Kau-

ran, or Jewrs, was her fellow to be found. No white Bula (Moham-
medan), no Vlachin (Greek), no slender Latiness (Roman Catholic),
could compare with her,

> And who on the hills hath seen the Vila—
> E'en the Vila, brother, must to her yield.

The swiftness of the Vila also affords a subject of comparison:
a fleet horse is said to be "Vilaish" or "swift as a Vita."

The Morlacchi of Dalmatia, as Sir Gardner Wilkinson informs
us, [b] believe also in the Vila. They describe her as a handsome female, who accompanies the, man who is her favourite everywhere he
goes, and causes all his undertakings to prosper. One thus favoured
is termed Vilénik. Another of their objects of belief is the Maçieh,
who appears in the form of a boy, with a cap on his head, and is
always laughing. Any one to whom he appears gets the power of
commanding him. If ordered to bring money, he usually steals it from
one of the neighbours, and if taxed with his dishonesty, he goes to
the sea and comes back dripping and with money.

NOTES

[a] Bowring, This version differs considerably from the German one of Talvi. We feel quite
    convinced that the English translator has mistaken the sense.
[b] Dalmatia and Montenegro, etc.

AFRICANS, JEWS

Loud from the hills the voice of riot comes,
Where Yumboes shout and beat their Jaloff drums.
–T. K.

THIS DIVISION of our work is somewhat miscellaneous, not being restricted to any particular race, or to any determinate part of the earth's surface. It contains merely such matters as appeared to us to be worthy of note, but which we could not include in any of the preceding sections.

AFRICANS

When evening's shades o'er Goree's Isle extend,
The nimble Yumboes from the Paps descend,
Slily approach the natives' huts, and steal,
With secret hand, the pounded coos-coos meal.
–T. K.

The Jaloff inhabitants of the mainland of Africa, opposite the isle of Goree, believe in a species of beings who have a striking and surprising correspondence with the Gothic Fairies. They call them Yumboes, and describe them as being about two feet high, of a white colour, as every thing preternatural is in Africa. It is remarkable that, acting on the same principle as the Greeks, who called their Furies Eumenides, and the Scots and Irish, who style the Fairies Good Neighbours, or Good People, the Africans call the Yumboes, Bakhna Rakhna, or Good People. The dress of the Yumboes exactly corresponds with that of the natives, and they imitate their actions in every particular. They attach themselves to particular families; and whenever any of their members die, the Yumboes are heard to lament them, and to dance, upon their graves. The Moors believe the Yumboes to be the souls of their deceased friends.

The chief abode of the Yumboes is a subterraneous dwelling on the Paps, the hills about three miles distant from the coast. Here they dwell in great magnificence, and many wonderful stories are told of those persons, particularly Europeans, who have been received and entertained in the subterraneous residence of the Yumboes: of how they were placed at richly furnished tables; how

302

nothing but hands and feet were to be seen, which laid and removed the various dishes; of the numerous stories the underground abode consisted of; the modes of passing from one to the other without stairs, etc., etc.

In the evening the Yumboes come down to the habitation of man, wrapped close in their *pangs*, [a] with only their eyes and nose visible. They steal to the huts, where the women are pounding in mortars the coos-coos, or corn, watch till the pounders are gone for sieves to searce the meal, and then slily creep to the mortars, take out the meal, and carry it off in their pangs, looking every moment behind them, to see if they are observed or pursued; or they put it into calabashes, and arranging themselves in a row, like the monkeys, convey it from hand to hand, till it is placed in safety.

They are also seen at night in their canoes, out fishing in the bay. They bring their fish to land, and, going to the fires kindled by the natives to keep away the wild beasts, they steal each as much fire as will roast his fish. They bury palm-wine, and when it becomes sour they drink of it till it intoxicates them, and then make a great noise, beating Jaloff drums on the hills. [b]

NOTES

[a] The Pang (Span. *pano,* cloth) is an oblong piece of cotton cloth, which the natives manufacture and wear wrapped round their bodies.

[b] For the preceding account of the Yumboes we are indebted to a young lady, who spent several years of her childhood at Goree. What she related to us she had heard from her maid, a Jaloff woman, who spoke no language but Jaloff.

JEWS

And the Mazikeen shall not come near thy tents.

It has long been an established article of belief among the Jews that there is a species of beings which they call Shedeem, Shehireem, or Mazikeen. These beings exactly correspond to the Arabian Jinn; and the Jews hold that it is by means of them that all acts of magic and enchantment are performed.

The Talmud says that the Shedeem were the offspring of Adam. After he had eaten of the Tree of life, Adam was excommunicated for one hundred and thirty years. "In all those years," saith Rabbi Jeremiah Ben E'liezar, "during which Adam was under excommunication, he begat spirits, demons, and spectres of the night, as it is written, 'Adam lived one hundred and thirty years, and begat children in his likeness and in his image,' which teaches, that till that time he bad not begotten them in his own likeness." In Berasbith Rabba, R. Simon says, "During all the one hundred and thirty years that Adam was separate from Eve, male spirits lay with her, and she bare by them, and female spirits lay with Adam, and bare by him."

These Shedeem or Mazikeen are held to resemble the angels in three things. They can see and not be seen; they have wings and can fly; they know the future. In three respects they resemble mankind: they eat and drink; they marry and have children; they are subject to death. it may be added, they have the power of assuming any form they please; and so the agreement between them and the Jinn of the Arabs is complete.

Moses Edrehi, a learned Jew of Morocco, has translated into Spanish for us several of the tales of the Mazikeen contained in the Talmud and Rabbinical writings. We select the following as specimens; and according to our usual custom, adhere strictly to our original.

The Broken Oaths

There was a man who was very rich, and who had but one only son. He bestowed upon him every kind of instruction, so that he became very leaned and of great talent.

Before his death the old man gave a great entertainment, and invited all the chief people of the city; and when the entertainment was over, he called his son, and made him swear, in the name of the great God of the whole universe that he never would travel or go out of his own country. He then left him the whole of his riches on this condition, and made him sign a paper to that effect, with sufficient witnesses, in the presence of all that company, and he gave the paper into the custody of one of the principal persons.

Some years after the death of his father, there came a very large ship from India, laden with merchandise of great value. The captain when he arrived inquired after the father of this young man, and the people said unto him that he was dead, but that he had left a son, and. they conducted the captain to the young man's dwelling. The captain then said unto him, "Sir, I have brought hither much property belonging to thy father, and as there is much property of thy father's still remaining, if thou wilt come with me, thou wilt be able to obtain much riches, for thou canst recover all that is owing unto thy father." He made answer unto the captain and said, that he could not travel, as he had taken an oath unto his father that he never would go out of the country. The captain, however, ceased not every day to persuade him, until at length he gave him his word that he would go with him. He then went unto the learned Rabbin that were at that time, to see if they would give him absolution respecting the oath be had sworn unto his father. But they counselled him not to leave the country. But his eagerness to acquire more riches was so great, that he would not hearken unto the counsel of any one. So he finally took his resolution, and went away with the captain.

Now, when they were in the midst of the sea, lo! the ship went to pieces, and all the merchandise that was on board was lost, and all the people were drowned, save only this young man, who got upon a plank. And the water carried him about from one place unto another, until it cast him upon the land. But here he was in danger of starving, and had nothing to eat but the herbs of the field, or to drink but the running water.

One day an exceeding large eagle drew near unto him, and seated himself on the ground before him. As he was now reduced to despair, and had little hopes of being able to preserve his life, and knew not where be was, be resolved to mount this eagle, and to sit upon his back. He accordingly mounted the bird, and the eagle flew with him until he brought him unto a country that was inhabited, where he left him. [a] When he saw that he was in a land where there were people, he was greatly rejoiced, and he immediately inquired where the great Rabbi of that country dwelt. But all the people that were there stood mocking at him, and cursing him, and saying that he should die, because be had broken the oath he had sworn unto his father. When he heard this be was greatly astonished at their knowing it, but he went to the house of the chief person among them who said unto him that he should abide in his house until they did him justice, because in that country they were all Mazikeen, and they wanted to kill him because he deserved death on account of the oath to his father, which he had broken. "Therefore," said he, "when they will sentence thee, and will lead thee forth to punishment, cry aloud and say, I call for justice before God and the king! The king will then do his utmost to deliver thee out of their hands, and thou wilt remain alive."

Accordingly, when he was tried before the senate, and before their princes and great men, he was found guilty, and sentenced to death, according to the law of God. And when they led him forth to be slain, he put his fingers before God, and before his majesty the king. [b] When they heard this, they took him before the king, who examined him, and saw that, in justice, he was worthy of death. But the king asked him if he had studied or knew the law of Moses, or had studied the Talmud, and various authors; and he saw that he was very learned, and a great Rabbi, and it grieved him much that he should be put to death. The king, therefore, begged that they would defer his execution until the following day, for he wished to give his case a little further consideration. At this they all held their peace, and departed.

Next day all the senators, governors, chief men, and all the people of the city, came together to see and hear the sentence of the king, and also to behold the death of this man, as it would be for them a very curious sight. Now, while they were all standing there assembled, before the king came forth from his palace to give his judgement, he called for this man who was condemned to death, and asked him if he was willing to remain with him and teach his children what he knew, as, in such case, he would do his utmost to deliver him from death. He made answer that he was willing. The king then went forth from his palace, and seated himself upon his throne of judgement, and called all the chief men, and all the people, and spake unto them in this sort:—

"Sirs, it is a truth that you have adjudged this man to death, which he deserves: but there is no rule without an exception, and I believe that this man hath not yet come to his time that he should die. For if it was the will of God that he should die, he would have died along with the rest of the people who were on board the same ship with him when the ship went to pieces, and not have escaped as he hath done. Again, if it was the will of God that he should die, he would not have reached the land, and an eagle would not have come and brought him hither amongst us. In like manner, God hath delivered him from you, for he might have been slain by you. He hath thus been delivered out of these manifold and great perils, and it therefore seemeth unto me that he should live; as for the sin that he hath committed, in breaking his oath, it is between him and God, who shall reward him for it one day or other. He shall therefore be free from us; and I ordain that no one shall touch him, or do him any evil; and whosoever troubleth him shall be put to death."

When they heard these words of the king, they all expressed themselves well pleased at his decision; and the man remained in the house of the king, teaching his children. He continued in the palace for three years, highly respected by every one, and greatly esteemed by the king for his talents and his capacity.

Now it came to pass that the king was obliged to set forth with an army, to war against one of the provinces of his kingdom which had rebelled. As he was on the point to set out, he called for this man, and gave him all the keys of his palaces and his treasures, and said unto him, "Behold! thou mayest view every thing that is in the land and in the palaces; but thou hast here a golden key of one palace which thou must beware of opening, for on the day that thou openest it I will slay thee." Then, charging the people to respect and attend to him, the king took his leave of him and departed. When the king was gone, he began to open and. examine all the palaces, and all the curiosities, which were such as he had never seen in his life, and all the treasures of the greatest riches that could be in the world; in short, he saw mountains upon mountains of diamonds of great weight, and. other things of various kinds, most admirable to behold. But when he had seen all, he was not satisfied; be wanted to see more. And as his desire was very great, he would open the other palace; and he thought he should suffer no injury thereby, so that he resolved to open it. Five or six times he drew nigh to open it, and as often he drew back in fear at length he took courage and opened it.

There were seven apartments, one within the other, and. every apartment was full of different rich and curious things. In the seventh apartment was the princess, with other women, all richly dressed, and very beautiful. When the princess saw him, she gave a sigh, and said, "Man, it grieveth me for thee! how art thou come hither? Where is thy regard for the advice of my father, who entreated thee not to open this palace, when he gave thee the keys of his palaces and his treasures, and straitly charged thee not to come hither? Know now that my father is coming, and that he will surely slay thee. But if thou wilt follow my counsel, and wilt espouse me,

I will save thee; but thou must give unto me thy oath, that thou wilt do it." He replied that he would, and he aware unto her, and gave it unto her in writing. She then said. unto him, "When my father asketh thee why thou hast opened the palace, thou shalt make answer, and say that thou desirest to marry me, and then he will let thee escape, and not slay thee."

He had scarcely ended speaking with her, when the king entered, with his sword drawn in his hand, to slay him. Then he threw himself on the ground, and began to entreat him, and. said that he was desirous to marry the princess. When the king heard this, he was rejoiced that he would remain there, and so teach his children all the knowledge he possessed; for he was of great capacity in everything. He therefore told him, that he would leave it to his daughter, whether she would have him or not. The king then asked his daughter, and she replied, "What your majesty doth for me is well done." The king then gave his consent for her marriage with him. The contract was made, and. notice was given to all the chief persons of the city, and the wedding was appointed. to be in two months.

When the appointed. time was come, all the chief men of all the provinces of the kingdom were invited, and. a great feast was made to celebrate the marriage of the princess; and they were married to their great joy and. happiness.

On the first night of their marriage, when the husband and the wife were alone, she said unto him, "Behold! I am not like one of you, and thou seest that, thanks be unto God! there is no defect in my body; if therefore, though we have been publicly married with the consent of my father, thou art not content to live with me as husband and wife, thou art at liberty, and no one shall know it; but if thou art content with all thy will, thou must swear unto me that thou wilt never leave me." He replied, that he was well content with everything; and. he aware unto her, and wrote it down on paper, and signed it with his hand, and gave it unto her; and they lived happily as man and wife for many years, and they had children; and his first-born he named Solomon, after the name of king Solomon.

Immediately after the marriage, the king caused it to be proclaimed. that his son-in-law should be the second person in the kingdom to give judgement, and to punish such as should be deserving of punishment. This the king did. with the consent of all the great men of the country.

But, after some years, this man began to be very anxious and melancholy; and his wife asked him many times what it was that ailed. him, but he would never tell her the cause: yet she persuaded him so much, that at length he told it unto her, and said, that when he looked upon his children he remembered the other children that he had, and his other wife, and that he yearned. to behold them once more. His wife replied, "My dear husband, let not this give thee any uneasiness, for if thou wishest to see them, thou canst see them." He answered, "If thou wilt do me this favour and grace, I shall thank thee much." She asked him how long he wished to stay with his wife and children, and he answered, three months; but she said, "No; I will give thee the space of a year, on condition, that as soon as the year is expired thou return again unto me." He answered, "If thou show me this favour, I will do all that thou wilt command me." She said, "Take an oath that thou wilt keep thy word." He then aware, and wrote it down on paper, and gave it unto her.

She then called one of her servants, and ordered him to convey him to his own house with all the speed he could make; and in the space of a few minutes he found himself in his own house with, his wife and children. The man then asked him if he had any commands for his lady? He replied, "I have nothing to do with thee or thy lady. I am now with my wife and. children; I know no other, and therefore I have no message to give." The servant then returned to his mistress; and. she asked him what his master had said, and if he had given him any message. He answered, "Madam, if I tell thee what he hath said, thou wilt not 'believe me." She then pressed. him, and he told her all. She said, "It doth not signify."

He remained, then, very happy with his family; but at the end of the year his wife sent a messenger unto him to call him back unto her, as the year was expired. But he answered that he would not, and. that he had nothing to do with them, as he was a man, and had nothing more to say with them. The messenger returned and. told his mistress, and she sent other messengers of greater dignity, for she said this one is not sufficient for him.. But he made the same reply that he had made unto the first. She then sent greater still, three or four times; and at last she was obliged to send her son Solomon. When he saw his son he embraced him, and asked him what he wanted. He told him that his mother had sent him, that he might come back with him, and that if he would not, she would come and avenge herself upon him. His father replied, that he had. no mind to depart from his house; that he would stay with his wife and children, who were human beings like himself. So when his son saw that there was no remedy, and. that he would not come with him, he returned unto his mother, and related the whole unto her.

His mother was then obliged to go herself with her great army. When they arrived at the city where the man dwelt, they said unto the princess that they would go up and slay the man that was her husband, and all the people of the city; but she answered, "No; they had. not permission to kill any one, as all the Hebrews, when they lie down to sleep at night, make their prayers unto God to protect and guard. them from all Mazikeen; so that we have no right or permission to touch them; and if we do them a mischief, we shall be chastised. for it by the God of Israel, who governeth the whole world. Do you, therefore, bide here without the city, and in the morning I and my son Solomon will arise and go unto the school of the Rabbin and the Sanhedrim, and if they will do me justice with him, well; if not, I will avenge myself upon him and upon them." They all made answer and said, "It is well said."

In the morning she arose with her son Solomon, and went unto the great school, where the divine Law was taught. They were consulting, when they heard the voice of one crying aloud, and saying, "Sirs, justice before God, and before you, upon such a one, my husband;" and all the people were amazed, and. were in astonishment when they heard the voice three times, and saw no one. They then sent for the man, who came unto them and. related the whole story, and said that he had no mind to go with her. They again heard the voice, which said, "Sirs, here are his oaths, signed. by himself, which he sware and. signed each time;" and then three written papers fell before them. They read them, and asked him if that was his signature. He said it was. They said unto him, "It is ill done to break so many oaths," and that there was no remedy, but that he should go with her to where he had lived so many years with her, and where she had saved him from death, and he had had children by her. "As for us, we advise thee to go with her, and if thou dost not, it will not come to good; for she is not an ordinary person, but is a princess, and merits attention, more especially as she hath right on her side." He answered. that he would give her Guet (a bill of divorce); but she made answer, that that would not be for her honour. In fine, he refused absolutely to go with her.

After a great deal of argument, and when she saw that there were no means to persuade him, she said, "Sirs, I am highly obliged and grateful to you; for I see that you do me the justice of God, and he will not accept it. You are free, and the sin will be upon his soul. Wherefore, sirs, since there is no remedy with him, I entreat that he will suffer me to take leave of him, and to embrace him." He replied that she might, and as soon as she embraced him she drew out his soul, and he died.. She then said, "Sirs, here is his son Solomon, who is one of yourselves. I will give him sufficient riches, and he shall be heir along with the children of his other wife, and you will make him among you a great Rabbi; for he is of sufficient ability, as you may see if you will examine him. Farewell."

So saying, she departed with her army. [c]

NOTES

[a] Comp. Lane, Thousand and One Nights, iii. p. 91.

[b] To signify that he appealed to them.

[c] From a rabbinical book called Mahasee Yerusalemee, i. e. History of a Hebrew of Jerusalem.—"Very old," says Moses Edrebi, "and known by the Hebrews to be true." "Moreover;' saith he of another tale, "it really happened, because every thing that is written in the Jewish books is true; for no one can print any new book without its being examined and approved of by the greatest and chiefest Rabbin and wise men of that time and city, and the proofs must be very strong and clear; so that all the wonderful stories in these hooks are true." The Jews are not singular in this mode of vouching for the truth of wonderful stories.

The Moohel

There was once a man who was exceedingly rich, but out of all measure avaricious, and who never had done a good deed in his life, and. never had given even the value of a farthing unto the poor.

It happened one winter's nights between the hours of twelve and one, that a man came and knocked loudly at the door of this miser. He opened the window, and saw a man at the door, and he asked him what it was he wanted. He. said that he wanted him to go with him to a village twelve miles distant from the town, to circumcise a young child that would be eight days old in the morning.

Now you must know, that this man of whom we treat was a Jew and a Moohel, that is, one whose office it is to circumcise the young children; and with all his avarice in money matters, he was not avaricious in his office, for he believed in the end of the world, and therefore he did this good action.

He accordingly agreed to go with the man, and he kindled a fire, and put his clothes before it, and. got ready the instruments he required for performing the ceremony. He then set out along with the strange man, whom he knew not, though it was winter, and dark and rainy; and they went along, journeying through the wilderness. This unfortunate Moohel, who did not know his way in the wilderness, and in the dark, every now and then fell over the stones on the way; but they still went on until they came to a great and lofty mountain in the midst of the wilderness, where people never passed, and where there are no people to be see; but only dark, dark mountains, that fill with terror those who look upon them.

The man who came with the Moohel now laid his hand on a great stone of the mountain, so large that five hundred persons could not remove or raise it; yet he raised it with only one hand. The place then opened, and they both descended. There were many flights of steps, and it was very deep within the earth, and below there was an entire city. They entered then into a palace that was very large and handsome; it had fine gardens, and there was a great deal of light, and music, and much dancing of men and women. When they saw this Moohel approach, they began to laugh and to mock at him; but the poor Moohel was greatly astonished at all the things that he saw, and as he stood looking on, he began to consider and reflect upon them; and then he saw that they were not human beings like us, and great fear came upon him; but be had no means of getting out, or of saving himself; so he constrained himself; and remained quiet.

Now the man who had brought him thither was one of their commanders, and a great personage among them. He took him then to the apartment of the lying-in woman, that he might view the child. The man then went away, and left him with the lying-in woman. But the woman groaned in great affliction, and began to weep. The Moohel asked her what ailed her? Then said the woman unto the Moohel, "How didst thou come hither? Knowest thou in what place thou art, and amongst whom thou art?" The Moohel replied that he did not, as he had not ventured to speak. The woman then explained, "Thou art in the land of the Mazikeen, and all the people that are here are Mazikeen; but I am a being like unto thyself; for when I was yet young and little, I was once alone in a dark place, and these people took me and brought me hither; and I was married to this husband, who is one of their great men, and who is, moreover, a Jew for there are different religions among them; and I also am a Jewess, and when this child was born, I spake unto my husband, and entreated of him, that he would get a Moohel to circumcise the, babe; and so he brought thee hither. But thou art in great danger here, and art lost; for thou wilt never be able to go out from here, and wilt be like one of them. Yet, as I have compassion for thee, and particularly as thou hast, out of kindness, come hither to circumcise the babe, and out of humanity, I will give thee a counsel that may be of service unto thee; and that is, when they ask thee to eat or to drink, take good heed not to touch anything, for if thou taste anything of theirs thou wilt become like one of them, and wilt remain here for ever."

The husband now came in, and they went to the congregation to perform the morning prayer. After the prayer, they returned to the house to perform the ceremony of circumcision. The Moohel took a cup of wine, and gave it to taste to the lying-in woman, to the babe, and to all who were invited to the ceremony, for this is the manner and the custom. But the man who had fetched the Moohel said unto him, "Thou also shouldst taste." The Moohel replied, that be could not, for he had dreamed an evil dream, and that he must fast; and by this excuse he escaped. But he waited for him till night, and then they brought him meat and drink; but he replied that he could not eat until he had passed two or three days fasting. When the man who bad brought him thither saw that he would neither eat nor drink for so long a time, he took compassion upon him, and said unto him, "What is the matter with thee, that thou wilt neither eat nor drink?"—"Sir," replied the Moohel, "I ask and desire no other thing but to go home unto my family; for this week we hold a feast, and I should be with my family. I therefore most humbly supplicate thee to take me unto my own house." He then began to beg and entreat him most earnestly, and the woman also entreated for him.

The man then said unto him, "Since thou desirest to go home unto thy house, come then with me; I will give thee a present for thy trouble. Come with me, where thou mayest see and take whatever will seem good unto thee." The Moohel answered, "I do not wish for anything. Thanks be to God! I am very rich—I want for nothing, but to return home unto my family."—"Nevertheless," said he, "come with me, till I show thee curious things that thou hast never seen in thy life." He was accordingly persuaded; he went with him, and he showed him divers apartments all full of silver, of gold, of diamonds, of all sorts of precious stones, and of other curious and magnificent things, such as he had never seen in his life.

He thus led him from. one chamber to another, and continually asked him if he wished for anything; for if he did, he might. take it. But he still refused, and would take nothing. At length they came to the last chamber, where there was nothing but bunches of keys hanging. The Moohel raised his eyes at seeing such a number of keys, and, lo! he beheld a bunch of keys that was his own. He began then to reflect deeply; and the man said unto him, "What dost thou stand gazing at? I have shown thee many precious and curious things, and yet thou didst not bestow so much attention upon them as upon these old keys, that are of little worth." "Be not offended, sir," answered the Moohel, "but these keys are so like mine, and I believe they are the same." He took the keys and began to examine them, and to point out each key separately to the man, who at length said unto him, "Thou art right, they are thy keys. Know that I am lord over the hearts of the people who never at any time do good; and as thou performest this good deed of circumcision, and riskest thy life in dangerous journeys, and goest with all sorts of people to do the commandment of the God of Israel, here, take the keys! From henceforward thy heart will be opened, [a] and will be good toward the poor, which will cause thee to live a long and a happy life with thy family. Come now with me; I will carry thee home to thy house and to thy family. Now shut thine eyes."

He shut his eyes, and instantly found himself in his own house amidst his family. He then began to distribute money to all the poor that were in the land, every week and every month. But the world is always curious to hear novelties and strange events, and the people, and even his own wife, as this was a very wonderful thing, pressed him and persuaded him, until at length he was obliged to relate the whole history of what had befallen him, from the beginning even unto the end; and it was a matter of great delight to all the world; and they did much good to the poor, and they all became rich, with great prosperity. And the Moohel lived very long, and spent a great and a happy life with his family, a pattern and an example unto the whole world. [b]

NOTES

[a] The moral here is apparent.

[b] From a very ancient rabbinical book called R. H. It is needless to point out its resemblance to German and other tales.

The Mazik-Ass

It came to pass in the countries of Africa, in a particular month, during which it is the usage and the custom of the Jews to rise in the night to say their prayers, that a servant, whose business it was to knock at the doors, and to call up the people, found one night an ass *(jumento)* in the street; and he mounted upon him, and went riding along and calling up the people. And, as he rode, lo! the ass began to swell and to increase in size, until he became three hundred yards in height, and reached up even unto the top of the loftiest tower of the church, upon which he set the man, and then went away; and on the morrow the man was found sitting upon the tower. Now, thou must know that this ass was one of the Mazikeen.

The Jews have, as it were, brought us back to Asia. As we proceed eastwards from Persia, where we commenced, India first meets our view, but of the numerous beings of its copious and intricate mythology, no class seems to belong to earth unless it be the Yakshas who attend on Kuveras, the Hindoo Plutos, and have charge of his enchanted gardens on the summit of Himalayas, and who bear some resemblance to the Dwarfs. There are also the misshapen Pisachas, who love to dwell in gloom; the, Vidhyadharas, *i. e.,* Masters of Magic, are said, to resemble the Jinn of the Arabs; and the dancing and singing Gandharvas and Apsaresas may be compared with the Nymphs of Grecian mythology.

Eastwards still lies China. Here there is a species of beings named Shinseën, who are said to haunt the woods and mountains, where, exempt from the passions and the cares of life, they dwell in a state of blissful ease; but still exercise an influence over human affairs. Sometimes they appear as old men with long beards; at other times as young maidens, sauntering amid rocks and. woods by moonlight. [a]

We do not recollect to have met, in our reading, with any other beings bearing a resemblance to what we term Fairies.

NOTE

[a] See Davis' translation of The Fortunate Union, i. 68

CONCLUSION

HERE, THEN, WE CONCLUDE. The task which we imposed on ourselves was to collect, arrange, classify, and give under one point of view the various ideas and legends respecting Fairies and similar beings of the popular creed, which lay scattered in a variety of books and a variety of languages. We have marked resemblances, traced coincidences, and offered etymologies. Many legends, especially German ones, we know, exist, which are not to be found. in this work; but, in general, they offer no new traits of popular lore, and most persons will, we apprehend, be content with what we have given.

The labours of MM. Grimm in this department of philosophy can never be too highly praised. They have been, in fact, the creators of it; and the German Mythology is a work of the most extensive learning, and written in the spirit of true philosophy. And this is no light praise; for of all subjects, Mythology appears to be the one on which imagination is most apt to run riot. Hence, it has been frequently almost brought into contempt by the wild vagaries of those who have presumed to write on it without judgement or common sense. Though all may not agree with the opinions or deductions in the preceding pages, we trust that they will find in them no traces of ill-regulated imagination.

As works of this kind have no bearing on material enjoyments, the number of those who will think lightly of them in these days will, of course, not be small. But in the view of sane reason and philosophy, the subject is by no means unimportant, nay, it is even more important than many of higher pretensions. To trace the corruption and degradation of the pure religion of the Gospel, has always been held to be a task worthy of the highest intellect: we should not, therefore, despise the present one, which is the same in kind though different in degree. We have seen that all these legendary beings and their characters and acts are remnants of ancient religious systems, the mental offspring of deep-thinking sages. It is surely, then, not uninteresting to trace them to their present form and condition. Even in a historic point of view they are not undeserving of attention. Thus, should our theory on the subject be correct, it is of importance to observe how the tribes around the Baltic, when they made conquests in the Roman Empire, brought with them the religious ideas of their forefathers, and left traces of them, which are discernible even at the present day. Again, nothing more interests the botanist than to find the same plants, modified by local circumstances, growing in widely-distant regions. The interest is similar when we find the same legends, modified also by circumstances, springing up in distant countries, and amongst tribes and nations who could hardly have had any communication.

This work is therefore to be regarded as a part of the philosophy of popular fiction. It is not by any means intended to be a work of mere amusement, and those who view or represent it in that light will do it manifest injustice. Many of the legends, no doubt, may possess attractions even for children; but the same is true of the narratives of Herodotus, and still more of those of the Old Testament, and therefore should not derogate from its real importance. At the same time, we have adopted a light and facile style, as that which we deemed best suited to the character of the subject and the taste of this country; but we trust that this will not lower either our subject or ourselves in the eyes of our readers. [a]

NOTE

[a] The legends from the German and other languages are, in general, faithfully translated, whence the style is, at times rude and negligent; English legends are for the most part, also, merely transcribed.

APPENDIX

THE FOLLOWING TALES are some of those which we contributed to the Irish Fairy Legends. Subjoined is a selection from the verses which we have written on various occasions, chiefly to oblige our lady-friends. They are inserted merely to show that the writer could compose well-rimed stanzas, while he lays no claim whatever to the title of poet.

The Harvest Dinner

It was Monday, and a fine October morning. The sun had been some time above the mountains, and the hoar frost and the dew-tops on the gossamers [a] were glittering in the light, when Thady Byrne, on coming in to get his breakfast, saw his neighbour Paddy Cavenagh, who lived on the other side of the road, at his own door tying his brogues.

"A good morrow to you, Paddy, honey," said Thady Byrne.

"Good morrow, kindly, Thady," said Paddy."

Why, thin, Paddy, avick, it isn't your airly risin', anyhow, that 'ill do you any harm this mornin'."

"It's thrue enough for you, Thady Byrne," answered Paddy, casting a look up at the sky; "for I b'leeve it 'a purty late in the day. But I was up, you see, murdherin' late last night."

"To be shure, thin, Paddy, it was up at the great dinner, yisterday, above at the big house you wor."

"Ay was it; an' a rattlin' fine dinner we had uv it too."

"Why, thin, Paddy, agrah, what's to all you now, but you'd jist sit yourself down here on this piece o' green sod, an' tell us all about it from beginnin' to ind."

"Niver say the word twist, man; I'll give you the whole full an' thrue account uv it, an' welcome."

They sat down on the roadside, and Paddy thus began.

"Well, you see, Thady, we'd a powerful great harvist uv it, you know, this year, an' the min all worked like jewels, as they are; an' the masther was in great sperits, an' he promis'd he'd give us all a grand dinner whin the dhrawin'-in was over, an' the corn all safe in the haggard. So this last week, you see, crown'd the business; an' on Satherday night the last shafe was nately tied an' sint in to the misthress, an' everything was flnisht, all to the tatchin' o' the ricks. Well, you see, jist as Larry Toole was come down from headin' the last rick, an' we war takin' away the laddher, out comes the misthress herself—long life to her—by the light o' the moon; an', 'Boys,' sez she, 'yez hav' flnish'd the harvist bravely, an' I invite yez all to dinner here to-morrow; an' if yez come airly, yez 'ill git mass in the big hall, widout the throuble o' goin' up all the ways to the chapel for it.'"

"Why, thin, did she raally say so, Paddy?"

"That she did—the divil the word o' lie in it."

"Well, go on."

"Well, if we didn't set up a shout for her, it 's no matther!"

"Ay, an' a good right yez had too, Paddy, avick."

"Well, you see, yistherday mornin'—which, God be praised, was as fine a day as iver come out of the sky—whin I tuk the beard off o' me, Tom Conner an' I set off together for the big house. An' I don't know, Thady, whether it was the fineness o' the day, or the thoughts o' the good dinner we wor to have, or the kindness o' the misthress, that med my heart so light, but I filt, anyhow, as gay as any skylark. Well, whin we got up to the house, there was every one o' the people that 's in the work, min, women and childher, all come together in the yard; an' a purty sight it was to luk upon, Thady: they wor all so nate an so clane, an' so happy."

"Thrue 'for you, Paddy, agrah; an' a fine thing it is, too, to work wid a raal gintleman like the masther. But till us, avick, how was it the misthress conthrived to get the mass for yez: shure Father Miley himself, or the codjuthor, didn't come over."

"No, in troth didn't they, but the misthress managed it betther nor all that. You see, Thady, there 'a a priest, an ould friend o' the family's, one Father Mulhall's on a visit, this fortnight past, up at the big house. He's as gay a little man as iver spoke, only he 's a little too fond o' the dhrop,—the more 'a the pity,—an' it's whispered about among the sarvints that by manes uv it he lost a parish he had down the counthry; an' he was an his way up to Dublin, whin he stopt to spind a few days wid his ould finds the masther an' misthress.

"Well, you see, the misthress on Satherday, widout sayin' a single word uv it to any livin' sowl, writes a letther wid her own hand, an' sinds Tom Freen off wid it to Father Miley, to ax him for a loan o' the vistmints. Father Miley, you know 's a mighty ginteel man intirely, and one that likes to obleege the quolity in anything that doesn't go agin' his juty; an' glad he was to hav' it in his power to sarve the misthress; an' he sint off the vistmints wid all his heart an' sowl an' as civil a letther, Tommy Freen says, for he hard the misthress readin' it, as ivir was pinned."

"Well, there was an alther, you see, got up in the big hall, jist bechune the two doors—if ivir you wor in it—ladin' into the store-room, an' the room the childher sleep in; and whin iviry thing was ready we all come in, an' the priest gev' us as good mass iviry taste as if we wor up at the chapel for it. The misthress an' all the family attinded thimsilves, an' they stud jist widinside o' the parlour-door; and it was raaly surprisin', Thady, to see how dacently they behaved thimsilves. If they wor all their lives goin' to chapel they cudn't have behaved thimsilves betther nor they did."

"Ay, Paddy, mavourneen; I'll be bail they didn't skit and laugh the way some people would be doin'."

"Laugh! not thimsilves, indeed. They'd more manners, if nothin' else, nor to do that. Well, to go an 'aid my story: whin the mass was ovir we whit sthrollin' about the lawn an' place tilt three o'clock come, an' thin you see the big bell rung out for dinner, an' may be it wasn't we that wor glad to hear it. So away wid us to the long barn where the dinner was laid out; an' 'pon my conscience, Thady Byrne, there's not one word o' lie in what I'm goin' to tell you; but at the sight o' so much vittles iviry taste uv appetite in the world lift me, an' I thought I'd ha' fainted down an the ground that was undher me. There was, you see, two rows o' long tables laid the whole linth o' the barn, an' table cloths spred upon iviry inch o' them; an' there was rounds o' beef, an' romps o' beef, an' ribs o' beef; both biled an' roast, an' there was ligs o' mootton, and han's o' pork, and pieces o' fine bacon, an' there was cabbage an' pratees to no ind, an'a knife an' fork laid for ivirybody; an' barrils o' beer an' porther, with the cocks in iviry one o' them, an' moogs an' porringirs in hapes. In all my born days, Thady dear, I nivir laid eyes on sich a load o' vittles."

"By the powers o' dilph! Paddy, ahaygar, an' it *was* a grand sight shure enough. Tare an' ayjirs! what ill loock I had not to be in the work this year! But go on, agra."

"Well, you see, the masther himself stud up at the ind uv one o' the tables, an' coot up a fine piece o' the beef for us; and right forenint him at the other ind, sot ould Paddy Byrne, for, though you know he is a farmer himself, yet the misthress is so fond uv him—he is sich a mighty dacint man—that she would by all manner o' manes hav' him there. Then the priest was at the head o' th' other table, an' said grace for us, an' thin fill to slashin' up another piece o' the beef for us: and forenint him sot Jim Murray the stchewart; an' shure enough, Thady, it was oursilves that played away in grand style at the beef an' the mootton, an' the cabbage, an' all th' other fine things. An' there was Tom Free; and all th' other sarvints waitin' upon us an' handin' us dhrink, jist as if we wor so many grand gintlemin that wor dinin' wid the masther. Well, you see, whin we wor about half doon, in walks the misthress hursilf, an' the young masther, an' the young ladies, an' the ladies from Dublin that 'a down on a visit wid the misthress, jist, as she said, to see that we wor happy and merry ovir our dinner; an' thin, Thady, you see, widout anybody sayin' a single word, we all stud up like one man, an' iviry man an' boy wid his full porringer o' porther in his hand dhrank long life an' success to the misthress and masther an' iviry one o' the family. I don't know for others, Thady, but for mysilf; I nivir said a prayer in all my life more from the heart; and a good right I had, shure, and iviry one that was there, too; for, to say nothin' o' the dinner, is there the likes uv her in the whole side o' the counthry for goodness to the poor, whethir they're sick or they're well. Wouldn't I mysilf. if it worn't but for her, be a lone an' desolate man this blissed day?"

"It's thrue for you, avick, for she brought Judy through it bet-ther nor any docther o' thim all."

"Well, to make a long story short, we et, an' we dhrank, an' we laughed, an' we talked, till we wor tirt, an' as soon as it grew dusk; we wor all called agin into the hail: an' there, you see, the mnisthress had got ovir Tim Connel, the blind piper, an' had sint for all the women that could come, an' the cook had tay for thim down below in the kitchen; an' they come up to the hail, an' there was chairs set round it for us all to sit upon, an' the misthress come out o' the parlour, an' 'Boys,' says she, 'I hope yez med a good dinnir, an' I 'ye bin thinkin' uv yez, you see, an' I 'ye got yez plinty o' partnirs, an' it's your own faults if yes don't spind a pleasint evinin'.' So wid that we set up another shout for the misthress, an' Tim sthruck up, an' the masther tuk out Nilly Mooney into the middle of the flure to dance a jig, and it was they that futted it nately. Thin the masther called out Dinny Moran, an' dhragged him up to one o' the Dublin young ladies, an' bid Dinny be stout an' ax her out to dance wid him. So Dinny, you see, though he was ashamed to make so free wid the lady, still he was afeard not to do as the masther bid him; so, by my conscience, he bowled up to her manfully, an' hild out the fist an' axed her out to dance wid him, an' she gev' him her hand in a crack, an' Dinny whipt her out into the middle o' the hail, forenint us all, an' pulled up his breeches an' called out to Tim to blow up 'The Rocks of Cashel' for thim. An' thin my jewil if you wor but to see thim! Dinny flingin' the jigs about as if they 'd fly from off him, an' the lady now here, now there, jist for all the world as if she was a spent, for not a taste o' n'ise did she make on the flure that ivir was hard; and Dinny callin' out to Tim to play it up fasther an' fasther, an' Tim almost workin' his elbow through the bag, till at last the lady was fairly tirt, an' Dinny thin clapt his hands an' up jumpt Piggy Reilly, an' she attacked him bouldly, an' danced down Dinny an' thin up got Johnny Regan an' put her down complately. An' sence the world was a world, I b'leeve there nivir was such dancin' seen."

"The sarra the doubt uv it, avick I 'm sartin'; they 're all o' thim sich rael fine dancers. An' only to think o' the lady dancin' wid the likes o' Dinny!"

"Well, you see, poor ould Paddy Byrne, whin he hears that the womin wor all to be there, in he goes into the parlor to the misthress, an' axes her if he might make so bould as to go home and fetch*his* woman.~So the misthress, you see, though you know Katty Byrne 's no great favourite wid hur, was glad ta obleege Paddy, an' so Katty Byrne was there too. An' thin ould Hugh Carr axt hur out to move a minnet wid him, an' there was Hugh, as stiff as if he dined on one o' the spits, wid his black wig an' his long brown coat, an' his blue stockin's, movin' about wid his hat in his hand, an' ladin' Katty about, an' lukin' so soft upon her; an' Katty, in her stiff mob-cap, wid the ears pinned down undher her chin, an' hum little black hat on the top uv her head; an' she at one corner curcheyin' to Hugh, an' Hugh at another bowin' to her, an' iviry body wundhenin' at thim, they moved it so iligantly."

"Troth, Paady, avourneen, that was well worth goin' a mile o' ground to see."

"Well, you see; whin the dancin' was ovir they tuk to the singin', an' Bill Carey gev' the 'Wounded Hussar,' an' the' Poor but Honest So'dger,' in sich style that yi'd have h'ard him up on the top o' Slee Roo; an' Dinny Moran an' ould Tom Freen gev' us the best songs they had, an' the priest sung the 'Cruiskeen Laun' for us gaily, an' one o' the young ladies played an' sung upon a thing widin in the parlor, like a table, that was purtier nor any pipes to listen to."

"An' didn't Bill giv' yes 'As down by Banns's Banks I sthrayed?' Shune that's one o' the best songs he has."

"An' that he did, till he med the very sates shake undher us; but a body can't remimber iviry thing, you know. Well, where was I? Oh, ay! You see, my dear, the poor little priest was all the night long goin' backwards an' forwards, iviry minit, bechune the parlor an' the hal; an' the sperits, you see, was lyin' opin on the sideboord, an' the dear little man he cudn't, for the life uv him, keep himself from it, so he kipt helpin' himself to a dhrop now an' a dhrop thin, till at last he got all as one as tipsy. So thin he comes out into the hall among us, an' goes about whispenin' to us to go home, an' not to be keepin' the family out o' their bids. But the misthress she saw what he was at, an' she stud up, an' she spoke out an' she said,' Good people,' sez she, 'nivir mind what the priest says to yez; yez are my company, an' not his, an' yes are heartily welcum to stay as long as yez like.' So whin he found he cud get no good uv us at all, he rowled off wid himself to his bid; an' his head, you see, was so bothered wid the liquor he'd bin taken', that he nivir once thought o' takin' off his boots, but tumbled into bed wid thim upon him, Tommy Freen tould us, whin he wint into the room to luk afther him; and divil be in Tim, when he h'ard it but he lilts up the 'Priest in his Boots;' and, God forgive us, we all burst out laughin', for shure who could hilp it, if it was the bishop himself?"

"Troth, it was a shame for yez, anyhow. But Paddy, agrah, did yez come away at all?"

"Why at last we did, afther another round o' the punch to the glory an' success o' the family. And now, Thady, comes the most surprisintest part o' the whole story. I was all alone, you see, for my woman, you know, cudn't lave the childher to come to the

dance; so, as it was a fine moonshiny night, nothim' 'ud sarve me but I must go out into the paddock, to luk afther poor Rainbow the plough bullock, that 's got a bad shouldher, and so by that manes, you see, I misst o' the cumpany, an' had to go home all alone by myself. Well, you see, it was out by the back gate I come, an' it was thin about twelve in the night, as well as I cud jidge by the Plough, an' the moon was shinin' as bright as a silver dish, and there wasn't a sound to be hard, barrin' the screechin' o' the ould owl down in the ivy-wall; an' I filt it all very pleasant, for I was sumhow rather hearty, you see, wid the dhrink I'd bin takin'; for you know, Thady Byrne, I'm a sober man."

"That's no lie for you, Paddy, avick. A little, as they say, goes a great way wid you."

"Well, you see, an I wint whistlin' to mysilf some o' the chunes they wor singin', and thinkin' uv any thin, shure, but the good people; whin jist as I come to the corner o the plantation, an' got a sight o' the big bush, I thought, faith, I seen sum things movin' backwards an' for'ards, an' dancin' like, up in the bush. I was quite sartin it was the fairies that, you know, resort to it, for I cud see, I thought, their little red caps an' green jackits quite plain. Well, I was thinkin', at first, o' goin' back an' gittin' home through the fields; but, says I to myself; says I, what sh'uld I be afeard uv? I'm an honest man that does nobody any harm; an' I h'ard mass this mornin'; an' it 's neither Holly eve nor St. John's eve, nor any other o' their great days, an' they can do me no harm, I 'm sartin. So I med the sign o' the crass, an' an I went in God's name, till I come right undher the bush; and what do you think they wor, Thady, afther all?"

"Arrah, how can I till? But you wor a stout man anyhow, Paddy, agrah!"

"Why, thin, what was it but the green laves o' the ould bush, an' the rid bunches o' the haves that war wavin' and shakin' in the moonlight. Well on I goes till I come to the cornir o' the Crab road, whin I happined to cast my eyes ovir tow'st the little moat in the Moatfield, an' there, by my sowl! (God forgive me for swaerin',) I seen the fairies in rael airnist."

"You did, thin, did you?"

"Ay, by my faith, did I, an' a mighty purty sight it was to see, too, I can tell you, Thady. The side o' the moat, you see, that luks into the field was opin, and out uv it there come the darlintest little calvacade o' the purtiest little fellows you ivir laid your eyes upon. They wor all dhrest in green huntin' frocks, wid nice little rid caps on their heads, an' they wor all mounted on purty little, long-tailed, white ponies, not so big as young kids, an they rode two and two so nicely. Well, you see, they tuk right acrass the field, jist abuv the san'pit, an' I was wundherin' in myself what they d do whim they come to the big ditch, thinkin' they 'd nivir get over it. But I'll tell you what it is, Thady. Misther Tom and the brown mare, though they. 're both o' thim gay good at either ditch or wall, they're not to be talked uv in the same day wid thim. They tuk the ditch, you see, big as it is, in full sthroke; not a man o' thim was shuk in his sate, nor lost his rank; it was pop, pop, pop, ovir wid thim; and thin, hurra, away wid them like shot acrass the High Field, in the direction o' the ould church. Well, my dear, while I was sthrainin' my eyes lukin' afther them, I hears a great rumblin' noise cumin' out o' the moat, an' whin I turned about to luk at it, what did I see but a great ould family coach-an'-six comin' out o' the moat, and makin' direct for the gate where I was stannin'. Well, says I, I 'in a lost man now, anyhow. There was no use at all, you see, in thinkin' to run for it, for they wor dhrivin' at the rate uv a hunt; so down I got into the gripe o' the ditch, thinkin' to snake off wid mysilf while they war op'nin' the gate. But, be the laws, the gate flew open widout a sowl layin' a finger to it, the very instant minuet they come up to it, an' they wheeled down the road jist close to the spot where I was hidin', an' I seen thin as plain as I now see you; an' a quare sight it was, too, to see; for not a morsel uv head that ivir was, was there upon one o' the horses, nor on the coachman neither, and yet, for all that, Thady, the Lord Lef'nint's coach cudn't ha' med a handier nor a shorter turn nor they med out o' the gate; an' the blind thief uv a coachman, jist as they wor ma-kin' the wheel, was near takin' the eye out o' me wid the lash uv his long whip, as he was cuttin' up the horses to show off his dhrivin'. I've my doubts that the schamer knew I was there well enough, and that he did it all a purpose. Well, as it passed by me, I peept in at the quolity widinside, an' not a head, no not as big as the head uv a pin, was there among the whole kit o' them, an' four fine futmin that war stannin' behind the coach war jist like the rest o' thim."

"Well, to be shure, but it *was* a quare sight."

"Well, away they wint tattherim' along the road, makin' the fire fly out o' the stones at no rate. So when I seen they 'd no eyes, I knew it was onpossible they could ivir see *me,* so up I got out o' the ditch, and afther them wid me along the road as fast as ivir I culd lay fut to ground. But whin I got to the rise o' the hill I seen they wor a great ways a-head o' me, an' they 'd taken to the fields, an' war makin' off for the ould church too. I thought they might have some business o' their own there, an' that it might not be safe for sthrangers to be goin' afther thim; so as I was by this time near my own house, I wint in and got quietly to bid, widout sayin' anyt'hing to the woman about it; an' long enough it was before I cud get to sleep for thinkin' o' them, an' that's the raison, Thady, I was up so late this mornin'. But wasn't it a sthrange thing, Thady?"

"Faith, an' shure it was, Paddy ahayger, as sthrange a thing as ivir was. But are you quite sartin an' shure that you seen thim?"

"Am I sartin an' shure I seen thim? Am I sartin an' shure I see the nose there on your face? What was to ail me not to see thim? Wasn't the moon shinin' as bright as day I An' didn't they pass widin a yard o' me? And did ivir any one see me dhrunk, or hear me tell a lie?"

"It 's thrue for you, Paddy, no one ivir did, and myself doesn't rightly know what to say to it?" [b]

NOTES

[a] As we have above given an etymon of *cobweb,* we will here repeat our note on the word *gossamer* in the Fairy Legends.

"Gossamers, Johnson says, are the long white cobwebs which fly in the air in calm sunny weather, and be derives the word from the Low Latin *gossapium.* This is altogether unsatisfactory. The gossamers are the cobwebs which may be seen, particularly of a still autumnal morning, in such numbers in the furze-bushes, and which are raised by the wind and floated through the air, as thus exquisitely pictured by Browne in his Britannia's Pastorals (ii. 2),

The milk-white gossamers not upwards snowed.

Every lover of nature must have observed and admired the beautiful appearance of the gossamers in the early morning, when covered with dew-drops, which, like prisms, separate the rays of light, and shoot the blue, red, yellow, and other colours of the *spectrum,* in brilliant confusion. Of King Oberon we are told—

A fiche mantle be did wear,

Made of tinsel gossamer,

Bestrew'd over with a few

Diamond drops of morning dew.

A much wore probable origin of *gossamer* than that proposed by Johnson is suggested by what baa been now stated. *Gossamer is,* we think, a corruption of *gorse,* or *gois samyt,* i. e. the samyt, or finely-woven silken web that lies on the *gorse* or furze. Voss, in a note on his Luise (iii. 17), says that the popular belief in Germany is, that the gossamers are woven by the Dwarfs.

[b] In the notes on this story Mr. Croker gives the following letter:—

"The accuracy of the following story I can vouch for, having heard it told several times by the person who saw the circumstances.

"About twenty years back, William Cody, churn-boy to a person near Cork, had, after finishing his day's work, to go through six or eight fields to his own house, about twelve o'clock at night. He was passing alongside of the ditch of a large field, and coming near a quarry, he heard a great cracking of whips on the other side. He went on to a gap in the same ditch, and out rode a little horseman, dressed in green, and mounted in the best manner, who put a whip to his breast, and made him stop until several hundred horsemen, all dressed alike, rode out of the gap at full speed, and swept round a glen. When the last horseman was clear off, the sentinel clapt spurs to his horse, gave three cracks of his whip, and was out of sight in a second.

"The person would swear to the truth of the above, as he was quite sober and sensible at the time. The place had always before the name of being very airy [the Scottish *eirie*]. *"Royal Cork Institution,* P. BATH. *June* 3, 1825."

The Young Piper

There was livin', it's not very long ago, on the borders o' the county Wicklow, a dacint honest couple, whose names wor Mick Flanagan and Judy Muldoon. These poor people wor blist, as the saying is, wid four childher, all buys: three o' them wor as fine, stout, healthy, goodlukin' childher as ivir the sun shone upon; an' it was enough to make any Irishman proud of the breed of his counthrymen to see thim about one o'clock on a find summer's day stannin' at their father's cabin-door, wid their beautiful, fine flaxen hair hangin' in curls about their heads, an' their cheeks like two rosy apples, an' a big, laughin' potato, smokin' in their hand. A proud man was Mick, o' these fine childher, an' a proud woman, too, was Judy; an' raison enough they had to be so. But it was far otherwise wid the remainin' one, which was the ouldest; he was the most miserable, ugly, ill-conditioned brat that ivir God put life into: he was so ill thriven, that he was nivir able to stand alone or to lave his cradle; he had long, shaggy, matted, curly hair, as black as the sut; his face was uv a greenish yollow colour; his eyes wor like two burnin' coals, an' wor for ever movin' in his head, as if they had the parpaitual motion. Before he was a twel'month ould he had a mouth full o' great teeth; his hands wor like kite's claws, and his legs wor no thicker nor the handle of a whip, and about as straight as a rapin' hook; to make the matther worse, he had the gut uv a cormorant, and the whinge, and the yelp, and the screech, and the yowl, was never out of his mouth.

The neighbours all suspicted that he was somethin' not right, more especialy as it was obsarved, that whin people, as they use to do in the counthry, got about the fire, and begun to talk o' religion and good things, the brat, as he lay in the cradle which his mother ginerally put near the fireplace that he might be snug, used to sit up, as they wor in the middle of their talk, and begin to bellow as if the devil was in him in right airnest: this, as I said, led the neighbours to think that all wasn't right wid him, an' there was a gineral consultashion held one day, about what id be best to do wid him. Some advised to put him out an the shovel, but Judy's pride was up at that. A purty thing, indeed, that a child of her's shud be put an a shovel, an' flung out on the dunghill jist like a dead kitten or a pisoned rat; no, no, she wouldn't hear to that at all. One ould woman, who was considhered mighty skilful an' knowin' intirely in fairy matthers sthrongly recomminded to put the tongs in the fire, an' to hate thim rid hot, an' thin to take his nose in thim, an' that that id, beyant all manner o' doubt, make him tell what he was, an' whare he come from (for the gineral supishion was, that he was changed by the good people); but Judy was too saft-harted, an' too fond o' the imp, so she wouldn't giv' into this plan neither, though iverybody said she was wrong; and may be so she was, but it's a hard thing, you know, to blame a mother. Well some advised one thing and some another, at last one spoke of sindin fur the priest, who was a very holy an' a very larned man, to see it; to this Judy uv coorse had no objection, but one thing or another always purvinted her doing so, an' the upshot o' the business was that the priest niver seen him at all. Well, things wint on in the ould way for some time longer. The brat continued yelpin' an' yowlin', an' aitin' more nor his three brothers put together, an' playin' all sorts uv unlucky thricks, for he was mighty mischievyously inclined, till it happened one day that Tim Carrol, the blind piper, goin' his rounds, called in and sot down by the fire to hav' a bit o' chat wid the woman o' the house. So afther some time, Tim, who was no churl uv his music, yoked an the pipes an' begun to bellows away in high style; whin the instant minnit he begun, the young fellow, who was lyin' as still as a mouse in his cradle, sot up, an begun to grin an' to twist his ugly phiz, an' to swing about his long tawny arms, an' to kick out his cracked legs, an' to show signs o' grate glee at the music. At last nothin' id sarve him but he must git the pipes into his own hands, an', to humour him, his mother axt Tim to lind thim to the child for a minnit. Tim, who was kind to childher, readily consinted; and, as Tim hadn't his sight, Judy herself brought thim to the cradle, an' wint to put thim an him, but she had no need, for the youth seemed quite up to the business. He buckled an the pipes, set the bellows undher one arm and the bag undher th' other, an' worked thim both as knowingly as iv he was twinty years at the thrade, an' lilted up "Sheela na Guira," in the finest style that iver was hard.

Well, all was in amazemint; the poor woman crast herself: Tim, who, as I tould you afore, was dark an' didn't well know who was playin,' was in grate delight; an' whin he hard that it was a littleprechaun, [an abridgment of Leprechaun] not aight years ould, that nivir seen a set of pipes in all his days afore, he wished the mother joy iv her son; offered to take him aff her han's iv she'd part wid him, swore he was a born piper, a nath'ral jainses, an' declared that in a little time more, wid the help uv a little good tachein' frum himsilf there wouldn't be his match in the whole counthry round. The poor woman was grately delighted to hear all this, particklarly as what Tim sed about nathral jainises put an ind to some misgivin's that war risin' in hur mind, laist what the naybours sed about his not bein' right might be only too thrue; an' it gratified hur too to think that her dear child (for she raely loved the whelp) wouldn't be forced to turn out an' big, but might airn dacent, honest bread fur himsilf. So whin Mick come home in the evenin' frum his work, she up an' she tould him all that happined, an' all that Tim Carrol sed; an Mick, as was nath'ral, was very glad to hear it, for the helpless condition o' the poor crather was a grate throuble to him; so nixt fair-day he tuk the pig to the fair of Naas, and wid what it brought he whipt up, the nixt holiday that come, to Dublin, an' bespoke a bran new set o' pipes o' the proper size fur him, an' the nixt time Tom Doolan whit up wid the cars, in about a fortnight after, the pipes come home, an' the minnit the chap in the cradle laid eyes on thim, he squealed wid delight, an' threw up his purty legs, an' bumped himsilf in his cradle, an' wint an wid a grate many comical thricks; till at last, to quite him, they gev him the pipes, an' immajetly he set to an' pulled away at "Jig Polthog," to th' admirashin uv all that hard him.

Well, the fame uv his skill an the pipes soon spread far an' near, for there wasn't a piper in the nixt three counties cud come near him at all, in Ould Maudha Roo, or the Hare in the Corn, or The Fox Hunther's Jig, or The Piper's Maggot, or any uv the fine ould Irish jigs, that make people dance whether they will or no: an' it was surprisin' to hear him rattle away The Fox Hunt; you'd raaly think you hard the hounds givin' tongue, an' the terriers yelpin' always behind, an' the huntsman an' the whippers-in cheerin' or correctin' the dogs; it was, in short, the very nixt thing to seein' the hunt itself.

The best uv him was, he was no way stingy uv his music, an' many's the merry dance the boys an' the girls o' the neighbourhood used to hav' in his father's cabin; an' he 'd play up music fur thim that, they sed, used, as it wor, to put quicksilver in their feet; an' they all declared they nivir moved so light an' so airy to any piper's playin' that ivir they danced to.

But besides all his fine Irish music, he had one quare chune uv his own, the oddest that iver was hard; fur the minnit he begun to play it iverything in the house seemed disposed to dance; the plates an' porringers used to jingle an the dhresser, the pots an' pot-hooks used to rattle in the chimbley, an' people used even to fancy they felt the stools movin' frum undher thim; but, how—iver it might be wid the stools, it is sartin that no one cud keep long sittin' an them, fur both ould and young always fell to caperin' as hard as ivir they cud. The girls complained that whin he begun this chime it always threw thim out in their dancin', an' that they nivir cud handle their feet rightly, fur they felt the flure like ice undher thim, an' thimsilves ready iviry minnit to come sprawlin' an their backs or their faces; the young bachelors that wanted to show aff their dancin' an' their new pumps, an' their bright red or green an' yellow garthers, swore that it confused thim so that they cud nivir go rightly through the heel-and-toe, or cover-the-buckle, or any nv their best steps, but felt thimsilves always bedizzied an' bewildhered, an' thin ould an' young id go jostlin' an' knockin' together in a frightful manner an' whin the anlooky brat had thim all in this way whirligiggin' about the flure, he'd grin an' he 'd chuckle an' he 'd chather, jist fur all the world like Jocko, the monkey, whin he 'a played off sum uv his roguery.

The oulder he grew the worse he grew, an' by the time he was noine year ould there was no stannin' the house for him; he was always makin' his brothers burn or scald thimsilves, or brake their shins ovir the pots an' stools. One time in harvist, he was left at home by himself; an' whin his mother come in she found the cat a horseback on the dog wid hur face to the tail, an' hur legs tied round him, an' the urchin playin' his quare chune to thim, so that the dog wint barking an jumpin' about, an' puss was miowin' fur the dear life, an' slappin' her tail backwards an' forwards, which whin it id hit agin the dog's chaps, he'd snap at it an' bite it, an' thin there was the philhiloo. Another time the farmer Mick worked wid, a mighty dacint kind uv a man, happened to call in, an' Judy wiped a stool wid her apron an' axed him to sit down an rest himself afther his walk. He was sittin' wid his back to the cradle, an' behind him was a pan o' blood, fur Judy was makin' hog's puddin's; the lad lay quite still in his nist, an' watched his opportunity till he got ready a hook at the hid uv a piece o' packthread an' he conthrived to fling it so handy that it cotcht in the bob o' the man's nice new wig, an' soused it in the pan o' blood. Another time his mother was comin' in from milkin' the cow, wid the pail an her head, an' the very minnit he saw her, he lilted up his infernal chune, an' the poor woman lettin' go the pail, clapped her hands aside an' begun to dance a jig, an' tumbled the milk all atop uv her husband, who was bringin' in some turf to bile the supper. In short there id be no ind to tellin' all his pranks, an' all the mischievyous tricks he played.

Soon afther, some mischances begun to happen to the farmer's cattle; a horse tuk the staggers, a fine vale calf died o' the blacklig, an' some uv his sheep o' the rid wather; the cows begun to grow vicious, an' to kick down the milkpails, an' the roof o' one hid o' the barn fell in; an' the farmer tuk it into his head that Mick Flannagan's onlooky child was the cause uv all the mischief. So, one day, he called Mick aside, an' sed to him, "Mick," sez he, "you see things are not goin' on wid me as they ought to go; an' to be plain an' honest wid you, Mick, I think that child o' yours is the cause uv it. I am raaly fallin' away to nothin', wid frettin', an' I can hardly sleep an my bed at night for thinkin' o' what may happen afore the mornin'. So I 'd be glad af you'd luk out fur work somewhare else; you 're as good a man as any in the whole counthry, there 'a no denyin' it, an' there's no fear but you'll have yer choice o' work." To this Mick med answer, and sed, "that he was sorry indeed for his losses, and still sorrier that he or his shud be thought to be the cause o' thim; that, for his own part, he wasn't quite aisy in his mind about that child, but he had him, an' so he must keep him;" an' he promised to luk out fur another place immajetly.

So nixt Sunday at chapil, Mick gev out that he was about lavin' the work at John Riordan's, an' immajetly a farmer, who lived a couple o' miles aff, an' who wanted a ploughman (the last one havin' jist left him), come up to Mick, an' offered him a house an' garden, an' work all the year round. Mick, who knew him to be a good employer, immajetly closed wid him. So it was agreed that the farmer shud sind his car to take his little bit o' furniture, an' that he shud remove an the following Thursday.

Whin Thursday come, the car come accordin' to promise, an' Mick loaded it, an' put the cradle wid the child an' his pipes an the top, an' Judy sat beside it to take care uv him, laste he shud tumble out an' be kilt; they dray the cow afore thim, the dog folled; but the cat, uv course, was lift behind: an' the other three childer wint along the road, pickin' haves and blackberries; for it was a fine day towst the latther ind uv harvist. They had to crass a river; but as it run through the bottom between two high banks, you didn't see it till you wor close up an it. The young fellow was lyin' purty quite in the bottom o' the cradle, till they come to the head o' the bridge, whin hearin' the roarin' o' the wather (for there was a grate flood in the river, as there was heavy rain for the last two or three days), he sot up in his cradle, an' luked about him; an' the minnit he got a sight ov the wather, an' found they wor goin' to take him acrass it, oh! how he did bellow, an' how he did squeal. "Whisht, alanna," sed Judy, "there 'a no fear o' yer; shure it 'a only ovir the stone bridge we 're goin'." "Bad luck to yer, ye ould rip," sez he, "what a purty thrick yuv played me, to bring me here;" an' he still wint an yellin', and the farther they got an the bridge, the loudher he yelled; till at last Mick cud hould out no longer; so givin' him a skelp o' the whip he had in his han', "Divil choke you, you crukked brat," sez he; "will you nivir stop bawlin'? a body can't hear their ears for you." Well, my dear, the instant minnit he felt the thong o' the whip, he jumped up in the cradle, clapped the pipes undher his arm, an' lept dane ovir the battlemints o' the bridge down into the wather. "Oh, my child! my child!" shouted Judy; "he's dane gone for ivir frum me." Mick an' the rest o' the childher 'run to the other side o' the bridge an' lukt down, an' they seen him comin' out from undher the arch o' the bridge, sittin crass-liggs an the top uv a big white-headed wave, an' playin' away an the pipes, jist as if nothin' had happened at all. The river was runnin very hard, so he was whirled away at a grate rate; but he played away as fast, ay, and faster nor the river run. They set aff as hard as they cud along the bank; but as the river med a suddint turn round the hill, about a hundred yards below the bridge, by the time they got there he was out o' sight, an' no one ivir led eyes an him sence; but the gineral belief is, that he wint home wid the pipes to his own relations—the good people—to make music fur thim.

The Soul Cages

Jack Dogherty lived on the coast of the county Clare. Jack was a fisherman, as his father and his grandfather before him had been. Like them, too, he lived all alone (but for the wife), and just in the same spot, too. People used to wonder why the Dogherty family were so fond of that wild situation, so far away from all human kind, and in the midst of huge scattered rocks, with nothing but the wide ocean to look upon. But they had their own good reasons for it.

The place was just, in short, the only spot on that part of the coast where anybody could well live; there was a neat little creek, where a boat might lie as snug as a puffin in her nest, and out from this creek a ledge of sunken rocks ran into the sea. Now, when the Atlantic, according to custom, was raging with a storm, and a good westerly wind was blowing strong on the coast, many's the richly-laden ship that went to pieces on these rocks; and then the fine bales of cotton and tobacco, and such like things; and the pipes of wine, and the puncheons of rum, and the casks of brandy, and the kegs of Hollands that used to come ashore. Why, bless you! Dunbeg Bay was just like a little estate to the Dohertys.

Not but that they were kind and humane to a distressed sailor, if ever one had the good luck to get to land; and many a time, indeed, did Jack put out in his little *corragh,* that would breast the billows like any gannet, to lend a hand towards bringing off the crew from a wreck. Bat when the ship was gone to pieces, and the crew were all lost, who would blame Jack for *picking* up all he could find? "And who's the worse of it?" said he. "For as to the king, God bless him!

everybody knows he 'a rich enough already, without gettin' what 'a floatin' in the say."

Jack, though such a hermit, was a good-natured, jolly fellow. No other, sure, could ever have coaxed Biddy Mahony to quit her father's snug and warm house in the middle of the town of Ennis, and to go so many miles off to live among the rocks, with the seals and sea-gulls for her next door neighbours. But Biddy knew what's what, and she knew that Jack was the man for a woman who wished to be comfortable and happy; for, to say nothing of the fish, Jack had the supplying of half the gentlemen's houses of the country with the Godsends that came into the bay. And she was right in her choice, for no woman ate, drank, or slept better, or made a prouder appearance at Chapel on Sundays than Mrs. Dogherty.

Many a strange sight, it may well be supposed, did Jack see, and many a strange sound did he hear, but nothing daunted him. So far was he from being afraid of Merrows, or such like beings, that the very first wish of his heart was fairly to meet with one. Jack had heard that they were mighty like Christians, and that luck had always come out of an acquaintance with them. Never, therefore, did he dimly discern the Merrows moving along the face of the waters in their robes of mist, but he made direct for them; and many a scolding did Biddy, in her own quiet way, bestow upon Jack for spending his whole day out at sea, and bringing home no fish. Little did poor Biddy know the fish Jack was after.

It was rather annoying to Jack that, though living in a place where the Merrows were as plenty as lobsters, he never could get a right view of one. What vexed him more was, that both his father and grandfather had often and often seen them; and he even remembered hearing, when a child, how his grandfather, who was the first of the family that had settled down at the Creek, had been so intimate with a Merrow, that, only for fear of vexing the priest, he would have had him stand for one of his children. This, however, Jack did not well know how to believe.

Fortune at length began to think that it was only right that Jack should know as much as his father and grandfather knew. Accordingly, one day, when he had strolled a little farther than usual along the coast to the northward, just as he was turning a point, he saw something, like to nothing he had ever seen before, perched upon a rock at a little distance out to sea: it looked green in the body, as well as he could discern at that distance, and he would have sworn, only the thing was impossible, that it had a cocked hat in his hand. Jack stood, for a good half hour, straining his eyes and wondering at it, and all the time the thing did not stir hand or foot. At last Jack's patience was quite worn out, and he gave a loud whistle and a hail, when the Merrow (for such it was) started up, put the cocked hat on its head, and dived down, head foremost, from the rock.

Jack's curiosity was now excited, and he constantly directed his steps toward the point; still he could never get a glimpse of the sea-gentleman with the cocked hat; and with thinking and thinking about the matter, he began at last to fancy he had been only dreaming. One very rough day, however, when the sea was running mountains high, Jack determined to give a look at the Merrow's rock, (for he had always chosen a fine day before,) and then he saw the strange thing cutting capers upon the top of the rock, and then diving down, and then coming up, and then diving down again. Jack had now only to choose his time, (that is, a good blowing day,) and he might see the man of the sea as often as he pleased. All this, however, did not satisfy him,—"much will have more;"—he wished now to get acquainted with the Merrow, and even in this he succeeded. One tremendous blustery day, before he got to the point whence he had a- view of the Merrow's rock, the storm came on so furiously that Jack was obliged to take shelter in one of the caves which are so numerous along the coast, and there, to his astonishment, he saw, sitting before him, a thing with green hair, long green teeth, a red nose, and pig's eyes. It had a fish's tail, legs with scales on them, and short arms like fins. It wore no clothes, but had the cocked hat under its arm, and seemed engaged thinking very seriously about something. Jack, with all his courage, was a little daunted; but now or never, thought he; so up he went boldly to the cogitating fish-man, took off his hat, and made his best bow.

"Your sarvint, sir," said Jack.—"Your servant, kindly, Jack Dogherty," answered the Merrow.—"To be shure, thin, how well your honour knows my name," said Jack.—"Is it I not know your name, Jack Dogherty? Why, man, I knew your grandfather long before he was married to Judy Began, your grandmother. Ah, Jack, Jack, I was fond of that grandfather of yours; he was a mighty worthy man in his time. I never met his match above or below, before or since, for sucking in a shellful of brandy. I hope, my boy," said the old fellow, "I hope you 're his own grandson."—"Never fear me for that," said Jack; "if my mother only reared me on brandy, 'tis myself that 'ud be a suckin infant to this hour."—"Well, I like to hear you talk so manly; you and I must be better acquainted, if it were only for your grandfather's sake. But, Jack, that father of yours was not the thing; he had no head at all, not he."—"I'm shure," said Jack, "sense your honour lives down undher the wather, you must be obleeged to dhrink a power to keep any hate in you, at all at all, in such a cruel, damp, cowld place. Well, I often hard of Christhens dhrinkin' like fishes;—and might I be so bould as to ax where you get the sperits?"—"Where do you get them yourself Jack?" said the Merrow, with a knowing look.—"Hubbub-boo," cries Jack, "now I see how it is; but I suppose, sir, your honour has got a fine dhry cellar below to keep them in."—"Let me alone for that," said the Merrow, with another knowing look.—"I'm shure," continued Jack, "it must be mighty well worth the luking at."—"You may say that, Jack, with your own pretty mouth," said the Merrow; "and if you meet me here next Monday, just at this time of the day, we will have a little more talk with one another about the matter."

Jack and the Merrow parted the beat friends in the world; and on Monday they met, and Jack was not a little surprised to see that the Merrow had two cocked hats with him, one under each arm. "Might I make so bould as to ask you, sir," said Jack, "why yer honour brought the two hats wid you to-day? You wouldn't, shure, be goin' to giv' me one o' them, to keep for the curosity of the thing?"—"No, no, Jack," said he, "I don't get my hats so easily, to part with them that way; but I want you to come down and eat a bit of dinner with me, and I brought you the hat to dive with."—"The Lord bless and presarve us cried Jack, in amazement, "would you want me to go down to the bottom of the salt say ocean? Shure I'd be smoothered and choked up wid the wather, to say nothin' of bein' dhrownded! And what would poor Biddy do for me, and what would she say?"—"And what matter what she says, you pinkeen you? Who cares for Biddy's squalling? It 'a long before your grandfather would have talked in that way. Many's the time he stuck that same hat on his head, and dived down boldly after me, and many's the snug bit of dinner, and good shellful of brandy, he and I had together, below under the water."—"Is it really, sir, and no joke?" said Jack; "why, thin, sorra' be from me for ivir and a day afther, if I'll be a bit a worse man nor my grandfather was! So here goes; but play me fair now. Here 's nick or nothin'!" cried Jack.—"That 's your grandfather all over," said the old fellow. "So come along, my boy, and do as I do."

They both left the cave, walked into the sea, and then swam a piece until they got to the rock. The Merrow climbed to the top of it, and Jack followed him, On the far side it was as straight as the wall of a house, and the sea looked so deep that Jack was almost cowed.

"Now, do you see, Jack," said the Merrow, "just put this hat on your head, and mind to keep your eyes wide open. Take hold of my tail, and follow after me, and you'll see what you'll see." In he dashed, and in dashed Jack after him boldly. They went and they went, and Jack thought they'd never stop going. Many a time did he wish himself sitting at home by the fireside with Biddy: yet, where was the use of wishing now, when he was so many miles as he thought below the waves of the Atlantic? Still he held hard by the Merrow's tail, slippery as it was. And, at last, to Jack's great surprise, they got out of the water, and he actually found himself on dry land at the bottom of the sea. They landed just in front of a nice little house that was slated very neatly with oyster-shells; and the Merrow, turning about to Jack, welcomed him down. Jack could hardly speak, what with wonder, and what with being out of breath with travelling so fast through the water. He looked about him, and could see no living things, barring crabs and lobsters, of which there were plenty walking leisurely about on the sand. Overhead was the sea like a sky, and the fishes like birds swimming about in it.

"Why don't you speak, man?" said the Merrow: "I dare say you had no notion that I had such a snug little concern as this? Are you smothered, or choked, or drowned, or are you fretting after Biddy, eh?" "Oh! not mysilf indeed," said Jack, showing his teeth with a good-humoured grin, "but who in the world 'ud ivir ha' thought uv seem' sich a thing?" "Well, come along my lad, and let's see what they've got for us to eat?"

Jack was really hungry, and it gave him no small pleasure to perceive a fine column of smoke rising from the chimney, announcing what was going on within. Into the house he followed the Merrow, and there he saw a good kitchen, right well provided with everything. There was a noble dresser, and plenty of pots and pans, with two young Merrows cooking. His host then led him into the *room,* which was furnished shabbily enough. Not a table or a chair was there in it; nothing but planks and logs of wood to sit on, and eat off. There was, however, a good fire blazing on the hearth—a comfortable sight to Jack. "Come, now, and I 'll show you where I keep—you know what," said the Merrow, with a sly look; and opening a little door, he led Jack into a fine long cellar, well filled with pipes, and kegs, and hogsheads, and barrels. "What do you say to that, Jack Dogherty?—Eh!—May-be a body can't live snug down under the water!" "The divil the doubt of that," said Jack, "anyhow."

They went back to the room, and found dinner laid. There was no table-cloth, to be sure—but what matter? It was not always Jack had one at home. The dinner would have been no discredit to the first house in the county on a fast-day. The choicest of fish, and no wonder, was there. Turbots, and soles, and lobsters, and oysters, and twenty other—kinds, were on the planks at once, and plenty of foreign spirits. The wines, the old fellow said, were too cold for his stomach. Jack ate and drank till he could eat no more: then, taking up a shell of brandy, "Here's to your honour's good health, sir," said he, "though beggin' your pardon, its mighty odd, that as long as we're acquainted, I don't know, your name yit." "That 's true, Jack," replied he; "I never thought of it before, but better late than never. My name is Coomara." "Coomara! And a mighty dacint sort of a name it is, too," cried Jack, taking another shellful: "here 's, then, to your good health, Coomara, and may you live these fifty years." "Fifty years!" repeated Coomara; "I 'm obliged to you, indeed; if you had said five hundred, it would have been something worth wishing." "By the laws, sir," said Jack, "yez live to a powerful great age here undlier the wather! Ye knew my grandfather, and he 'a dead and gone betther nor sixty years. I 'm shure it must be a mighty healthy place to live in." "No doubt of it; but come, Jack, keep the liquor stirring."

Shell after shell did they empty, and to Jack's exceeding surprise, he found the drink never got into his head, owing, I suppose, to the sea being over them, which kept their noddles cool. Old Coomara got exceedingly comfortable, and sang several songs; but Jack, if his life had depended on it, never could remember any of them. At length said he to Jack, "Now, my dear boy, if you follow me, I 'll show you my curiosities!" He opened a little door, and led Jack into a large room, where Jack saw a great many odds and ends that Coomara had picked up at one time or another. What chiefly took his attention, however, were things like lobster-pots, ranged on the ground along the wall.

"Well, Jack, how do you like my curiosities?" said old Coo. "Upon my sowkins, sir," said Jack, "they 're mighty well worth the lukin' at; but might a body make so bould as to ax what thim things like lobster-pots are?" "Oh, the soul-cages, is it?" "The what, sir?" "These things here that I keep the souls in." "Arrah! what sowls, sir? " said Jack in amazement: "shure the fish ha' got no sowls in them?" "Oh, no," replied Coo, quite coolly, "that they haven't; but these are the souls of drowned sailors." "The Lord presarve us from all harm!" muttered Jack," how in the world did you conthrive to get thim?" "Easily enough. I've only when I see a good storm coming on, to set a couple of dozen of these, and then, when the sailors are drowned, and the souls get out of them under the water, the poor things are almost perished to death, not being used to the cold; so they make into my pots for shelter, and then I have them snug, and fetch them home, and keep them here dry and warm; and is it not well for them, poor souls, to get into such good quarters?"

Jack was so thunderstruck he did not know what to say, so he said nothing. They went back into the dining-room, and had some more brandy, which was excellent, and then, as Jack knew that it must be getting late, and as Biddy might be uneasy, he stood up, and said he thought it was time for him to be on the road.

"Just as you like, Jack," said Coo, "but take a *doch an durrus* before you go; you've a cold journey before you." Jack knew better manners than to refuse the parting glass. "I wondher" said he, "will I ivir be able to make out my way home." "What should all you," said Coo, "when I show you the way?" Out they went before the house, and Coomara took one of the cocked hats, and put it on Jack's head the wrong way, and then lifted him up on his shoulder that he might launch him up into the water. "Now," says he, giving him a heave, "you 'll come up just in the same spot yon came down in; and, Jack, mind and throw me back the hat." He canted Jack off his shoulder, and up he shot like a bubble—whirr, whirr, whiz—away he went up through the water, till he came to the very rock he had jumped off where he found a landing-place, and then in he threw the hat, which sunk like a stone.

The sun was just going down in the beautiful sky of a calm summer's evening. The evening star was seen brightly twinkling in the cloudless heaven, and the waves of the Atlantic flashed in a golden flood of light. So Jack, perceiving it was getting late, set off home; but when he got there, not a word did he say to Biddy of where he had spent his day.

The state of the poor souls cooped up in the lobster-pots, gave Jack a great deal of trouble, and how to release them cost him a great deal of thought. He at first had a mind to speak to the priest about the matter; but what could the priest do, and what did Coo care for the priest? Besides, Coo was a good sort of an old fellow, and did not think he was doing any harm. Jack had a regard for him too, and it also might not be much to his own credit if it were known that he used to go dine with the Merrows under the sea. On the whole, he thought his best plan would be to ask Coo to dinner, and to make him drunk, if he was able, and then to take the hat and go down and turn up the pots. It was first of all necessary, however, to get Biddy out of the way; for Jack was prudent enough, as she was a woman, to wish to keep the thing secret from her.

Accordingly, Jack grew mighty pious all of a sudden, and said to Biddy, that he thought it would be for the good of both their souls if she was to go and take her rounds at Saint John's Well, near Ennis. Biddy thought so too, and accordingly off she set one fine morning at day dawn, giving Jack a strict charge to have an eye to the place. The coast being clear, away then went Jack to the rock to give the appointed signal to Coomara, which was, throwing a big stone into the water; Jack threw, and up sprang Coo. "Good morrow, Jack," said he; "what do you want with me?" "Jist nothin' at all to spake about, sir," replied Jack; "only to come and take pot-luck wid me, now that Biddy's out of the way; if I might make so free as to ax you, an' shure it 's myself that's afther doin' so." "It's quite agreeable, Jack, I assure you; what 's your hour?" "Any time that 's most convanient to yoursilf, sir: say one o'clock, that you may go home, if you wish it, wid the daylight." "I'll be with you," said Coo, "never fear me."

Jack went home and dressed a noble fish dinner, and got out plenty of his best foreign spirits, enough for that matter to make twenty men drunk. Just to the minute came Coo, with his cocked hat under his arm. Dinner was ready; they sat down, and ate and drank manfully. Jack thinking of the poor souls below in the pots, plied old Coo well with brandy, and encouraged him to sing, hoping to put him under the table, but poor Jack forgot that he had not the sea over his own head now to keep it cool. The brandy got into it and did his business for him, and Coo reeled off home, leaving his entertainer as dumb as a haddock on a Good Friday.

Jack never woke till the next morning, and then he was in a sad way. "Tis no use at all for me thinkin' to make that ould Rapperee dhrunk," said Jack; "an' how in this world can I help the poor sowis out o' the lobster pots." After ruminatin nearly the whole day, a thought struck him. "I have it," said he, slapping his thigh; "I'll be bail Coo nivir saw a dhrop o' raal potyeen as ould as he is, an' that's the thing to settle him! Och! thin isn't it well that Biddy won't be home these two days yit; I can have another twist at him." Jack asked Coo again, and Coo laughed at him for having no better head; telling him, he 'd never come up to his grandfather. "Well, but thry me agin," said Jack, "and I'll be bail to dhrink you dhrunk and sober and dhrunk agin."—"Any thing in my power," said Coo, "to oblige you."

All this dinner, Jack took care to have his own liquor watered, and to give the strongest brandy he had to Coo. At last, says he, "Pray, sir, did you ivir dhrink any potyeen? any raal mountain-jew-?"—"No," says Coo; what 's that, and where does it come from?"— "Oh! that 's a sacret," said Jack, "but it 'a the right stuff; nivir believe me agin if it isn't fifty times better nor brandy or rum either. Biddy's brother jist sint me a present of a little dhrop, in exchange for some brandy and as you're an ould frind o' the family, I kep it to thrate you wid."—"Well, let 'a see what sort of thing it is," said Coo.

The potyeen was the right sort, it was first-rate, and had the real smack on it. Coo was delighted with it; he drank and he sang, and he laughed and he danced, till he fell on the floor fast asleep.

Then Jack, who had taken good care to keep himself sober, snapt up the cocked hat, ran off to the rock, leaped in, and soon arrived at Coo's habitation.

All was as still as a churchyard at midnight—not a Merrow young or old, was there. In he went and turned up the pots, but nothing did he see, only he heard, he thought, a sort of a little whistle or chirp as he raised each of them. At this he was surprised, till he recollected what the priest had often said. that nobody living could see the soul, no more than they could see the wind or the air. Having now done all he could do for them he set the pots as they were before, and sent a blessing after the poor souls to speed them on their journey wherever they were going. He now began to think of returning; he put on the hat (as was right,) the wrong way; but 'when he got out, he found the water so high over his head that he had no hopes of ever getting up into it now that he had not old Coomara to give him a lift. He walked about looking for a ladder, but not one could he find, and not a rock was there in sight. At last he saw a spot where the sea hung rather lower than anywhere else, so he resolved to try there. Just as he came to it, a big cod happened to put down his tail. Jack made a jump and caught hold of it, and the cod, all in amazement, gave a bounce and pulled Jack up. The minute the hat touched the water, pop away Jack was whisked; and up he shot like a cork, dragging the poor cod, that he forgot to let go, up with him tail foremost. He got to the rock in no time, and without a moment's delay hurried home rejoicing in the good deed he had done. But, meanwhile, there was fine work at home; for our friend Jack had hardly left the house on his soul-freeing expedition, when back came Biddy from her soul-saving one to the well. When she entered the house and saw the things lying *thrie-na heelah* on the table before her—"Here 's a purty job," said she, "that blackguard of mine—what ill luck I had ivir to marry him—he's picked up some vagabone or other, while I was prayin' for the good of his sowl; and they've bin dhrinkin' up all the potyeen that my own brother gev' him, and all the sperits, to be shure, that he was to have sould to his honour." Then hearing an outlandish kind of grunt, she looked down and saw Coomara lying under the table. "The blessed Vargin help an' save me," shouted she, "if he hasn't made a rael baste of himself. Well, well, well to be shure, I often hard till of a man makin' a baste of himself wid dhrink, but I niver saw it afore! Oh hone, oh hone,—. Jack, honey, what 'ill I do wid you, or what 'ill I do widout you? How can any dacint woman ivir think of livin' wid a baste?"

With such like lamentations, Biddy rushed out of the house and was going, she knew not where, when she heard the well known voice of Jack, singing a merry tune. Glad enough was Biddy to find him safe and sound, and not turned into a thing that was like neither fish nor flesh. Jack was obliged to tell her all; and Biddy, though she had half a mind to be angry with him for not telling her before, owned that he had done a great service to the poor souls. Back they both went most lovingly to the house, and Jack wakened up Coomara; and perceiving the old fellow to be rather dull, he bid him not be cast down, for 'twas many a good man's case; said it all came of his not being used to the potyeen, and recommended him, by way of cure, to swallow a hair of the dog that bit him. Coo, however, seemed to think he had had quite enough: he got up, quite out of sorts, and without having the good manners to say one word in the way of civility, he sneaked off to cool himself by a jaunt through the salt water.

Coomara never missed the souls. He and Jack continued the best friends in the world; and no one, perhaps, ever equalled Jack at freeing souls from purgatory; for he contrived fifty excuses for getting into the house below the sea, unknown to the old fellow; and then turned up the pots, and let out the souls. It vexed him, to be sure, that he could never see them; but as he knew the thing to be impossible, he was obliged to be satisfied. Their intercourse continued for several years. However, one morning, on Jack's throwing in a stone, as usual, he got no answer. He flung another, and another; still there was no reply. He went away, and returned the next morning; but it was to no purpose. As he was without the hat, he could not go down to see what had become of old Coo; but his belief was, that the old man, or the old fish, or whatever he was, had either died, or had removed away from that part of the country. *)

*) We must here make an honest confession. This story had no foundation but a German legend. [see Nixies—Germany] All that is not to be found there is our own pure invention. Yet we afterwards found that it was well-known on the coast of Cork and Wicklow. "But," said one of our informants, "It was things like flower-pots he kept them in." So faithful is popular tradition is these matters! In this and the following tale there are some traits by another hand which we are now unable to discriminate.

Barry of Cairn Thierna

Fermoy, though now so pretty and so clean a town, was once as poor and as dirty a village as any in Ireland. It had neither barracks, nor church, nor school, nor anything to admire. Two-storied houses were but few: its street (for it had but one) was chiefly formed of miserable mud cabins; nor was the fine scenery around sufficient to induce the traveller to tarry in its paltry, dirty inn, beyond the limits actually required.

In those days it happened that a regiment of foot was proceeding from Dublin to Cork. One company, which left Caher in the morning, had, with 'toilsome march,' passed through Mitchelstown, tramped across the Kilworth mountains; and, late of an October evening, tired and hungry, reached Fermoy, the last stage but one to their quarters. No barracks, as we have said, were then built there to relieve them; and every voice was raised, calling to the gaping villagers for the name and residence of the billet-master.

"Why, thin, can't ye be aisy, now, and let a body tell you," said one. "Shure, thin, how can I answer you all at onst," said another. "Anan!" cried a third, affecting not to understand the sergeant, who addressed him. "Is it Mr. Consadine you want replied a fourth, answering, *à l' Irlandaise,* the question, by asking another. "Bad luck to the whole breed and seed of the sogers!" muttered a fifth villager, between his teeth. "It 'a come to ate poor people that work for their bread, out of house and home, yez are?' "Whisht, Teigue, can't you, now?" said his neighbour, jogging the last speaker; "there 'a the house, gintlemen. You see it there, yondher, forenint you, at the bottom of the sthreet, wid the light in the winddy; or, stay, shure it 'a mysilf id think little of runnin' down 'odd you, poor crathurs! for 'tis tirt and wairy yez must be afther the road."—"That 's an honest fellow," said several of the dust-covered soldiers; and away scampered Ned Flynn, with all the men of war following close at his heels.

Mr. Consadine, the billet-master, was, as may be supposed, a person of some, and on such occasions as the present, of no small consideration in such a place as Fermoy. He was of a portly build, and of a grave and slow movement, suited at once to his importance and to his size. Three inches of fair linen were at all times visible between his waistband and waistcoat. His breeches-pockets were never buttoned; and, scorning to conceal the bull-like proportions of his chest and neck, his shirt-collar was generally open, as he wore no cravat; and a flaxen bob-wig commonly sat fairly on his head, and squarely on his forehead. Such, then, was Mr. Consadine, billet-master-general and barony sub-constable, who was now just getting to the end of his eighth tumbler, in company with the proctor, who at that moment had begun to talk of coming to something like a fair settlement about his tithes, when Ned Flynn knocked.

"See who's at the door, Nilly," said the eldest Miss Consadine, raising her voice, and calling to the barefooted servant girl. "Tis the sogers, sir, is come!" cried Nelly, running back into the room without opening the door. "I hear the jinketin' of their swoords and bagnets on the pavin' -stones."—"Divil welcome them at this hour o' the night," said Mr. Consadine, taking up the candle, and moving off to the room on the opposite side of the hail, which served him for an office.

Mr. Consadine's own pen, and that of his son Tom were now in full employment. The officers were sent to the inn; the sergeants, corporals, etc., were billeted on those who were on indifferent terms with Mr. Consadine; for, like a worthy man as he was, he leaned as light as he could on his friends. The soldiers had nearly all departed for their quarters, when one poor fellow, who had fallen asleep, leaning on his musket against the wall, was awakened by the silence, and starting up, he went over to the table at which Mr. Consadine was seated, hoping his worship would give him a good billet. "A good billet, my lad," said the billet-master-general, "that you shall have, and on the biggest house in the whole place. Do you hear, Tom! make out a billet for this honest man upon Mr. Barry of Cairn Thierna." "On Mr. Barry of Cairn Thierna!" said Tom, with a look of amazement. "Yes, to be sure, on Mr. Barry of Cairn Thierna—the great Barry!" replied his father, giving a nod. "Isn't he said to keep the grandest house in this part of the counthry?—or stay, Tom, jist hand me over the paper, and I'll write the billet myself."

The billet was made out accordingly; the sand glittered on the signature and broad flourishes of Mr. Consadine, and the weary grenadier received it with becoming gratitude and thanks. Taking up his knapsack and firelock, he left the office, and Mr. Consadine waddled back to the proctor to chuckle over the trick he had played on the soldier, and to laugh at the idea of his search after Barry of Cairn Thierna's house. Truly had he said no house could vie in capacity with Mr. Barry's; for like Allan A-Dale's, its roof was the blue vault of Heaven, with its crescent so pale.

Barry of Cairn Thierna was one of the chieftains who, of old, lorded it over the barony of Barrymore, and for some reason or other, he had become enchanted on the mountain of Cairn Thierna, where he was known to live in great state, and was often seen by the belated peasant.

Mr. Consadine had informed the soldier that Mr. Barry lived a little way out of the town, on the Cork road; so the poor fellow trudged along for some time with eyes right and eyes left, looking for the great house; but nothing could he see only the dark mountain of Cairn Thierna before him, and an odd cabin or two on the road-side. At last he met a man, of whom he asked the way to Mr. Barry's. "To Mr. Barry's?" said the man; "what Barry is it you want?" "I can't say exactly in the dark," returned the soldier. "Mr. What's-his-name, the billet-master, has given me the direction on my billet; but he said it was a large house, and I think he called him the great Mr. Barry." "Why, sure, it wouldn't be the great Barry of Cairn Thierna you 're asking after?" "Aye," said the soldier, "Cairn Thierna—that 's the place. Can you tell me where it is?" "Cairn Thierna!" repeated the man—"Barry of Cairn Thierna! I'll show you the way, and welcome; but it 's the first time in all my born days that ever I h'ard of a soger bein' billeted on Barry of Cairn Thierna. 'Tis a quare thing, anyhow, for ould Dick Consadin to be sindin' you up there," continued he; "but you see that big mountain before you—that's Cairn Thierna. Any one will show you Mr. Barry's when you get to the top of it, up to the big hape of stones."

The weary soldier gave a sigh as he walked forwards toward the mountain; but he had not proceeded far when he heard the clatter of a horse coming along the road alter him, and, turning his head round, he saw a dark figure rapidly approaching. A tall gentleman, richly dressed, and mounted on a noble gray horse, was soon at his side, when the rider pulled up, and the soldier repeated his inquiry after Mr. Barry of Cairn Thierna. "Why, I'm Barry of Cairn Thierna, myself," said the gentleman, "and pray what 's your business with me, friend." "I have got a billet on your house, sir," replied the soldier, "from the billet-master of Fermoy." "Did you, indeed," said Mr. Barry; "well, then, it is not very far off; follow me and you shall be well taken care of, depend upon it."

He turned off the road, and led his horse up the steep side of the mountain, followed by the soldier, who was astonished at seeing the horse proceed with so little difficulty, where he was obliged to scramble up, and could hardly find or keep his footing. When they got to the top, there was a house, sure enough, far beyond any house in Fermoy. It was three stories high, with fine windows, and all lighted up within, as if it was full of grand corn-party. There was a hall-door too, with a flight of stone steps before it, at which Mr. Barry dismounted, and the door was opened to him by a servant-man, who took his horse round to the stable. Mr. Barry, as he stood at the door, desired the soldier to walk in, and, instead of sending him down to the kitchen, as any other gentleman would have done, brought him into the parlour, and desired to see his billet. "Ay," said Mr. Barry, looking at it and smiling, "I know Dick Consadine well—he 's a merry fellow, no doubt, and, if I mistake not, has got some capital good cows down on the inch-field of Carrickabrick; a sirloin of beef would be no bad thing for supper, my man, eh?"

Mr. Barry then called out to some of his attendants, and desired them to lay the cloth, and make all ready, which was no sooner done than a smoking sirloin of beef was placed before them. "Sit down, now, my honest fellow," said Mr. Barry, "you must be hungry after your long day's march." The soldier with a profusion of thanks for such hospitality, and acknowledgments for such condescension, sat down and made, as might be expected, an excellent supper; Mr. Barry never letting his jaws rest for want of helping until he was fairly unable to eat more. Then the boiling water was brought in, and such a jug of whiskey punch as was made! Take my word for it,—it did not, like honest Robin Craig's, require to be hung out on the bush to let the water drain out of it.

They sat together a long time, talking over the punch, and the fire was so good, and Mr. Barry himself was so free a gentleman, and had such fine conversation about everything in the world, far or near, that the soldier never felt the night going over him. At last Mr. Barry stood up, saying it was a rule with him that every one in his house should be in bed by twelve o'clock, "And," said he, pointing to a bundle which lay in one corner of the room, "take that to bed with you, it's the hide of the cow I had killed for your supper; give it to the billet-master when you go back to Fermoy, in the morning, and tell him that Barry of Cairn Thierna sent it to him. He will soon understand what it means, I promise you; so, good night, my brave fellow; I wish you a comfortable sleep and every good fortune; but I must be off and away out of this long before you are stirring." The soldier gratefully returned his host's good wishes, and went off to the room which was shown him, without claiming, as every one knows he had a right to do, the second best bed in the house.

Next morning the sun awoke him. He was lying on the broad of his back, and the skylark was singing over him in the beautiful blue sky, and the bee was humming close to his ear among the heath. He rubbed his eyes; nothing did he see but the clear sky, with two or three light morning clouds floating away. Mr. Barry's fine house and soft feather bed had melted into air, and he found himself stretched on the side of Cairn Thierna, buried in the heath, with the cowhide which had been given him, rolled up under his head for a pillow. ")

"Well," said he, "this bates cockfighting, anyhow! Didn't I spind the plisantest night I iver spint in my life with Mr. Barry last night? And what in the world has becom' of the house, and the hall door with the steps, and the very bed that was undher me?" He stood up. Not a vestige of a house or any thing like one, but the rude heap of stones on the top of the mountain, could he see; and ever so far off lay the Blackwater, glittering with the morning sun, and the little quiet village of Fermoy on its banks, from whose chimneys white wreaths of smoke were beginning to rise upwards into the sky. Throwing the cowhide over his shoulder, he descended, not without some diffi-culty, the steep side of the mountain, up which Mr. Barry had led his horse the preceding night with so much ease; and he proceeded along the road, pondering on what had befallen him.

When he reached Fermoy, he went straight to Mr. Consa-dine's, and asked to see him. "Well, my gay fellow," said the official Mr. Consadine, recognising, at a glance, the soldier; "what sort of an entertainment did you meet with from Barry of Cairn Thierna?" "The best of good thratement, sir," replied the soldier; "and well did he spake of you, and he disired me to give you this cowhide as a token to remimber him by." "Many thanks to Mr. Barry for his generosity," said the billet-master, making a low bow, in mock solemnity; "many thanks indeed, and a right good skin it is, wherever he got it."

Mr. Consadine had scarcely finished the sentence, when he saw his cow-boy running up the street, shouting and crying aloud, that the best cow in the Inch-field was lost and gone, and nobody knew what had become of her, or could give the least tidings of her.

The soldier had spread out the skin on the ground for Mr. Consadine to see it; and the cow-boy looking at it, exclaimed—"That is her hide, wherever she is; I'd take my Bible oath to the two small white spots, with the glossy black about thim; and there's the very place where she rubbed the hair off her shouldher last Martinmas." Then clapping his hands together, he literally sang "the tune the old cow died of." This lamentation warn stopped short by Mr. Consadine: "There is no manner of doubt about it," said he. "It was Barry that kilt my best cow, and all he has left me is the hide o' the poor baste to comfort myself with; but it will be a warnin' to Dick Consadine, for the rest of his life, nivir again to play off his thricks upon thravellers."

---

* It is not very likely that the inventor of this legend knew anything about the Amadigi of B. Tasso, yet in that poem we meet this circumstance more than once. In c. ii., when night falls on the young knight Alidoro, in the open country, he finds a pavilion pitched beside a fountain, with lights in it, and hears a voice which invites him to enter it. He there sups and goes to sleep in a rich bed, and on awaking in the morning (iii. 38) finds himself lying in the open air. Another time (c. viii) be comes to a fair inn, in a wild region, where he is entertained and his wounds are dressed by a gentle damsel, and on awaking in the morning he finds himself lying under a tree. The tent and inn were the work of his protectress, the Fairy Silvana. Another Fairy, Argea, entertains (c. xxxiii.) a king, queen, knight and ladies, in a stately palace. At night they retire to magnificent chambers, and in the morning they find themselves lying in a mead, some under trees, others on the sides of a stream, with more of the beauties of the ladies displayed than they could have desired.

Aileen a Roon

(Ellen my love)

Carrol O'Daly is the Lochinvar of Ireland. He and Ellen Cavanagh were intimate from childhood. The result was love; but Ellen's father insisted on her marrying a wealthier suitor. On the wedding-night Carrol came disguised as a harper, and played and sung this air, which he had composed for the occasion. Ellen's tenderness revived in full force; she contrived to make her father, the bridegroom, and the guests drink to excess, and by morning she and Carrol were beyond pursuit.

The following lines were written one evening to gratify a lady who wished to have the writer's idea of what Carrol might have sung. The air is generally known under the name of Robin Adair—

> What are the joys wealth and honours bestow?
> Do they endure like true love's steady glow?
> Shadows of vanity,
> Mists of the summer sky,
> Soon they disperse and *fly,*
> Aileen a roon!
> Time was when Aileen tripped light as the fawn,
> Spying young Carrol approach in the dawn,
> Ere the sun's early beam
> Glittered on lake and stream,—
> Oh! that was bliss supreme,
> Aileen a roon!
> Or when mild even's star beamed in the west,
> Bringing to nature the season of rest—
> At that sweet hour to rove,
> Down by yon spreading grove,
> Breathing forth vows of love,
> Aileen a roon!

Aileen forgets, but her Carrol more true,
As these past scenes memory brings to his view.
Heaves many a heavy sigh,
Breaking his heart is nigh—
And canst thou let him die?
Aileen a roon!

Rousseau's Dream

These verses are adapted to the well-known air. They were suggested by a passage from Rousseau's works, quoted by Alison in his Essay on Taste. Though real names are mentioned, the scenery and subject are purely ideal.

Calmly at eve shone the sun o'er Lake Leman,
Bright in his beam lay the watery expanse,
Softly the white sails reflected his gleaming,
Groves, banks, and trees their slow shadows advance.
Cool from the mountains the summer-gale breathed,
Laden with fragrance the lake it came o'er;
Leman, exulting, danced joyous beneath it,
Light crisped waves gently roll to the shore.
At that soft hour on the blue Leman rowing,
Slowly a sage urged his bark by a grove,
Silently musing, his lofty mind glowing,
Viewing earths pomp and the glories above
As o'er the lake the long shadows extended,
Whispering the breeze, lulled each sense to repose;
Calm he reclined, and as slumber descended,
Visions of bliss to his fancy arose.
Heaven to his view seemed arrayed in new glory,
Earth breathed forth fragrance and basked in the ray
Clad in loose raiment, more white than the hoary
Front of Mont Blanc, came a son of the day.
Lightly his wand o'er the slumberer extending,
While with new joy laughed the earth, sky, and lake;
Love in his accents with soft pity blending,
Shedding content, thus the bright vision spake:—
"Hither I come, from ray cloud-crowned station,
Touched with thy grief; to shed balm o'er thy mind '
I am the Spirit to whom, at creation,
Charge was by Heaven o'er this region assigned.
List to my accents, thou hunted by malice!

Let what I utter sink deep in thy breast:
Fly from mankind, to the lakes, hills, and valleys,
Thus, thus alone, shall thy spirit find rest.
"But if again to the world thou now fliest,
Thou should return, and again meet thy foes,
Think on this hour, when for comfort thou sighest,
And the bright scene will dispel all thy woes."
Gone was the vision: eve's star now was glancing,
Cold came the breeze o'er the blue curling stream;
Waked from his slumber, his heart with joy dancing,
Homeward he turned, and still mused on his dream.

Alexander Selkirk's Dream

Composed one day when confined to bed by a cold and unable to read

O'ER the isle of Juan Fernandez
Cooling shades of evening spread,
While upon the peaks of Andes
Still the tints of day were shed.
From the sea-beat shore returning
Homeward hied the lonely man,
O'er his cheerless fortune mourning,
As through past days memory ran.
Soon his brief repast was ended
And he sought his lowly bed;
Balmy slumber there descended,
Shedding influence o'er his head.
Then a vision full of gladness
Came, sent forth by Him supreme,
Who his suffering servants' sadness
Oft dispelleth in a dream.
*

In his view the lively dream sets
Hills and vales in verdure bright;
Where the gaily-prattling streamlets
Sparkle in the morning-light.
Hark! the holy bell is swinging,
Calling to the house of prayer;
Loud resounds the solemn ringing
Through the still and balmy air.
Youths and maids from glen and mountain
Hasten at the hallowed sound,
Old men rest by shady fountain,
Children lay them on the ground.
Now the pious throng is streaming
Through the temple's portal low;
Rapture in each face is beaming
Pure devotion's genuine glow.
Fervently the hoary pastor,

Humbly bent before his God,
Supplicates their heavenly Master
Them to lead on Sion's road;
Owns that all have widely erred
From the true, the narrow way,
That with Him we have no merit,
And no claim of right can lay.
Loud then rise in choral measure
Hymns of gratitude and praise,
As, inspired with solemn pleasure,
Unto Heaven their strains they raise.
Now the grave discourse beginneth,
Which, ungraced by rhetoric's arts,
Quick the rapt attention winneth,
While it glorious truths imparts;
While it tells how kind is Heaven
To the race of him who fell;
How of old the Son was given
To redeem from pains of hell;
How the Holy Spirit abideth
In their hearts that hear his call;
How our God for all provideth,
How His mercy's over all;
How, beyond the grave extending,
Regions lie of endless bliss;
How our thoughts on that world bending,
We should careless be of this.
Once again the raised hymn pealeth
Notes of joy and jubilee,
Praising Him who truth revealeth,
Dweller of Eternity!
*

Night's dim shades were now retreating,
Over Andes rose the day
On the hills the kids' loud bleating
Lingering slumber chased away.
Birds their merry notes were singing,
Joyous at the approach of morn—
Morn that, light and fragrance flinging,

Earth doth cherish and adorn.
Waked by Nature's general chorus
Selkirk quits his lonely couch,
While o'er heaven run colours glorious,
Heralding the sun's approach.
Still the vision hovers o'er him,
Still the heavenly strains he hears,
Setting those bright realms before him
Where are wiped away all tears.
All this vain and transitory
State of mankind here on earth,
Weighed with that exceeding glory,
Now he deems as nothing worth.
Low he bends in adoration,
As the sun ascends the sky;
Doubt and fear and lamentation
With the night's last shadows fly.

A Moonlight Scene

Conceived and commenced when passing Oven Putney Bridge
on a fine moonlight night in summer

THE moonbeams on the lake are glancing,
The nimble bark is now advancing,
That for this grove is bound.
Ye gentle clouds, ah! hear a lover,
And hasten not the moon to cover
And darkness pour around.
Doth fancy sport, or do l hear her,
As nearer still she comes and nearer,
Cutting the billows bright? -.
How still! scarce even a light breeze flying!
Earth, water, air, at peace are lying
Beneath the calm moonlight.
My heart beats high, my soul rejoices,
Methinks l hear their merry voices—
She soon will reach the shore.—
Ah me! my hopes, my hopes are failing,
Yon sable cloud is onwards sailing—
The moon it covers o'er.
Now o'er the lake they dubious wander,
And on some part remote may strand her,
Unless they aid obtain—
l'll wave a signal from the summit
Of you high bank, and haply from it
Some guidance they may gain.
The cloud moves on, the moonlight beameth
And o'er the lovely lady streameth,
Upon her lofty stand.
With joyful shout the boatmen greet her,
Her anxious lover hastes to meet her,
And eager springs to land.

Lines

Written in a Lady's Album

IN those blest days, when free from care,
And happy as the birds in air,
I roamed the hills and dales,
By purling rills oft passed the day,
Or on green banks recumbent lay,
Listening the shepherds' tales,
My fancy, rising on the wing,
Would visions fair before me bring,
Of castles high, and towers,
With knights in radiant panoply,
And ladies of the beaming eye,
Within their fragrant bowers;
Or lead me thence away to shades
Of woods, and show me, in the glades,
The cottages serene,
Where Peace dwelt with Content, among
The happy, gay Arcadian throng
That tenanted the scene.
But whether cot or tower arose
In vision, at the dawn or close
Of summer-days, to me,
The lovely form of woman still
Shone bright by dale, by mend, by rill,
Amid my extacy.
I saw her robed in every grace
With youth, with loveliness of face,
And virtue's gentle eye;
And from her tongue heard accents fail,
That would the rudest heart enthral,
And raise emotions high.
But like the Eastern prince, who loved
The pictured form of one that moved
In life full many a year

Ere he beheld the light, I deemed
The lovely form of which I dreamed
Would ne'er to me appear.

And years came on, and years went by,
And yet I never found me nigh
My youthful vision bright.
I said,—I might as well, I ween,
Expect to see the Fairy-queen
Descend, to bless my sight.
But often, when we hope it least,
And when our search has well nigh ceased,
Good fortune will befall:
So I one evening saw a maid,
Who every grace and charm displayed
That decked my *Ideal*.
Her portrait here I need not show,
For, reader, thou must surely know
That peerless, gentle maid:
To her these lines I consecrate;
And if she smiles I'll deem, elate,
My toil far overpaid.

To Amanda

[These are the verses quoted in the Introduction to the "Tales and Popular Fictions." The author was very young when he wrote them; and Amanda was, like Beatrice and Laura, a mere *donna di mente,* having no real existence.]

As when a storm in vernal skies
The face of day doth stain,
And o'er the smiling landscape flies,
With mist and drizzling rain;
If chance the sun look through the shower
O'er flowery hill and dale,
Reviving Nature owns his power,
And softly sighs the gale:
So when, by anxious thoughts oppressed,
My soul sinks in despair,
When smiling hope deserts my breast,
And all is darkness there
If chance Amanda's form appear,
The gloom is chased away,
My soul once more her soft smiles cheer,
And joy resumes his sway.
Then, dear Amanda, since thy smile
Has power all gloom to charm,
Oh! ever thus my cares beguile,
And guard my soul from harm.
Let Hymen's bands our fates unite,
What bliss may then be ours!—
Our days will glide, like streamlets bright,
O'erhung with fragrant flowers.

Lines

Written in Rome in the Spring of 1842.

FAIR Tibur, once the Muses' home,
Before us lay; around
Was spread the plain which mighty Rome
Oft saw with victory crowned.
The sun rode high, the sky was clear,
The lark poured forth his strain,
And flowers, the firstlings of the year,
Shed fragrance o'er the plain.
A gentle lady turned on me
Her bright expressive eyes,
And bade the flame of poesy
Within my bosom rise.
'Twas then I felt, I felt, alas!
How Time has dealt with me,
And how the rays of fancy pass,
And vanish utterly.
For time has been when such a view
And mandate of the fair,
With images of brightest hue,
Had fill'd the land and air:
While now I strive, and strive in vain,
To twine poetic flowers,
Since from me Time away has ta'en
Imagination's powers.
Then lady, be thou gentle still,
Let pity sway thy breast;
Accept for deeds the fervent will
To honour thy behest,

A Farewell

FAREWELL! farewell! the parting hour
Is come, and I must leave thee!
Oh! ne'er may aught approach thy bower
That might of bliss bereave thee!
But ever a perennial rill
Of joy, so brightly flowing,
Keep each fair thought in fragrance still
Within thy pure mind blowing.
For life all charm had lost for me,
My thoughts were only sadness,
When fortune led me unto thee
To taste once more of gladness.—
I've seen the sullen shades of night
Fair nature's face concealing,
And marked how scattered rays of light
Came morn's approach revealing.
The light increased, the orb of day
Clomb to the mountain's summit;
And vale and plain, and stream and bay,
Drew life and lustre from it.
And as it towered in majesty,
Light all around it shedding,
It seemed a monarch, seated high,
Bliss through his realms wide spreading.
All nature joyed; I felt my heart
Distend, and fill with pleasure;
For heavenly light and warmth impart
A bliss we cannot measure.
This glorious sun to me art thou,
Whose light all gloom dispelleth,
Before whose majesty I bow
When he his power revealeth.
Thy golden locks, thine eyes so blue,
Thy smile so sweetly playing,
Were those first shafts of light that flew,
The gloom of night warraying.

But when, more intimately known,
I found not only beauty,
But genius, taste, and truth, thine own,
Combined with filial duty:
Then rose the sun, o'er all my soul
In full effulgence beaming,
And tides of joy began to roll
Beneath his radiance gleaming.—
Time still his noiseless course pursues
With unremitting vigour,
And lovely Spring each year renews
The waste of Winter's rigour.
Were mine the power, thus, like Time,
To wake again life's flowers,
And days recall of youthful prime
Passed in the Muses' bowers;
Then, lovely maiden! fancy-free,
Rich in each mental treasure,
In me thou wouldst a votary see—
Thy will would be my pleasure.
But while such bliss might not be mine,
A friendship pure and holy
I offered at the hallowed shrine,
To which my heart turned solely.—
When distant from thee many a mile,
High waves between us swelling,
I'll think upon thy lovely smile,
Of pure emotion telling.
The sky will show me thy blue eye;
The whispering breeze of even
Recall that voice, whose melody
Oft lapped my soul in heaven!
The sinking sun thy ringlets' gold
Will show; but memory only
The treasures of thy mind unfold
To me when musing lonely.
Oh! may I hope that memory,
That power for ever changing,
Will make thee sometimes think on me,

O'er distant mountains ranging?
Say me not nay; let Fancy cheat
My soul with bland illusion;
And let not Doubt my vision sweet
Dispel by rude intrusion.

Verses

Written at Bath 1840, for a little boy who kept an album, and was a great admirer of Robin Hood and his Merry men.

HAD the kind Muse, young friend, on me
Her pleasing gifts bestowed,
And taught to tread of poesy
The smooth and flowery road;
Then should the deeds of Robin Hood,
And Little John, so bold,
And of the Friar, stout and good,
In numbers high be told.
The merry greenwood should resound
With feats of archery,
And antlered deer along should bound
So light and gracefully!
But vain the hopes: 'gainst Fate's decrees
To struggle I must cease;
I only can write histories
Of England, Rome, and Greece.

Father Cuddy's Song

In the legend of Clough Na Cuddy.

QUAM pulchra sunt ova,
Cum alba et nova
In stabulo scite leguntur;
Et à Margery bells,
Quae festiva puella!
Pinguis lardi cum frustis coquuntur.
Ut belles in prato
Aprico et lato
Sub sole tam laete renident,
Ova tosta, in mensa
Mappa bene extensa,
Nitidissima lance consident.

TRANSLATION.
Oh! 'tis eggs are a treat,
When so white and so sweet
From under the manger they 're taken,
And by fair Margery,
Och! 'tis she's full of glee,
They are fried with fat rashers of bacon.
Just like daisies all spread
O'er a broad sunny mead,
In the sunbeams so beauteously shining,
Are fried eggs fair displayed
On a dish, when we've laid
The cloth and are thinking of dining.

The Praises of Mazenderan

[The object of this version was to give a correct idea of the animated anapastic measure in which the Shib-Nameh is written. Our knowledge of Persian was extremely slight; but a friendly Orientalist gave us a faithful line-for-line translation, which we versified, and he and Ram Mohun Roy then compared our version with the original.]

His band from the lute hath its melody drawn,
And thus rose the song of Mazenderân:—
May Mazenderan, the land of my birth,
Its hills and its dales, be e'er famed o'er the earth:
For evermore blooms in its gardens the rose,
On its hills nods the tulip, the hyacinth blows;
Its air ever fragrant, its earth flourishing,
Cold or heat is not felt,—'tis perpetual spring.
The nightingale's lays in the gardens resound;
On the sides of the mountains the stately deer bound,
In search evermore of their pastime and food;
With fragrance and colour each season's bedewed;
Its streams of rose-water unceasingly roll,
Whose perfume doth gladness diffuse o'er the soul
In November, December, and January,
Pull of tulips the ground thou mayest everywhere see;
The springs, unexhausted, flow all through the year;
The hawk at his chase everywhere doth appear.
The region of bliss is adorned all o'er
With dinars, with rich stuffs, and with all costly store;
The idol-adorers with fine gold are crowned,
And girdles of gold gird the heroes renowned.
Whoe'er hath not dwelt in that region so bright,
His soul knows no pleasure, his heart no delight.

Index

Bakhna Rakhna, *302*

cross, *44, 153, 160, 184, 192*

fairies, *9, 10, 19, 22, 28, 32, 35, 37, 39, 46, 49, 50, 51, 52, 59, 61, 63, 64, 75, 76, 77, 78, 79, 80, 85, 86, 87, 89, 90, 94, 97, 100, 101, 102, 106, 121, 122, 123, 124, 126, 139, 150, 153, 157, 160, 161, 162, 164, 174, 176, 189, 190, 191, 192, 193, 196, 197, 198, 199, 214, 215, 250, 252, 269, 273, 338, 339*

fairy, *22, 26, 36, 38, 41, 45, 50, 51, 52, 57, 61, 62, 63, 69, 72, 73, 74, 75, 76, 77, 79, 80, 84, 85, 88, 90, 91, 92, 93, 94, 95, 96, 97, 100, 101, 106, 116, 121, 122, 123, 128, 133, 134, 150, 152, 153, 157, 158, 159, 161, 178, 193, 194, 248, 252, 258, 266, 269, 344*

farisees, *46, 47*

fary, *53, 55, 56*

fata, *241, 242, 243, 254*

Hinzelmann, *115, 130*

lob, *72, 98*

lubber, *62, 95*

Luck of Eden Hall, *25, 27*

lutin, *274, 279*

mermaids, *216*

monkey, *59, 259, 347*

neck, *20, 92, 215, 270, 368*

ninny, *259*

nymphs, *82, 88, 91, 93, 232, 233, 234, 237, 295*

oaf, *100*

Ogier le Danois, *66*

ouph, *100*

pawkey, *59*

pixies, *43*

pouke, *58, 98*

puck, *60*

pucker, *259*

Robin Goodfellow, *19, 23, 25, 60, 61, 85, 101*

Robin Hood, *57, 61, 390*

St. Peter's suster, *99*

witch, *62, 63, 69, 79*

Paper books

VAMzzz Publishing is located in the very centre of old Amsterdam, in The Netherlands. Our publishing company creates high quality revised editions of five star occult, witchcraft, Gothic and esoteric classics, mostly written in the Fin de siècle-period and early 20th century.

As a publisher, we deeply respect the writer of any book we choose, so we join our forces (top level graphic design & thirty years of occult studies) to produce enchanting volumes which maximize the reading pleasure and inform, often with extra added information. In contrast to the current trend of digital screen addiction, we think, this variety of literature needs to be presented on paper. *No e-books, but real books!*

Apart from republications of valuable but forgotten books, we are also in the preparation of new publications on topics such as self-healing, magic, new astrology and more.

Previews of all books including a complete table of contents can be viewed on www.vamzzz.com. More books will be added to the list. *VAMzzz Publishing* strives to publish new volumes every month. Please visit our website regularly for the latest updates.

VAMzzz Publishing
P.O. Box 3340
1001 AC Amsterdam
The Netherlands
contactvamzzz@gmail.com
www.vamzzz.com

Recommended

Fairy Mythology
Romance and
Superstition of Various
Countries 1
by Thomas Keightley
404 pages, Paperback,
ISBN 9789492355096

The term "Fairy" covers all kinds of nature spirits and Elementals all over the world. Not just the tiny sugar sweet creatures hovering around flowers. Thomas Keightley collected an impressive amount of mostly European, and nowadays often "extinct" folklorist data on these invisible realm's inhabitants, and compiled these in *Fairy Mythology* (1870). In its revised edition, this massive work of over 800 pages, is republished in two volumes to meet modern reading standards. Volume 2 covers the Fairy-lore of the British Isles, Ireland, Southern Europe, Eastern Europe and some Jewish and African lore. Volume 1 deals extensively with Scandinavia, Iceland, Feroer, the Orkneys, Shetland Islands, Rugen, Germany and Switserland. In volume 1 the origins of the term Fairy are traced and oriental and medieval romance, Edda's and Sagas are examined before we explore Fairy-species as Elle-maids, Trolls, Nisses, Elves, Dwarfs, Necks, Mermaids, Nixes, Heinzelmänchen, Watermen or Wassermänchen, Hödeken, Changeling, Wild women and Little people. An invaluable work of resource for those interested in old European folklore or nature magic.

Taboo, Magic, Spirits
A study of primitive elements in Roman religion
by Eli Edward Burriss
200 pages, Paperback, ISBN 9789492355034

In Ancient Rome Mana was the term used for a mysterious, magical medium, which could be helpful or harmful (Taboo). Just like the Chinese qi, it could empower the positive and the negative. Contents: Mana, Magic and Animism – Positive and Negative Mana (Taboo) – Miscellaneous Taboos – Magic Acts: The General Principles – Removing Evils by - Magic Acts – Incantation and Prayer– Naturalism and Animism.

Chaldean Magic
It's Origin and Development
by François Lenormant
454 pages, Paperback, ISBN 9789492355027

The essentials of magic in Chaldea are presented inside a context of comparison or contrast to Egyptian, Median, Turanian, Finno-Tartarian and Akkadian magic, mythologies, religion and speech. Interesting is the Chaldean demonology, with its incubus, succubus, vampire, nightmare and many Elemental spirits, most of them coalesced with the primal powers of nature.

Unicorn
A mythological investigation
by Robert Brown Jr.
124 pages, Paperback, ISBN 9789492355072

Brown Jr. believes the unicorn to be a lunar symbol, and draws on mythology from a wide range of sources all over the world to build his case. The author discusses the heraldic use of the unicorn, relates the creature to ancient goddesses like Astarte, Hecate en the Gorgon Medusa, and provides the reader with lost esoteric Moon-lore.

Là-Bas
A Journey into the Self
by Joris-Karl Huysmans
378 pages, Paperback, ISBN 9789492355058

The plot of *Là-Bas* concerns the novelist Durtal, who is disgusted by the emptiness and vulgarity of the modern world. He seeks relief by turning to the study of the Middle Ages. Through his contacts in Paris, Durtal discovers that Satanism is not a thing of the past but alive and kicking in turn of the century France. The novel culminates with a description of a black mass.

Devil-worship in France
Or The Question of Lucifer
by Arthur Edward Waite
240 pages, Paperback, ISBN 9789492355065

In *Devil-Worship in France,* Waite attempts to discern what is genuine from what is fake in the evidence of 19th century Satanism. To get the answers he spends a great deal of time investigating the French Masonic echelon, debunking a "conspiracy of falsehood" and determining what should be understood by Satanism and what not. Huysmans' diabolical novel *Là-Bas* (1891) inspired Waite to write this sceptical analysis.

Testament of Solomon
A First Century AD Grimoire
76 pages, Paperback, ISBN 9789492355041

A first century AD grimoire, and therefore the oldest, and least known, of all grimoires (magical instruction books) in the occult tradition. The book describes health inflicting demons of zodiacal decans, summoned by King Solomon, and how he controlled them to use their forces to build his temple and more. Translated by F. C. Conybeare, appeared first in the *Jewish Quarterly Review* of October, 1898.

Amazons - *Two publications in one book -*
I. The Amazons by Guy Cadogan Rothery
II. Religious Cults Associated With the Amazons
      by Florence Mary Bennett
328 pages, Paperback, ISBN 9789492355089

Contents I: The Amazons of Antiquity – Amazons
in Far Asia – Modern Amazons of the Caucasus –
Amazons of Europe – Amazons of Africa – Amazons of
America – The Amazon Stones.
Contents II: The Amazons in Greek legend – The Great
Mother – Ephesian Artemis – Artemis Astrateia and
Apollo Amazonius – Ares.

Aradia
Gospel of the Witches
by Charles Godfrey Leland
174 pages, Paperback, ISBN 9789492355010

This wonderful book describes the creation according to
Italian witch-lore. We also read about the witch-meeting
or sabbath (treguenda) and the book contains many
original magical recipes, like spells for love and good
fortune. Diana is further connected to the Moon and
the fairy world.

Etruscan Magic & Occult Remedies
(Two volumes in one book)
Charles Godfrey Leland
628 pages, Paperback, ISBN 9789492355003

Part One of the book gives us a complete and detailed
insight in the Etruscan and Roman rooted pantheon of
the Tuscan Streghe (witches). Part Two describes many
of their spells, incantations, sorcery and several lost
divination methods. Much information in this book,
Leland received first hand from the Tuscan witches
Maddalena and Marietta.

Ophiolatreia
Rites and Mysteries of Serpent Worship
Author: Hargrave Jennings
186 pages, Paperback, ISBN 9789492355126

An account of the rites and mysteries connected with the origin, rise and development of serpent worship in various parts of the world, enriched with interesting traditions, and a full description of the celebrated serpent mounds & temples, the whole forming an exposition of one of the phases of phallic, or sex worship.

Voodoos and Obeahs
Phases of West India Witchcraft
by Joseph J. Williams
374 pages, Paperback, ISBN 9789492355119

This work goes into great depth concerning the New World-African connection and is highly recommended if you want a deep understanding of the dramatic historical background of Haitian and Jamaican magic and witchcraft, and the profound influence of imperialism, slavery and racism on its development. Williams includes numerous quotations from rare documents and books on the topic.